1986
YEAR BOOK OF
INFECTIOUS DISEASES

1986

The Year Book of INFECTIOUS DISEASES

Editor
Sheldon M. Wolff, M.D.

Associate Editors
Sherwood Gorbach, M.D.
Gerald Keusch, M.D.
Mark Klempner, M.D.
David Snydman, M.D.

Year Book Medical Publishers, Inc.
Chicago • London

Printed in U.S.A.

International Standard Book Number: 0-8151-9375-0

International Standard Serial Number: 0743-9261

.

The editor for this book was Jane A. Toomey, and the production manager was H. E. Nielsen. The Managing Editor for the YEAR BOOK series is Caroline Scoulas.

The Year Book Series

Anesthesia: Drs. Miller, Kirby, Ostheimer, Saidman, and Stoelting

Cancer: Drs. Hickey, Clark, and Cumley

Cardiology: Drs. Harvey, Kirkendall, Laks, Resnekov, Rosenthal, and Sonnenblick

Critical Care Medicine: Drs. Rogers, Allo, Dean, Gioia, McPherson, Michael, and Traystman

Dentistry: Drs. Cohen, Hendler, Johnson, Jordan, Moyers, Robinson, and Silverman

Dermatology: Drs. Sober and Fitzpatrick

Diagnostic Radiology: Drs. Bragg, Keats, Kieffer, Kirkpatrick, Koehler, Miller, and Sorenson

Digestive Diseases: Drs. Greenberger and Moody

Drug Therapy: Drs. Hollister and Lasagna

Emergency Medicine: Dr. Wagner

Endocrinology: Drs. Schwartz and Ryan

Family Practice: Dr. Rakel

Hand Surgery: Drs. Dobyns and Chase

Hematology: Drs. Spivak, Bell, Ness, Quesenberry, and Wiernik

Infectious Diseases: Drs. Wolff, Gorbach, Keusch, Klempner, and Snydman

Medicine: Drs. Rogers, Des Prez, Cline, Braunwald, Greenberger, Wilson, Epstein, and Malawista

Neurology and Neurosurgery: Drs. DeJong, Currier, and Crowell

Nuclear Medicine: Drs. Hoffer, Gore, Gottschalk, Sostman, and Zaret

Obstetrics and Gynecology: Drs. Pitkin and Zlatnik

Ophthalmology: Dr. Ernest

Orthopedics: Dr. Coventry

Otolaryngology–Head and Neck Surgery: Drs. Paparella and Bailey

Pathology and Clinical Pathology: Dr. Brinkhous

Pediatrics: Drs. Oski and Stockman

Plastic and Reconstructive Surgery: Drs. McCoy, Brauer, Haynes, Hoehn, Miller, and Whitaker

Podiatric Medicine and Surgery: Dr. Jay

Psychiatry and Applied Mental Health: Drs. Freedman, Lourie, Meltzer, Nemiah, Talbott, and Weiner

Pulmonary Disease: Drs. Green, Ball, Menkes, Michael, Peters, Terry, Tockman, and Wise

Rehabilitation: Drs. Kaplan and Szumski

Sports Medicine: Drs. Krakauer, Shephard, and Torg, Col. Anderson, and Mr. George

Surgery: Drs. Schwartz, Jonasson, Peacock, Shires, Spencer, and Thompson

Urology: Drs. Gillenwater and Howards

Vascular Surgery: Drs. Bergan and Yao

Table of Contents

The material in this volume represents material reviewed up to February 1985.

Journals Represented

American Heart Journal
American Journal of Cardiology
American Journal of Diseases of Children
American Journal of Epidemiology
American Journal of Gastroenterology
American Journal of Medicine
American Journal of Surgery
Annals of Internal Medicine
Annals of Surgery
Antimicrobial Agents and Chemotherapy
Archives of Diseases in Childhood
Archives of Internal Medicine
Archives of Ophthalmology
Archives of Surgery
Blood
British Medical Journal
Chest
Digestive Diseases and Sciences
Epidemiologic Reviews
European Journal of Clinical Pharmacology
Gastroenterology
Human Pathology
Infection and Immunity
Intensive Care Medicine
International Journal of Gynecological Pathology
International Journal of Law and Psychiatry
Journal of the American Academy of Dermatology
Journal of the American Medical Association
Journal of Clinical Investigation
Journal of Experimental Medicine
Journal of Infectious Diseases
Journal of Neurosurgery
Journal of Pediatrics
Journal of Urology
Lancet
Medicine
Nature
New England Journal of Medicine
Obstetrics and Gynecology
Pediatric Infectious Disease
Pediatrics
Proceedings of the National Academy of Sciences
Quarterly Journal of Medicine
Retina
Reviews of Infectious Diseases
Science
Southern Medical Journal
Surgery
Thorax
Urology
Western Journal of Medicine

Publisher's Preface

The 1986 YEAR BOOK OF INFECTIOUS DISEASES is a new YEAR BOOK devoted to a subject of long-standing interest and investigation. Infections have been discussed in the YEAR BOOK OF MEDICINE since the first edition of the PRACTICAL MEDICINE YEAR BOOKS was published in 1901. Despite antibiotics and modern technology, infectious diseases remain a problem. Literature on the subject continues to grow remarkably as researchers and clinicians report their efforts to gain control over the agents of infection.

For those familiar with the YEAR BOOK series, 1985 marked the eighty-fifth anniversary of the original PRACTICAL MEDICINE YEAR BOOKS. To mark this milestone, the YEAR BOOKS were issued with a more contemporary cover design, and the format for the contents was modified to identify the article titles, authors' names, and journal citations more readily by isolating this information as a discrete block of copy. The substance of the YEAR BOOKS—the abstracts of scholarly articles with substantive editorial comments—was not changed. The YEAR BOOKS continue to survey a broad spectrum of the world's medical literature, abstracting significant articles and providing perspective on them via editorial commentary. Development of YEAR BOOKS is a complex process requiring 12 months to survey literature and several more months to write abstracts and prepare comments. We continually work to reduce this lag period to the minimum necessary.

We are most pleased to welcome Sheldon Wolff and his associates as Editors of the YEAR BOOK OF INFECTIOUS DISEASES, and we hope it will become a valuable resource and a welcome addition to your library.

Introduction

Legionnaires' disease, toxic shock syndrome, and acquired immunodeficiency syndrome are all recently recognized clinical entities that have an infectious agent as their cause. Despite the development of powerful antimicrobial agents and new vaccines, infectious diseases continue to occupy a major place in almost all areas of clinical medicine. In support of such a statement, one need only review (as we have done for this book) the thousands of journal articles that are published each year in the general area of infectious diseases. Selecting the articles that we believed to be worthy of inclusion in this volume was not an easy task. Despite our best efforts, I am sure that one can point to important articles that have not been included in this volume, or point out selections that will not stand the "test of time." Although the editors all practice in the area of general infectious diseases, we each have our areas of special interest, which undoubtedly are reflected in our selections. Nonetheless, we attempted to cover, in the broadest sense, the areas of infectious diseases that were clinically relevant.

The clinical applications of the "new" biologies, such as recombinant DNA technology, will surely have a great impact on all areas of medicine and especially on infectious diseases. The availability of large quantities of specific microbial antigens should lead to better diagnostic tests and powerful new vaccines. Monoclonal antibodies should aid in diagnosis and in immunotherapy. The production of mediators and cellular components will lead to better understanding of host responses and defenses, and to reconstitution of deficient patients. With this rapidly expanding knowledge base will come more new information, making future volumes of the YEAR BOOK exciting to anticipate.

The preparation of this volume has been an educational experience for the editors, and we hope our readers will feel the same. We acknowledge with gratitude the efforts of the editorial staff of Year Book Medical Publishers, who abstracted our selections with such care and clarity.

Sheldon M. Wolff, M.D.

1 Bacterial Infections

Sepsis and Endocarditis

How Important Are Dental Procedures as a Cause of Infective Endocarditis?

Warren G. Guntheroth (Univ. of Washington)
Am. J. Cardiol. 54:797–801, Oct. 1, 1984   1–1

Data on eighteen pediatric patients who had infective endocarditis (IE) over a 25-year period were reviewed to detect causes of "failed" chemoprophylaxis. The patients were aged 3–28 years at the onset of illness. The average age was 14 years. All the patients had congenital heart disease, and they were counseled about the importance of prophylaxis against IE. In no case was the onset of IE preceded by a dental procedure. The most common causative organisms were *Streptococcus viridans* and *Staphylococcus*. Patients survived 13 episodes of IE, although 2 of them had persistent hemiparesis. One death followed a second episode of IE. Routine prophylaxis consisted of 2 gm of orally given penicillin V given 30–60 minutes before dental procedures and 500 mg every 6 hours for a total of 8 doses. A review of the literature left no doubt that dental extractions can produce bacteremia, but studies of the duration of bacteremia have given conflicting results. The prevalence of dental extractions preceding IE was only 3.6% for 1,322 cases.

Bacteremia was associated with 40% of 2,403 reported dental extractions, but it also was found in 38% of patients after mastication and in 11% of patients with oral sepsis and no intervention. The cumulative exposure to "physiologic" sources of bacteremia in a hypothetical month ending with a single dental extraction is nearly 1,000 times greater than from the extraction. There is general agreement that chemoprophylaxis has never proved to be effective in clinical trials, and current American Heart Association recommendations for parenteral chemoprophylaxis are impractical, inconvenient, and uncomfortable. Use of a single oral dose of amoxicillin appears to be much simpler and probably relatively effective. Scrupulous oral and dental hygiene undoubtedly is more important than any chemoprophylactic regimen in preventing infective endocarditis. It may be wise to continue the use of oral antibiotics in invasive dental procedures and to use sensitivity-based antibiotics to cover such procedures as genitourinary operation.

Right-sided Infective Endocarditis as a Consequence of Flow-Directed Pulmonary Artery Catheterization: Clinicopathologic Study of 55 Autopsied Patients
Katherine M. Rowley, K. Soni Clubb, G.J. Walker Smith, and Henry S. Cabin (Yale Univ.)
N. Engl. J. Med. 311:1152–1156, Nov. 1, 1984   1–2

Isolated cases of infective endocarditis have been described in association with use of a flow-directed pulmonary artery catheter. A review was made of data on 142 consecutively autopsied patients in 1982–1983. Thirty-two male and 23 female patients, mean age 59 years, had had flow-directed pulmonary artery catheterization during the final hospital stay.

Fifteen of the 55 catheterized patients, including the 4 with right-sided infective endocarditis, also had a central venous pressure line in place. Nine patients had a temporary transvenous right ventricular pacemaker. About half the catheterized patients and 3 of the 87 noncatheterized patients had right-sided endocardial lesions. The most common was subendocardial hemorrhage and sterile thrombi. The valve lesions were most frequent on the pulmonic valve cusps. Nineteen catheterized patients had positive blood cultures, and 11 had positive cultures when the catheter was in place. Right-sided infective endocarditis developed in 4 of these 11 patients. Four other catheterized patients had infected left heart lesions. Twenty-one noncatheterized patients had bacteremia, but none had autopsy evidence of infective endocarditis.

Many endocardial lesions produced by flow-directed pulmonary catheters may be incidental autopsy findings, but infective endocarditis can develop. Infected vegetations probably are a direct result of catheter-induced endocardial damage in these cases with concurrent or subsequent bacteremia. The risk of endocarditis is especially high in debilitated patients who have bacteremia or are at risk for bacteremia.

► This study is the human analogue of experimental catheter-induced bacterial endocarditis which has been examined in the rabbit model. The longer the flow-directed catheter remained in place, the greater the risk of complications. Two-dimensional echocardiography has recently been shown to be useful in making a diagnosis antemortem (Tsao, M.M.P., and Katz, D.: *Rev. Infect. Dis.* 6:783–790, 1984).—D.S.

Gonococcal Endocarditis: A Case Series Demonstrating Modern Presentation of an Old Disease
Genaro C. Fernandez, Alan J. Chapman, Jr., Roberto Bolli, Steven D. Rose, Michael E. O'Meara, Jerry C. Luck, Craig M. Pratt, and James B. Young (Houston)
Am. Heart J. 108:1326–1334, November 1984   1–3

Previously, the gonococcus accounted for a substantial proportion of cases of infective endocarditis, but only 25 well-documented cases have been reported in the English medical literature since 1942. Three cases reported involved the aortic valve and required emergency valve replacement, and 1 case involved the tricuspid valve.

Man, 35, had developed rhinorrhea and a cough 5 weeks before admission, followed by a swollen, tender, right ankle and then similar involvement of the left ankle, knees, elbows, and wrists. The arthritis improved with Indocin therapy, but dyspnea worsened. The patient had been treated for gonococcal urethritis 3 years earlier. The temperature was 99.3 F, and mild respiratory distress was present. A systolic ejection murmur was clearest at the left sternal border. Right-sided pleuritic chest pain and a pleural friction rub appeared 10 days after admission when cardiomegaly and a right lower lobe infiltrate were found. Jugular venous distention and a loud, holosystolic murmur were present 3 days later. Echocardiography showed a tricuspid valve vegetation, and intravenous vancomycin therapy was instituted. Blood cultures yielded *Neisseria gonorrhoae* on the 15th hospital day, and penicillin then was administered. The patient improved clinically. Cultures of the throat, urethra, and rectum were negative for gonorrhea.

Neisseria gonorrhoeae can damage previously healthy cardiac valves and can produce acute bacterial endocarditis. Echocardiography is a useful approach to suspected gonococcal endocarditis. It may also provide useful hemodynamic information. Prompt valve replacement often is necessary, and penicillin therapy is essential. The gonococcus is no longer a frequent cause of subacute infective endocarditis.

Pneumococcal Bacteremia at Medical-Surgical Hospital for Adults Between 1975 and 1980
F.L. Ruben, C.W. Norden, and Y. Korica (Univ. of Pittsburgh)
Am. J. Med. 77:1091–1094, December 1984   1–4

Review was made of 72 episodes of pneumococcal bacteremia occurring in an adult medical-surgical hospital between 1975 and 1980, spanning the period in 1977 when 14-valent pneumococcal vaccine was licensed. The 10–14 episodes occurring yearly accounted for up to 5% of all bacteremias. The estimated annual incidence of pneumococcal bactermia was 1 episode in every 1,000 patients discharged. Episodes were relatively frequent from January through March.

The mean patient age was 61 years. Sixteen of the 72 episodes were hospital acquired, occurring within an average of 9 days after hospital admission. Chest x-ray films showed no infiltrate in 18% of the patients. All but 13% had an underlying illness, and 43% had ultimately fatal disorders. Six patients were asplenic. Antimicrobial therapy was given to all but 6 patients. Complications included 9 episodes of respiratory failure, 8 of meningitis, and 9 of pleural effusion or empyema. Overall, 57% of the patients survived the episode and were discharged from the hospital; 28 deaths were caused directly by the infection or by complications. Five of the 6 asplenic patients died.

All 3 patients who received 14-valent pneumococcal vaccine survived, whereas 11 of 32 nonvaccinated patients seen in the same period died.

Ten of the 15 pneumococcal isolates tested in the last 2 years of the review period were types included in the vaccine. Apparently, about half of the patients in whom pneumococcal bacteremia developed could have been immunized in a hospital-based vaccination program.

Pneumococcal vaccine should be used liberally in view of the severity of pneumococcal bacteremia that develops despite treatment and the tendency for patients having underlying disease to be affected. Asplenic persons have the highest priority for vaccination.

Changing Pattern of Neonatal Streptococcal Septicemia
Linda Spigelblatt, Jacques Saintonge, Raymond Chicoine, and Michel Laverdière (Univ. of Montreal)
Pediatr. Infect. Dis. 4:56–58, January 1985   1–5

Most studies of neonatal septicemia have shown a persistently high incidence of group B streptococcus and *Escherichia coli* as causal organisms (table). Broughton et al. reported a marked increase in viridans streptococcal infection in neonates in 1977–1980. The incidence of such infection in 1977–1982 was determined at the authors' institution when 11,509 live births occurred. Thirty-four neonates had 35 positive blood cultures for streptococci. Viridans streptococci were cultured in 19 instances, group B streptococci in 12, and group D enterococci in 4. Six of the cultures yielding viridans streptococci were mixed. Eleven of the infants with viridans streptococcal infection were considered to be septic. The infants with viridans streptococcal infection and those with group B streptococcal infection were similar with regard to maternal illness, chorioamnionitis, prematurity, and birth weight. The latter infants had a comparatively earlier onset of symptoms and a higher incidence of both respiratory distress and leukopenia.

This survey confirms an increase in the occurrence of viridans streptococcal bacteremia in neonates. Viridans streptococcus was the most frequently isolated pathogen in neonates in this study. Viridans streptococcus may be a less virulent organism than group B streptococcus in newborn infants. Viridans infection probably is transmitted vertically from mother to infant. Viridans streptococcus is associated with bacteremia in obstetric-gynecologic patients, and it is a common inhabitant of the female genitourinary tract. The viridans streptococcus should be considered a pathogen in ill neonates.

Surgical Aspects of *Clostridium septicum* Septicemia
Timothy M. Pelfrey, Robert P. Turk, James B. Peoples, and Dan W. Elliott (Wright State Univ.)
Arch. Surg. 119:546–550, May 1984   1–6

The unique association between *Clostridium septicum* infections and concurrent malignant neoplasms was shown previously. A survey was made of the incidence of cancer, especially that of the gastrointestinal

ORGANISMS IDENTIFIED IN NEONATAL SEPTICEMIA IN THE LAST 50 YEARS

Organisms	No. of Patients							
	Dunham (1927–1932)	Nyhan (1933–1957)	McCracken (1953–1964)	Gluck (1957–1965)	Jeffery (1967–1975)	Broughton (1970–1976)	Broughton (1977–1980)	Spigelblatt (1977–1982)
Beta-hemolytic streptococcus	15[a]	29[b]	10[a]	1[c]	13[c]	119[c]	83[c]	12[c]
Staphylococcus	11	12	19	5	6	NR	NR	5
Enterococcus		1	2	14	1	NR	NR	4
Viridans streptococcus		1		2	1	15	41	19
Escherichia coli	10	34	16	42	8	76	37	5
Other Gram negatives[d]		14	15	43	13	99	41	2
Mixed		4				NR	NR	
Others	3	11	12	10	5	NR	NR	2
Total	39	106	74	117	47	309	202	49

[a]Lancefield group not reported.
[b]Lancefield Group A (21), Group B (6), Group D (1), and Group F (1).
[c]Lancefield Group B.
[d]Includes *Klebsiella-Enterobacter, Pseudomonas, Proteus, Citrobacter,* and *Salmonella.* NR, not reported.
(Courtesy of Spigelblatt, L., et al.: Pediatr. Infect. Dis. 4:56–58, January 1985.)

tract, in 8 patients seen between 1978 and 1982. The diagnosis of C. *septicum* sepsis was made in ante mortem blood culture studies. Seven of the 8 patients had an occult malignancy in the gastrointestinal tract, and the eighth patient was thought to be preleukemic. Three patients had primary abdominal complaints on hospital admission, and the diagnosis of a malignancy was made prior to onset of sepsis. Four patients had gangrene of an extremity; 3 of these patients died of sepsis prior to diagnosis of malignancy. Another patient with gas gangrene of an extremity survived with administration of hyperbaric oxygen; he had no occult malignancy, but blood dyscrasia was present. Of the 4 patients treated medically, 1 survived with antibiotic treatment, but the other 3 died of sepsis. Four patients had an operation, in 3 directed at the primary cause of C. *septicum*; 2 of the 4 survived.

Of 144 reports of C. *septicum* septicemia, the disease in 72% was associated with malignant neoplasms. A disruption in the gastrointestinal tract mucosa induced by tumor infiltration or the ulcerating effects of chemotherapy or radiation therapy may serve as a portal of entry for C. *septicum*. Administration of appropriate therapy depends on early, accurate diagnosis. Sepsis caused by C. *septicum* must be suspected in patients with known existing or previously treated gastrointestinal tract or hematologic malignant neoplasms who have gastrointestinal tract symptoms and sepsis and in those who have nontraumatic gas gangrene of an extremity. Medical therapy consists of intravenously administered penicillin G sodium, up to 25 million units daily in divided doses. Surgical therapy includes debridement or amputation, and celiotomy in those with abdominal signs of a primary malignant neoplasm. Patients recovering from C. *septicum* sepsis should undergo an appropriate search for underlying malignancy.

Plasmid Pattern Analysis for Differentiation of Infecting From Noninfecting *Staphylococcus epidermidis*

Gordon L. Archer, Adolf W. Karchmer, Nahum Vishniavsky, and J. Linda Johnston
J. Infect. Dis. 149:913–920, June 1984   1–7

The problem of differentiating clinically significant from insignificant bacterial isolates is difficult in the case of *Staphylococcus epidermidis*, since it is the most common contaminant of routine cultures. The authors tested the effectiveness of the plasmid pattern as a marker for differentiating infecting from noninfecting S. *epidermidis* isolates. Plasmid patterns were determined for S. *epidermidis* organisms isolated from two or more blood cultures from each of the 36 infected and 15 uninfected patients. The skin flora of 9 patients who underwent cardiac surgery (CS) were cultured before and after operation; the skin flora from 3 patients with S. *epidermidis*-related prosthetic valve endocarditis (SE-PVE) were also cultured during therapy. Infections in the 36 patients include prosthetic valve endocarditis in 26, cerebrospinal fluid shunt or ventriculostomy infections in 6, intravenous catheter sepsis in 2, urinary tract infection in 1, and osteomyelitis in 1.

In 32 of the 36 patients with documented *S. epidermidis* infection, identical plasmid patterns were seen among sequential or paired isolates from each patient. The plasmid pattern from a given patient was unique to that patient. The plasmid pattern analysis of paired isolates from patients with SE-PVE remained stable over time, even during antibiotic therapy. None of the isolates from 10 controls had the same plasmid pattern; each isolate differed from the other by at least two plasmid bands. These reflected the variety of plasmid patterns among colonizing coagulase-negative staphylococci cultured from skin flora of uninfected CS patients.

Plasmid pattern analysis may be useful in the diagnosis of *S. epidermidis* infections. Since all contaminants examined had different plasmid patterns, and since 32 of 36 patients with *S. epidermidis*-related infections had plasmid pattern identity in all isolates from sequential cultures, the sensitivity and specificity of the test were 89% and 100%, respectively. However, plasmid pattern analysis has several potential pitfalls. The power of the test to distinguish between two isolates decreases directly with the number of plasmid bands and the diminishing difference in molecular size between two bands. Also, the quick-lysis technique used for preparation of the crude lysates can convert covalently closed circular DNA to open circular and linear DNA, a procedure resulting in the appearance of more bands than there are plasmids on the electrophoretic gel.

▶ Molecular epidemiology is creeping into the lives of all of those concerned with infectious diseases. When wedded to the often difficult task of assigning clinical significance to the isolation of *S. epidermidis,* molecular epidemiology becomes a powerful clinical tool for the treatment of the individual patient. The superiority of this method over antibiograms or biochemical reactions when distinguishing various *S. epidermidis* isolates makes the tasks of simplifying the method and standardizing its interpretation a high priority. I, for one, await the routine availability of this tool in the clinical microbiology laboratory.—M.K.

Respiratory Tract

Parapneumonic Effusions and Empyema in Hospitalized Children: A Retrospective Review of 227 Cases

Bishara J. Freij, Helen Kusmiesz, John D. Nelson, and George H. McCracken, Jr. (Univ. of Texas, Dallas)
Pediatr. Infect. Dis. 3:578–591, November 1984   1–8

A review was made of data on 227 children treated for parapneumonic effusion or empyema in a 19-year period. The etiologic agents are shown in the table. Cases were most frequent in the winter and spring months. A causative agent was identified in three-fourths of all patients. Most of the children were otherwise healthy. The most common finding on chest radiography apart from pleural effusion was pneumatocele, which was most often associated with *Staphylococcus aureus* infection. Pneumo-

FREQUENCY OF PATHOGENS

No. of Cases

Etiology	January 1964–June 1973	July 1973–December 1982	Total
Staphylococcus aureus	43 (34)*	23 (23)	66 (29)
Streptococcus pneumoniae	27 (22)	22 (22)	49 (22)
Haemophilus	15 (12)	25 (25)	40 (18)
Other bacteria	8 (6)	10 (10)	18 (8)
Sterile	32 (26)	22 (22)	54 (24)
All cases	125 (100)	102 (100)	227 (100)

*Numbers in parentheses, percentage of cases.
(Courtesy of Freij, B.J., et al.: Pediatr. Infect. Dis. 3:578–591, November 1984.)

thorax was seen in 13% of all cases but most frequently in children with *S. aureus* empyema. Lung abscesses were found in 13 cases, including 7 cases of *S. aureus* empyema.

Patients generally received a β-lactam antibiotic initially. Children with *S. aureus* empyema generally were treated for the longest periods. Closed chest tube drainage was used in two thirds of the cases. Sixteen patients had multiple thoracenteses without chest tube placement. About half the patients had chest tubes removed within 5–7 days. The mortality was 8%. Eleven of the 19 deaths occurred in children with *S. aureus* empyema. Most deaths occurred in infants. Pleural fluid superinfection occurred in 7% of patients having closed chest tube drainage. Bronchopleural fistula complicated 3% of the cases. Three children had a relapse of empyema after closed chest tube drainage.

Thoracentesis is indicated when a pleural effusion is found in association with pneumonia in a child. If empyema is diagnosed, intercostal chest tube drainage should be strongly considered. Repeat thoracentesis may be helpful in equivocal cases. Appropriate antibiotic therapy and thorough surgical drainage are necessary to prevent loculation and formation of a restrictive pleural peel. Other infected sites must be sought, especially in cases of *Hemophilus* infection.

Laboratory Diagnosis of Pneumonia Due to *Streptococcus pneumoniae*
Carl A. Perlino (Emory Univ.)
J. Infect. Dis. 150:139–144, July 1984   1–9

Various techniques have been used to increase the diagnostic accuracy of sputum examination in suspected pneumococcal pneumonia. The author determined the diagnostic reliability of the Quellung reaction of the sputum and the gram-stained directed sputum culture (SC) for bacteriologic diagnosis of pneumonia due to *Streptococcus pneumoniae,* compared with detection of pneumococcal polysaccharide in the sputum by counterim-

POSITIVITY OF CIE, QUELLUNG REACTION, AND
DIRECTED SPUTUM CULTURE IN 21 DEFINITE
CASES OF PNEUMOCOCCAL PNEUMONIA*

Test	No. positive (%)
CIE	17 (81.0)
Quellung reaction	18 (85.7)
Directed culture	17 (81.0)

*Pneumococcal pneumonia was defined by positive blood or pleural fluid cultures for pneumococci.
(Courtesy of Perlino, C.A.: J. Infect. Dis. 150:139–144, July 1984.)

munoelectrophoresis (CIE) and isolation of pneumococci from cultures of blood or pleural fluid (BPF). Sputum specimens were obtained from 211 adults with community-acquired bacterial pneumonia. Initially, detection of CIE-positive sputum and BPF-positive cases were considered to indicate definite pneumococcal infection.

Among 119 CIE-positive cases, the Quellung reaction and SC were positive for 117 and 96 specimens, respectively. However, 52 false positive results with the Quellung reaction (27) and SC (25) were obtained from 92 CIE-negative sputums, suggesting that CIE is a less sensitive indicator of pneumococcal infection than was originally assumed. The Quellung reaction, SC, and CIE were positive in similar numbers of BPF-positive cases (table). A positive Quellung reaction was always confirmed by a positive CIE or SC in these 21 cases. When the data for all 211 cases were assessed, a positive Quellung reaction was confirmed by a positive CIE, sputum culture, or blood culture in 134 (93.1%) of 144 positive tests. A positive SC was confirmed by a positive CIE, Quellung reaction, or blood culture in 116 (95.9%) of 121 positive cases, whereas CIE was positive for only 117 (81.3%) of 144 sputum samples positive by the Quellung reaction and for only 96 (79.3%) of 121 SC-positive specimens. These data support the diagnostic reliability of both the Quellung reaction and SC, and the use of both tests gave results superior to those obtained with any one test alone. Patients with a positive test for pneumococcal infection occasionally had other potential pathogens identified from the sputum culture, i.e. *Hemophilus influenzae* and *Staphylococcus aureus*.

Routine use of both the Quellung reaction and SC provides an accurate diagnosis of pneumococcal infection, and CIE of sputum is a less sensitive indicator. However, isolation of potential pathogens from sputum cultures with positive tests for pneumococcal infection may be significant and raises the possibility of mixed infection. Compared with CIE, the Quellung reaction and SC are rapid and simple to perform and relatively inexpensive.

▶ What we really need is a simple, rapid, accurate test for pneumococcal pneumonia, or indeed for any microbial pathogen. Can you imagine treating diabetic acidosis without having rapid blood sugar results? The CIE is fairly rapid, however, as shown in this study, it is not particularly accurate and it does not account for other pathogens in the same sputum. The Quellung reaction is certainly rapid, but it requires a skilled technician with appropriate reagents in the laboratory at the time of admission. It also fails to identify other pathogens. Culture is the gold standard, but it is a retrospective confirmation rather than a prospective guide to treatment. Our microbiology laboratories still work in the 1880s, when Robert Koch developed these microbial isolation techniques.—S.G.

Clinical and Microbiologic Features of *Branhamella catarrhalis* Bronchopulmonary Infections
Nicholas J. Slevin, John Aitken, and Peter E. Thornley (Christchurch, New Zealand)
Lancet 1:782–784, April 7, 1984   1–10

Branhamella catarrhalis (formerly *Neisseria catarrhalis*), an oropharyngeal commensal, is recognized as a lower respiratory tract pathogen in patients with generalized immunosuppression and chronic chest disease. A review was made of the clinical and microbiologic features in 101 patients with *B. catarrhalis* bronchopulmonary infection diagnosed by the presence of gram-negative intracellular diplococci in sputum and growth of more than 20 colonies of *B. catarrhalis* in quantitative culture at a 10^{-7} dilution. Overall, 94 patients had either a chronic chest disease or were current or previous smokers, 59 had a cause of generalized immunosuppression, and 17 had a high risk of aspiration from the oropharynx; only 7 patients were nonsmokers with no chronic chest disease, and 4 patients had no apparent risk factors. Clinical features included purulent sputum in 67 of 71 patients (94%), fever of more than 37 C in 30 of 57 patients (53%), leukocytosis greater than 11×10^9/L in 16 of 44 patients (36%), and transient patchy pulmonary shadowing seen on chest x-ray examination in 17 of 54 patients (31%). *Branhamella catarrhalis* infection contributed to 4 of 6 deaths. It was the only pathogen isolated from the sputum in 71 patients, and in 30 others was associated with other bacterial pathogens. Antibiotic sensitivity studies showed all 10 isolates of *B. catarrhalis* tested to be sensitive to oxytetracycline; all 82 tested were sensitive to cefuroxine, 93 of 96 were sensitive to erythromycin, and 85 of 95 were sensitive to cotrimoxazole. Beta-lactamase was produced by 38 of 99 isolates.

A history of chronic chest disease or smoking was associated with *B. catarrhalis* bronchopulmonary infection in this series. The presence of purulent sputum, fever, leukocytosis, and transient opacity in the chest radiograph constitute evidence of pathogenicity. In vitro susceptibility studies show that erythromycin, tetracycline, and cotrimoxazole should be the preferred antibiotics in treatment of *B. catarrhalis* infection.

▶ There may be no such thing as a nonpathogenic commensal. Given the right circumstances in the right patient, almost any organism may be capable of causing disease. In this series, *B. catarrhalis* infection is well-documented by quantitative culture and is strongly associated with abnormal hosts. In such patients, isolation of this organism should be taken seriously and not dismissed as normal oropharyngeal flora.—G.K.

Association of Aminoglycoside Plasma Levels With Therapeutic Outcome in Gram-Negative Pneumonia

Richard D. Moore, Craig R. Smith, and Paul S. Lietman (Johns Hopkins Univ.)
Am. J. Med. 77:657–662, October 1984   1–11

Gram-negative bacilli other than *Hemophilus* probably are the most frequent cause of nosocomial pneumonia. It has been suggested that high serum aminoglycoside levels may be necessary for successful therapeutic results. Plasma aminoglycoside levels were related to the outcome in 37 cases of gram-negative pneumonia from four prospective, double-blind trials of gentamicin, tobramycin, and amikacin. The initial intravenous dose of gentamicin and tobramycin was 2 mg/kg; that of amikacin, 8 mg/kg. All drugs were given at eight-hour intervals for maintenance, in doses adjusted for renal function. Goal maintenance plasma levels 1 hour after infusion were 5–10 μg/ml for gentamicin and tobramycin and 20–40 μg/ml for amikacin. All patients also received methicillin, nafcillin, penicillin, or cephalothin. The average patient age was 63 years. Nearly half the patients had underlying chronic pulmonary disease, and about half had a rapidly fatal underlying illness.

Fifty-four percent of patients survived and improved clinically. Twelve others died during antibiotic therapy. *Klebsiella* was the most common infecting organism. The mean duration of aminoglycoside therapy was 7 days. Gentamicin was used in 13 patients, tobramycin in 18, and amikacin in 6. The outcome was better when patients had a maximal peak plasma level of gentamicin or tobramycin of 7 μg/ml; of amikacin, 28 μg/ml (table). The association was not due simply to a longer duration of treatment. The peak plasma aminoglycoside level was the most important factor in outcome on stepwise logistic regression analysis. Nephrotoxicity occurred in 35% of successfully treated patients and in 35% of those in whom treatment failed.

These findings show the importance of achieving and maintaining ad-

	MAXIMAL PEAK PLASMA LEVELS*	
	≥7 μg/ml † ≥28 μg/ml ‡	<7 μg/ml † <28 μg/ml ‡
Success	14 (78%)	6 (32%)
Failure	4 (22%)	13 (68%)

*With use of Fisher's exact test, differences between groups were significant at level of P<.006.
†For gentamicin and tobramycin
‡For amikacin
(Courtesy of Moore, R.D., et al.: Am. J. Med. 77:657–662, October 1984.)

equate plasma aminoglycoside levels throughout the treatment of gram-negative pneumonia. Adequate 1-hour postinfusion drug levels may improve the chance for a successful therapeutic outcome in these cases.

▶ This paper illustrates an often repeated axiom, which is respected more in theory than in practice; namely, it is more important to overtreat with an aminoglycoside antibiotic, risking some toxicity, than to play it safe with a low dose and subtherapeutic blood levels. The authors make the same point in a companion paper published in the *Journal of Infectious Diseases* (149:443–448, 1984) which deals with plasma levels of aminoglycosides in patients with gram-negative bacteremia.—S.G.

The Concept of Pertussis as a Toxin-Mediated Disease
Margaret Pittman (Bethesda, Md.)
Pediatr. Infect. Dis. 3:467–486, Sept.–Oct. 1984   1–12

Pertussis is a toxin-mediated disease initiated by *Bordetella pertussis* on the cilia of the respiratory tract mucosa. The bacteria attach to and multiply among the cilia, but they do not invade tissues or the blood. The organism liberates an exotoxin that produces most if not all the symptoms of pertussis and induces prolonged immunity. Pertussis toxin increases susceptibility to many agents, including histamine, serotonin, lipopolysaccharide endotoxin, cold, and bacterial and viral diseases. It produces various metabolic changes such as hypoglycemia and refractoriness to epinephrine and induces lymphocytosis-leukocytosis. The pathologic changes of pertussis result from altered functions of toxin-sensitized cells, not from histologic damage. The affected cells include lymphocytes, other leukocytes, cardiac cells, and pancreatic islet cells. Altered glucose metabolism is a prominent aspect of pertussis. Other cellular effects of the toxin presumably produce paroxysms and neurologic disturbances. Functional cell changes in vitro are irreversible, and restoration of tissue function in vivo appears to require renewal of the cells. This explains why bacterial therapeutic agents are ineffective in pertussis.

Pertussis immunization protects against the disease. The present whole cell pertussis vaccine confers protective immunity, but protection against colonization is shorter than against the disease. Identification of pertussis toxin as the reactive and protective antigen holds promise for development of a toxoid, possibly combined with one or two other components of *B. pertussis* that would be as effective and nonreactive as diphtheria toxoid. *Bordetella pertussis* is an obligatory parasite and pathogenic only for human beings; it is not chronically carried. It should therefore be possible to eradicate the organism, as was done with smallpox virus.

▶ In the current storm over the use and complications of the pertussis component of diphtheria-tetanus toxoid pertussis (DTP), the need to develop a better immunogen is of major importance. This paper reviews the pathogenesis of pertussis, particularly the role of an exotoxin with multiple biologic effects. It is valuable for American physicians to refamiliarize themselves with the organism and the disease it causes; for if DTP immunization is stopped, as it was in England, there would be danger of epidemics of whooping cough occurring once again. This review will not only help the physician to follow future developments in pertussis immunization, but also help answer important questions about the disease and the current vaccine.—G.K.

Gastrointestinal

Unidentified Curved Bacilli in the Stomach of Patients With Gastritis and Peptic Ulceration
Barry J. Marshall and J. Robin Warren (Perth, Australia)
Lancet 1:1311–1315, June 16, 1984

Helicobacter

1–13

Curved or spiral bacteria have long been recognized in the stomach. Biopsy specimens were obtained from intact areas of antral mucosa in 100 consecutive patients seen for gastroscopy to confirm an association between these organisms and gastritis. Spiral or curved bacilli were demonstrated in specimens from 58 patients. Their presence correlated closely with both gastric and duodenal ulcer (table). Most patients with peptic ulcer also had gastritis.

The bacteria were readily distinguished from contaminant organisms and debris. Silver staining was the most sensitive means of detecting them. Gastritis was present in all but 2 of 57 biopsy specimens showing bacteria. The correlation remained when ulcer patients were excluded. Bacilli cultured from 11 biopsy specimens were gram-negative, flagellate, and microaerophilic, apparently a new species related to *Campylobacter*. Many negative cultures were discarded too soon. Growth of the curved bacteria was evident as 1-mm nonpigmented colonies within 3 days.

No well-defined clinical syndrome has been associated with the presence of pyloric *Campylobacter*. The only endoscopic finding associated with histologic gastritis and the presence of pyloric *Campylobacter* was peptic

ASSOCIATION OF BACTERIA WITH ENDOSCOPIC DIAGNOSES

Endoscopic appearance*	Total	With bacteria	p
Gastric ulcer	22	18 (77%)	0·0086
Duodenal ulcer	13	13 (100%)	0·00044
All ulcers	31	27 (87%)	0·00005
Oesophagus abnormal	34	14 (41%)	0·996
Gastritis†	42	23 (55%)	0·78
Duodenitis†	17	9 (53%)	0·77
Bile in stomach	12	7 (58%)	0·62
Normal	16	8 (50%)	0·84
Total	100	58 (58%)	

*More than one description applies to several patients, e.g., 4 patients had both gastric and duodenal ulcers.
†Refers to endoscopic appearance, not histologic inflammation.
(Courtesy of Marshall, B.J., and Warren, J.R.: Lancet 1:1311–1314, June 16, 1984.)

ulcer. The organism is likely to be etiologically related to chronic antral gastritis and probably to peptic ulceration.

▶ Several authors from different parts of the world have now confirmed the initial observations of Marshall and Warren, that the *Campylobacter*-like organism is present in some cases of gastric or duodenal ulceration. What remains to be solved is the nature of its association with disease. The *Campylobacter*-like organisms are found in the gastric mucosa of normal people, hence establishing their position in the normal intestinal flora. It may be that the *Campylobacter*-like organisms accumulate preferentially in sites of mucosal ulceration due to an alteration in the epithelial barrier. In an effort to establish their pathogenicity, future studies must consider response to specific antimicrobial therapy, antibody levels, and duplication of the pathologic events in an appropriate animal model. In short, Koch's postulates must be satisfied before we can accept the etiologic role of this organism in gastric or duodenal ulcer.—S.G.

Enteropathogenic *Escherichia coli* of Classic Serotypes Associated With Infant Diarrhea: Epidemiology and Pathogenesis
Myron M. Levine (Baltimore) and Robert Edelman (Bethesda)
Epidemiol. Rev. 6:31–51, 1984.   1–14

Enteropathogenic *Escherichia coli,* the first recognized diarrheogenic class of *E. coli,* emerged in the 1950s as the chief cause of outbreaks of diarrhea in infant nurseries and as a cause of sporadic infant diarrhea. Strains within the O55, O111, and O127 serogroups are particularly associated with infant diarrhea. Enteropathogenic *E. coli* are present in large numbers in both the small bowel and colon in infants with diarrhea. Sensitive serologic techniques demonstrate responses to the enteropathogenic *E. coli* strain isolated from the stool. Studies in volunteers showed unequivocally that enteropathogenic *E. coli* strains from patients with diarrhea, selected solely by serotype, are diarrheogenic. Both institutional and community outbreaks caused by enteropathogenic *E. coli* continue to be recognized. Pathognomonic histologic findings have been described in both animal models and in biopsy specimens obtained from infants with diarrhea caused by enteropathogenic *E. coli* strains O119 and O125.

The role of enteropathogenic *E. coli* as a cause of endemic sporadic diarrheal disease in the community remains controversial. The predilection of enteropathogenic *E. coli* diarrheal disease to occur in very young infants is a striking feature. Reservoirs of infection that have been suggested include infants and young children with either clinical or asymptomatic infection; asymptomatic adult carriers, including mothers and persons handling infants; and animals. Modes of transmission may include direct contact from contaminated hands, contaminated weaning foods or formula, and fomites. Identification of the bacterial products responsible for the enteroadhesiveness of enteropathogenic *E. coli* may lead to the development of immunogens for oral immunization. Research also is centering on attempts to prepare attenuated strains for use in live vaccines for oral administration.

▶ Enteropathogenic *E. coli,* the first identified *E. coli* causing enteric disease, later were discredited as a cause of human illness because the enteropathogenic *E. coli* serotypes were found in as many asymptomatic as symptomatic patients. Careful clinical investigation has now clearly documented their importance as agents of disease, especially in the infant younger than age 1 year. Pathogenesis appears to depend on a unique adherence mechanism and the production of a toxin similar to *Shigella* toxin (see the paper by O'Brien et al., abstract 1–16), suggesting potential targets for vaccine development. Meanwhile, the etiologic workup of acute diarrhea in the young infant should include serotyping *E. coli* for enteropathogenic *E. coli* strains.—G.K.

Sporadic Cases of Hemorrhagic Colitis Associated With *Escherichia coli* 0157:H7: Clinical, Epidemiologic, and Bacteriologic Features
Chik H. Pai, Rhonda Gordon, Harry V. Sims, and Lawrence E. Bryan (Calgary, Alberta)
Ann. Intern. Med. 101:738–742, December 1984   1–15

Escherichia coli 0157:H7 now is recognized as a cause of hemorrhagic colitis, producing severe crampy abdominal pain, watery and then grossly bloody diarrhea, and little or no fever. The organism was isolated from 19 (15%) of 125 patients with grossly bloody diarrhea seen in a 6-month period in 1983 at 3 hospitals in Calgary; it was also found in 1 sibling with nonbloody diarrhea. There was no apparent clustering of patients geographically or in time. Illness appeared to be associated with the consumption of hamburgers by 15 patients. It usually was self-limited, but hemolytic-uremic syndrome developed in 3 children shortly after the onset of diarrhea; another had *Clostridium difficile* toxin-associated diarrhea after treatment with antibiotics for urinary tract infection. The organism was excreted only briefly in the stools of adults, but for a longer time in children. All of the isolates produced verotoxin. Cytotoxic activity was present in stool filtrates. All of the isolates were susceptible in vitro to all antimicrobials used routinely to test for gram-negative organisms.

Hemorrhagic colitis caused by *E. coli* 0157:H7 may be more frequent than previously thought, suggesting that patients with grossly bloody diarrhea be promptly evaluated for infection by this organism. The detection of free cytotoxin in stool filtrates may be an effective diagnostic procedure. Early stool collection is important. Prompt identification of *E. coli* 0157:H7 requires an antiserum for serotyping, but no such antiserum is available commercially. In the present study, a crude anti-0157 serum prepared in rabbit was fairly specific. Hemolytic-uremic syndrome is a frequent complication of hemorrhagic colitis in children, making an etiologic diagnosis especially important. Invasive diagnostic procedures are not necessary when this usually self-limited illness is the cause of excessive blood in the stools.

▶ This is yet another form of *E. coli* diarrhea, distinct from the enterotoxigenic, enteropathogenic, invasive, and adherent forms already described. In a patient with bloody diarrhea, a search for the organism can be undertaken. We know now, however, that many patients present without gross blood in the stool. Since there is no simple isolation procedure that distinguishes this organism from other *E. coli* in the intestinal flora, many cases are bound to be missed. Recently, we have come to recognize the important association with this infection and the hemolytic-uremic syndrome, adding importance to this organism, especially since it seems to be acquired through our food chain.—S.G.

Shiga-Like Toxin-Converting Phages From *Escherichia coli* Strains That Cause Hemorrhagic Colitis or Infantile Diarrhea
Alison D. O'Brien, John W. Newland, Steven F. Miller, Randall K. Holmes, H. Williams Smith, and Samuel B. Formal
Science 226:694–696, Nov. 9, 1984   1–16

Toxin-converting bacteriophages are released spontaneously from *Escherichia coli* strains, and some strains of *E. coli* produce a cytotoxin that seems identical to the *Shigella* dysenteriae 1-like (Shiga-like) toxin. The *E. coli* 0157:H7 strain 933, which causes hemorrhagic diarrhea and produces large amounts of Shiga-like toxin, harbors 2 different toxin-converting phages, 933J and 933W. *Escherichia coli* K-12 acquired the ability to produce a high titer of Shiga-like toxin after lysogenization by either of the bacteriophages isolated from the 0157:H7 strain. One of these phages, 933J, is closely related to another Shiga-like toxin-converting phage from an *E. coli* 026 isolate associated with infantile diarrhea, with respect to morphology, virion polypeptides, DNA restriction fragments, lysogenic immunity, and heat stability. However, there were differences in host range.

A family of Shiga-like toxin-converting phages apparently exists in nature. There is preliminary evidence that phages belonging to the family of Shiga-like toxin-converting phages also are present in some strains of *E. coli*. How the converting phages control production of Shiga-like toxin remains to be established. Converting phages could contain either the toxin structural genes or the regulatory elements that act on toxin structural genes already present in the host bacterium. The strong correlation between production of high levels of Shiga-like toxin and the ability of *E. coli* to produce bloody diarrhea or hemorrhagic colitis in people emphasizes the potential medical relevance of the Shiga-like toxin-converting phages.

▶ Strains of *E. coli* that cause infantile diarrhea (enteropathogenic *E. coli*) and the recently described hemorrhagic colitis due to *E. coli* 0157:H7 also produce a toxin similar or identical to *Shigella* (Shiga) toxin. Toxin production appears to be a function of the presence of a phage in the bacterium which carries necessary genes similar to the well known story of *Corynebacterium diphtheriae*. If this phage has a wide host range, more clinical examples of culture-negative Shiga-like disease may result. For the future, assay for toxin may become a critical diagnostic test.—G.K.

Aeromonas hydrophila and *Plesiomonas shigelloides* as Causes of Intestinal Infections
Scott D. Holmberg and J.J. Farmer III (Centers for Disease Control, Atlanta)
Rev. Infect. Dis. 6:633–639, Sept.–Oct. 1984   1–17

Aeromonas and *Plesiomonas* are gram-negative facultative anaerobic bacilli of the family Vibrionaceae, organisms ubiquitous in fresh and brackish water in the United States. *Aeromonas hydrophila* and *Plesiomonas shigelloides* have been isolated more often in persons with diarrhea, and the bulk of evidence reviewed supports their ability to cause gastrointestinal disease in healthy persons. Pathogenesis of disease due to these noninvasive bacteria is unclear but may involve an enterotoxin. *Aeromonas hydrophila* produces at least one hemolysin, but little is known of *Plesiomonas* toxins.

Gastroenteritis from these organisms usually is mild and self-limited, with watery, nonbloody diarrhea. Extraintestinal complications including sepsis can occur in immunosuppressed patients, malignancy, or patients with hepatobiliary disease. Various selective mediums for growth of these organisms have been described. Healthy persons do not routinely require antimicrobial therapy, only replacement of fluids and electrolytes lost in diarrheal stools. Antimicrobials are reserved for patients with chronic diarrhea, those who are seriously ill, and those at risk of extraintestinal complications. Tetracycline, trimethoprimsulfamethoxazole, chloramphenicol, and aminoglycosides have been consistently active against *A. hydrophila* in vitro. Isolates of *P. shigelloides* have been resistant to penicillin, ampicillin, and carbenicillin.

The emergence of multiple drug-resistant *A. hydrophila* in aquatic reservoirs may be a future hazard. Further work is needed to determine sources of infection and risk factors for illness, and to monitor the possible emergence of drug-resistant strains.

▶ Two more organisms to add to the list of bona fide enteric pathogens.—G.K.

Non-01 *Vibrio cholerae* Gastroenteritis in Northern California
Surinder Kumar, Michael L. Shorenstein, Nicholas Niven, and Miguel Stroe (Santa Cruz, Calif.)
West. J. Med. 140:783–784, May 1984   1–18

Cholera rarely occurs in the United States, and when diagnosed, a history of foreign travel or of ingestion of raw seafood is usually elicited. A patient in northern California had a non-01 *Vibrio cholerae* infection with a classic cholera-like syndrome, but no history of eating raw seafood or of traveling abroad.

Male, 18, a surfer, complained of nausea, vomiting, diarrhea, and abdominal cramps of 10 days' duration. There was no history of ingesting raw seafood or of foreign travel. The patient was afebrile and severely dehydrated with postural hypotension. Analysis of serum electrolyte levels indicated anion-gap metabolic acidosis and prerenal azotemia. Diarrhea workup was initiated. Stool specimens were light green and watery, but findings on microscopic examination were negative. Sigmoidoscopy showed mild mucosal congestion. Culture of stool specimens yielded a vibrio on thiosulfate-citrate bile salt medium; this organism was later classified as non-01 cholera. Fluid replacement was started intravenously with 24-hour infusion volumes over the first 3 days totaling 7,765 ml, 9,800 ml, and 10,800 ml, respectively, with concomitant outputs of 5,900 ml, 7,740 ml, and 7,800 ml, mostly in the form of massive diarrhea. Doxycycline was administered in an oral dose of 100 mg every 12 hours. Recovery was uneventful. Non-01 *V. cholerae* was isolated from the sea water where the patient surfed and from 2 nearby freshwater creeks as well.

This case report describes an unusual exposure to *V. cholerae* related to offshore surfing near an area of sewage effluent. Non-01 *V. cholerae* gastroenteritis, although rare in the United States, is increasingly being recognized as a clinical entity that can produce an acute diarrheal syndrome similar to classic *V. cholerae* or *V. parahaemolyticus* gastroenteritis.

▶ Since 1978 the United States has become one of the endemic nations for cholera. Typical *Vibrio cholerae* 01, Biotype E1 Tor, has become established along the Gulf of Mexico coast and cases have occurred regularly. Non-01 *V. cholerae* are also found in bays and estuaries, and cause a mild diarrheal disease associated with eating raw oysters from contaminated waters. This patient is unusual because of the clinical presentation of cholera gravis with a non-01 cholera vibrio and the lack of an epidemiologic exposure except for surfing. In view of the increasing number of vibrios associated with human disease, clinical microbiology laboratories may need to upgrade their ability to isolate and identify these organisms (for an excellent review see Morris, Jr., J.G., and Black, R.E.: *N. Engl. J. Med.* 312:343–350, 1985).—G.K.

Infections With *Campylobacter jejuni* and *Campylobacter*-like Organisms in Homosexual Men
Thomas C. Quinn, Steven E. Goodell, Cynthia Fennell, San-Pin Wang, Michael D. Schuffler, King K. Holmes, and Walter E. Stamm (Seattle)
Ann. Intern. Med. 101:187–192, August 1984   1–19

Homosexual men are predisposed to intestinal infections because of specific sexual practices and exposure to many sexual partners within a community of men in whom several enteric pathogens are hyperendemic, and in some because of acquired immunodeficiency. Homosexual men attending a sexually transmitted diseases clinic were studied to determine the prevalence, clinical manifestations, and histopathologic features of *Campylobacter* infections among them. Included, were 158 homosexual men with intestinal symptoms suggestive of proctitis, proctocolitis, or enteritis, and, as controls, 75 asymptomatic homosexual men, 75 heterosexual men, and 75 heterosexual women.

Campylobacter jejuni was isolated in 6% of symptomatic homosexual men and in 3% of asymptomatic homosexual men (table). *Campylobacter*-like organisms were isolated from 16% of symptomatic homosexual men

Isolation of Campylobacter Species and Campylobacter-Like Organisms
From Homosexual Men With and Patients Without Gastrointestinal
Tract Symptoms Attending a Sexually Transmitted Disease Clinic

Patients with Positive Cultures

	Symptomatic Homosexual Men ($n = 158$)	Asymptomatic Homosexual Men ($n = 75$)	Asymptomatic Heterosexual Men ($n = 75$) and Women ($n = 75$)
		n	
C. jejuni	10	2	0*
C. fetus fetus	1	0	0
Campylobacter-like organisms	26†	6	0‡
Type 1	18	6	0
Type 2	4	0	0
Type 3	1	0	0
Untyped	3	0	0

*$P = .004$, Fisher's exact test, comparing prevalence of *C. jejuni* in homosexual men with that in heterosexual men and women.

†$P = .05$, Fisher's exact test (1 tail), comparing prevalence of *Campylobacter*-like organisms in symptomatic homosexual men and in asymptomatic homosexual men.

‡$P = .001$, Fisher's exact test, comparing prevalence of *Campylobacter*-like organisms in symptomatic and asymptomatic homosexual men with that in heterosexual men and women.

(Courtesy of Quinn, T.C., et al.: Ann. Intern. Med. 101:187–192, August 1984.)

and 8% of the asymptomatic homosexual men. In the symptomatic group, additional pathogens caused anorectal or intestinal infections in 50% of those with *C. jejuni* infections and in 69% of those with *Campylobacter*-like infections. The sexual practice of anilinctus was significantly greater among men infected with *Campylobacter* species (10 of 13) or *Campylobacter*-like organisms (23 of 31) than among men without enteric infections. Infections with *C. jejuni* and *Campylobacter*-like organisms were usually associated with symptoms such as diarrhea, abdominal cramps, tenesmus, and hematochezia, as well as signs of proctocolitis (e.g., mucosal ulcerations and bleeding) seen on sigmoidoscopy, increased numbers of leukocytes in rectal smears, acute nonspecific inflammatory changes seen in rectal biopsy specimens, and a serum antibody response to the infecting organism.

The findings suggest that *Campylobacter*-like organisms may cause proctocolitis in some homosexual men; however, other infectious causes of proctocolitis are likely. Infections with these organisms are usually associated with signs and symptoms of acute proctocolitis with acute nonspecific rectal inflammation identified in the biopsy specimen.

▶ These *Campylobacter*-like organism are undoubtedly missed by most hospital microbiology laboratories because of at least 2 distinct characteristics; they are extremely fastidious, and they require immediate, direct plating for optimal recovery. Many of the *Campylobacter* culture media contain cephalothin which inhibits these organisms. In addition, these strains do not grow at 42 C which is used in some laboratories for preferential growth of *C. jejuni*. Because they are fastidious and prefer a microaerophilic environment, early discarding of the culture or relatively aerobic conditions may also interdict routine isolation of these *Campylobacter*-like organisms. Another issue concerning the virulence of these organisms is "the company they keep," since other pathogens often are present in the same fecal specimen. Indeed, 69% of patients with *Campylobacter*-like organisms has other recognizable pathogens and who knows how many unrecognized pathogens in the same stool sample. This is an intriguing report that deserves further study.—S.G.

Typing Scheme for *Clostridium difficile:* Its Application in Clinical and Epidemiologic Studies
Soad Tabaqchali, Diane Holland, Sheila O'Farrell, and Robert Silman (St. Bartholomew's Hosp., London)
Lancet 1:935–938, Apr. 28, 1984.   1–20

Clostridium difficile is well known to be the primary cause of pseudomembranous colitis and antibiotic-associated colitis. There are several reports of clusters of such cases in hospitals. However, the important questions of whether cross-infection occurs and if patients acquire the organism from the hospital environment, are still unanswered because a suitable system for typing this organism is lacking. A bacteriophage typing scheme is being developed by Sell et al. Wüst et al. have applied various existing methods used in the typing of other bacterial species to investigate strains obtained from a hospital outbreak of diarrhea caused by *C. difficile*. The authors have developed a method based on the incorporation of sulfur-35-labeled methionine into bacterial proteins and their separation by sodium dodecylsulfate-polyacrylamide gel electrophoresis (SDS-PAGE). This procedure gives rise to patterns of radiolabeled proteins which can be visualized on autoradiography.

In all, 250 strains of *C. difficile* were isolated from patients and the environment of 4 hospitals; 170 strains from St. Bartholomew's Hospital, 44 strains from Whipps Cross Hospital, London, derived mainly from routine fecal specimens, 20 selected strains from Birmingham General Hospital, and 16 strains from Addenbrooke's Hospital, Cambridge. Twelve *Clostridium* species were investigated with the patterns of bacterial proteins from each being distinct. Among the 250 strains of *C. difficile* examined by this method, there were 9 distinct groups: group X was the most common (83 strains), but groups A, B, C, D, and E were also present in high numbers; groups W, Y, and Z were much less common. There were only 5 strains that did not fall within any of the groups. Therefore, 98% of the strains investigated could be placed within the 9 standard groups.

In investigating the outbreaks of antibiotic-associated diarrhea in the oncoogy and orthopedic wards in St. Bartholomew's Hospital, the authors showed for the first time that the same strain was isolated from patients and their environment. This finding provides strong evidence that there is cross-infection between patients and that the organism is hospital-acquired. It also emphasizes that *C. difficile* is an infectious agent and isolation precautions should be instituted, particularly in areas where patients are at risk. Closure of the oncology and orthopedic wards in St. Bartholomew's Hospital was enforced to ensure decontamination. The finding that certain groups (X and E) were associated with outbreaks of pseudomembranous and antibiotic-associated colitis, whereas others (A, B, C, and D) were isolated mainly from mothers and newborn infants, suggests that certain strains may have greater virulence. Further studies are necessary to understand the discrepancy between the symptomless carriage of *C. difficile* in infants and the devastating results of pseudomembranous colitis.

▶ The availability of a typing scheme for *C. difficile* makes it possible to study the epidemiology and virulence of this organism. It appears that certain strains predominate in the hospital environment, whereas other strains, perhaps less virulent, are found in asymptomatic carriers. Beside the specific information about this organism, the described method provides an important tool for investigating epidemiology and virulence of several other important pathogens for which current typing methods are either unavailable or cumbersome.—S.G.

Percutaneous Aspiration and Drainage for Suspected Abdominal Infection
Timothy L. Pruett, Ori D. Rotstein, Jeffrey Crass, Mathis P. Frick, Anna Flohr, and Richard L. Simmons (Univ. of Minnesota)
Surgery 96:731–737, October 1984   1–21

Eighty-four patients underwent computed tomography (CT)–guided percutaneous aspiration (PCA) or percutaneous drainage (PCD) in 1981–1984. Fifty-five patients who were suspected on clinical grounds of having an infected fluid collection had a total of 66 procedures. The PCA with a 22-gauge needle was followed by catheter insertion for drainage using a modified Seldinger technique. In 5 cases a catheter was not placed because the site aspirated was too thick to be drained. A 8.3 F pigtail catheter was used in most cases. Contrast sinography was performed before gravity drainage was instituted. The catheters usually were irrigated 2–3 times daily with sterile saline, but antibiotic instillation was not routinely performed.

Only 3 patients had a noninfectious cause for an abdominal fluid collection. A positive diagnosis was not made in 11% of 66 attempts at diagnostic aspiration. The overall success rate of PCA-PCD was 47% where no operation was necessary. Catheter drainage was maintained for as long as 91 days. Nine patients had more than 1 catheter placed. Solid organ abscesses and collections just below the fascia were most successfully treated. Simple pancreatic pseudocysts were successfully treated if drainage continued until the cavity was totally obliterated. Five other patients were palliated by PCD. All but 1 of 26 simple, well-defined, nonfungal collections without enteric communication were totally cured by PCA-PCD. The reasons for failure are listed in the table. Two patients required operation for bleeding caused by transhepatic passage of the needle or catheter.

Percutaneous aspiration-drainage has an important role in the manage-

---

REASONS FOR FAILURE OF PCA/D

Cause of failure	Cases
Organized hematoma or retroperitoneal phlegmon	10
Enteric fistula	9
Fungal infection—not localized or too thick	9
Infected tumor	5*
Bleeding	2
Recurrence	2*
Total	37

*Same patient.
(Courtesy of Pruett, T.L., et al.: Surgery 96:731–737, October 1984.)

---

ment of abdominal infections. The diagnostic yield is high, and excessive morbidity has not resulted from catheter placement for 1–2 days. A catheter can be left in place until the potential space is obliterated if good drainage occurs and there is no enteric source contaminating the space. An abscess fed by a leaking viscus can be controlled if it can be converted to a low output, narrow tract enterocutaneous fistula.

► This paper notes a high failure rate (over 50%) of percutaneous drainage, which is somewhat higher than other reports. The reason is probably due to case selection since over half of the patients in this series had a noninfectious cause for the abdominal collection. In fact, their results with bacterial infections were rather good. The lesson is that this procedure works very well for patients with bacterial intra-abdominal abscess, but less well for other types of intra-abdominal lesions.—S.G.

Risk of Infection After Penetrating Abdominal Trauma

Ronald Lee Nichols, Jeffrey W. Smith, Daniel B. Klein, Donald D. Trunkey, Ronald H. Cooper, Michael F. Adinolfi, and John Mills
N. Engl. J. Med. 311:1065–1070, Oct. 25, 1984   1–22

The risk factors involved in the development of infection in patients operated on for abdominal trauma are not well understood. A prospective study of these factors was undertaken in a series of 145 patients admitted with penetrating abdominal trauma and gastrointestinal perforation distal to the duodenum in 1979–1982. Patients received either 2 gm of cefoxitin intravenously every 6 hours and placebo given intravenously every 8 hours, or 600 mg of clindamycin given intravenously every 6 hours and 1.7 mg/kg of body weight of gentamicin given intravenously every 8 hours in a double-blind design. The treatment groups were similar in age, sex, and extent of injury.

The incidence and types of infectious complications were similar in the two treatment groups. About one fifth of the patients in both groups were infected. Major trauma-related infections occurred in 9% of the patients in both groups. Hospitalization was significantly prolonged by infection in both treatment groups. Adverse reactions to treatment also were comparably frequent in the two groups. The factors associated with postoperative infection included ostomy formation at operation, shock at admission, number of intra-abdominal organs involved, amount of blood or blood products required at operation, and age of patient. The severity of injury correlated well with the risk of postoperative infection developing.

Comparable results were obtained with cefoxitin alone and combined clindamycin and gentamicin treatment in patients with penetrating abdominal trauma and gastrointestinal perforation in this study. The risk of infection depends chiefly on whether soilage of the peritoneum has occurred. In such cases the risk increases with the severity of trauma, increasing age, and presence of left colon injury.

► The two antibiotic regimens, cefoxitin alone or clindamycin and gentamicin, perform equally well in this group of severely injured patients. This point has been established previously by other groups. The importance of this paper, however, is the identification of risk factors that predict outcome. The "modified trauma index score" proposed by these authors is somewhat different from the schema suggested by Dellinger et al. abstract 1–24. I suspect that either scoring system would be useful as a predictor. The important point is that patients entered into such a trial should be assessed with regard to severity whenever conclusions are to be drawn relating to intervention strategies.— S.G.

Intraleukocytic Sequestration as a Cause of Persistent *Staphylococcus aureus* Peritonitis in Continuous Ambulatory Peritoneal Dialysis
Brian P. Buggy, Dennis R. Schaberg, and Richard D. Swartz (Univ. of Michigan)
Am. J. Med. 76:1035–1040, June 1984   1–23

Peritoneal infection is a serious limitation to continuous ambulatory peritoneal dialysis. Four recent patients had peritonitis caused by *Staphylococcus aureus,* which either persisted or rapidly relapsed after the cessation of intraperitoneal therapy with vancomycin or cephalothin and tobramycin. Four more recent patients with *S. aureus* peritonitis and persistently cloudy dialysate, abdominal pain, and dialysate leukocytosis after 4 to 6 days of intraperitoneal treatment with vancomycin and tobramycin were changed to vancomycin-rifampin therapy, and promptly responded clinically and bacteriologically.

In 2 of the initial patients, the peritoneal dialysis effluent was cultured before and after the addition of lysostaphin, an enzyme that lyses only extracellular staphylococci. Most bacteria in the effluent survived this treatment in both instances, suggesting that viable organisms survived within polymorphonuclear leukocytes in the peritoneal fluid. Decreased polymorphonuclear leukocyte bactericidal activity was demonstrated in the effluent. Increased growth occurred when 95% of the polymorphonuclear cells in the effluent were still viable. The response to rifampin supports the sequestration of viable staphylococci within polymorphonuclear leukocytes, since this drug readily penetrates these cells. The organism was sensitive to the antibiotics initially used in all 8 cases.

Intraleukocytic sequestration of *S. aureus* was the apparent direct cause of persistent peritonitis in these patients. There was no evidence of the catheter itself or an intra-abdominal abscess being responsible. A defect in macrophage function might also be a factor. Rifampin may be useful when *S. aureus* causes persistent peritonitis despite treatment with the usual antistaphylococcal antibiotics.

▶ What is it that permits some microorganisms to thrive in the unusually hostile intracellular environment of phagocytes and what strategies can we devise to eliminate microorganisms from this protected environment? These are two exceedingly important areas in infectious diseases which deserve intensive investigation. In this paper, the authors were faced with 4 patients undergoing continuous ambulatory peritoneal dialysis whose intraperitoneal *S. aureus* infections were not cured by vancomycin or cephalothin and tobramycin therapy. Since *S. aureus* is one of the pathogens that can persist intracellulary, the strategy of introducing a bioactive antibiotic into the infected host cell to overcome this microbial advantage was employed. Rifampin, which accumulates in polymorphonuclear leukocytes probably by its lipid solubility, was added to the therapeutic regimen and the patients were cured. While this observation does not prove that it was the ability of the rifampin to penetrate polymorphonuclear leukocytes that made the difference, enthusiasm continues to be generated about modifying the intracellular environment in order to tip the balance in favor of the host cell. A recent paper (Sibley, L.D., et al.: *Nature* 315:416–419, 1985) suggests that another modification of the intracellular environment (e.g., the pH in the microorganism containing vacuole) may be important to the intracellular survival of *Toxoplasma gondii*. Stay tuned.—M.K.

Surgical Infection Stratification System for Intra-Abdominal Infection: Multicenter Trial

E. Patchen Dellinger, Margaret J. Wertz, Jonathan L. Meakins, Joseph S. Solomkin, Maria D. Allo, Richard J. Howard, and Richard L. Simmons
Arch. Surg. 120:21–29, January 1985   1–24

A surgical infection stratification (SIS) system combining an anatomical category and an acute physiologic score (APS) has been proposed to compare treatment groups objectively in trials. The system was applied to 187 patients treated for established intra-abdominal infection at 5 centers in North America. The patients had proved abscess or peritonitis arising from the stomach or duodenum, small or large bowel, or appendix or representing postoperative complications. The APS reflects the deviation from normal of 33 routinely determined laboratory variables or physical findings.

Overall mortality was 24%. The rate of "successful" treatment with a single operation and a single course of antimicrobial therapy was 48%. Four fifths of deaths occurred in the presence of infection. The best predictors of survival or death were the APS, malnutrition, and patient age. The APS was clearly the most important predictive variable, followed by malnutrition. Eight-four percent of predictions of survival or death were correct. *Escherichia coli* and *Bacteroides fragilis* were the most frequent isolates from operative cultures. The average hospital period for surviving patients was 30 days.

The relatively simple SIS system can be applied to patients with intra-abdominal infection in multicenter studies. Severity of illness, malnutrition, and age are more important than the anatomical origin of infection in determining the outcome in these cases. The SIS system is expected to help improve diagnostic and therapeutic approaches to intra-abdominal infection.

▶ This is an important paper since it proposes a unified scoring system for judging risk factors and outcome in patients with intra-abdominal infections. Only by using such a scoring system can the variables in this condition be assessed with regard to various interventions such as antibiotics or other treatment modalities. Some criticisms of their statistical approach were included in the commentary accompanying the paper. In addition, the requirement to assess 33 variables places a burden on the surgeon unless he has an experienced research nurse to record these entries. Finally, the presence of shock on the first day seems to be a strong predictor, although other factors clearly are important. If the paper had contained a table of odds ratios, it would have been easier for readers to interpret the relative importance of each of the variables. These issues notwithstanding, this paper is a significant contribution to the vexing assessment of clinical trials of intra-abdominal sepsis.—S.G.

Genitourinary

Bacteriuria in the Catheterized Patient: What Quantitative Level of Bacteriuria is Relevant?
Randall P. Stark and Dennis G. Maki (Univ. of Wisconsin, Madison)
N. Engl. J. Med. 311:560–564, Aug. 30, 1984   1–25

The studies of Kass indicated that a noncatheterized patient with more than 10^5 organisms per milliliter of clean-voided urine is likely to continue to have the organism in similar or higher concentration in a culture obtained a day later. The present study attempted to determine the critical concentration of organisms in a single urine culture from a catheterized patient that will predictably persist or increase in subsequent cultures without intercurrent suppressive antimicrobial therapy. A total of 110 adults, each of whom had an indwelling catheter inserted in a hospital, were assessed serially for an average of 7 consecutive days. Mean age was 55 years. Most patients were being monitored after operation or because of an acute life-threatening illness. Most had risk factors for nosocomial

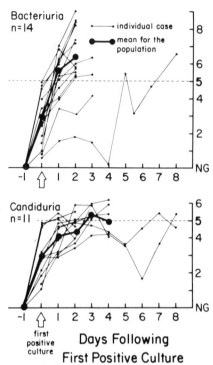

Fig 1–1.—Rate of progression of bacteriuria and candiduria in 25 catheterized patients once any microorganisms were detectable in a urine culture. The numbers on the ordinate are the logs of the number of organisms per milliliter. Analysis was restricted to the 25 evaluable cases of low-level catheter-associated bacteriuria ($<10^5$ organisms per milliliter), 24 of which showed progression to high-level bacteriuria ($>10^5$ organisms per milliliter). It is apparent that when any organisms appeared in catheter urine, low-level bacteriuria progressed very rapidly to levels exceeding 10^5 organisms per milliliter in 12 of the 14 cases within 2 days. Candiduria progressed less rapidly. In 9 of 11 cases, a concentration exceeding 10^5 organisms per milliliter was reached within 3 days. Progression in 12 of 24 cases overall occurred during antimicrobial therapy, including 9 of the 11 cases of candiduria. (Courtesy of Stark, R.P., and Maki, D.G.: N. Engl. J. Med. 311:560–564, Aug. 30, 1984. Reprinted by permission of *The New England Journal of Medicine*.)

urinary tract infection. Two thirds of the patients eventually received systemic antimicrobial therapy.

Bacteriuria was identified in 51 patients, and 34 had high-level bacteriuria with more than 10^5 organisms per milliliter. In 10 instances, the initial culture showed high-level bacteriuria. Low-level bacteriuria or candiduria progressed to high levels in 96% of the instances, usually within 3 days of initial culture, in the absence of suppressive antimicrobial therapy. Only 27% of cases without growth and with at least 2 days of evaluable follow-up progressed to high-level bacteriuria. Bacteriuria progressed very rapidly (Fig 1–1), whereas candiduria progressed less rapidly.

The urinary tract of the catheterized patients is highly vulnerable to infection once small numbers of organisms gain access. Counts considerably less than 10^5/ml may be considered clinically relevant. A criterion of 10^2/ml might be valid if it can be easily and reproducibly detected. Low-level bacteriuria should not be disregarded, although routine treatment is not advisable, particularly for patients who are asymptomatic and not immunosuppressed.

▶ The dangers of generalizing from the specific clinical setting in which data are collected to the general patient population are emphasized in this important paper on the level of "significant bacteruria" in catheterized patients. While 10^5 organisms per milliliter surely provokes higher attention and, usually, the institution of antibiotic therapy, we need to remember that this criterion was largely established in voided "clean catch" urine specimens from healthy women. The extraordinary frequency (>90%) of progression from low-level bacteriuria (10^0–10^4) to high-level bacteriuria (>10^5) in catheterized patients will likely lower the threshold for "significant bacteriuria" in this setting. It also reemphasizes the need to remove urinary catheters at the earliest possible moment and the necessary of attention to detail in handling these systems in order to prevent the introduction of any organisms into the catheter-compromised urinary tract.—M.K.

The Effect of Covert Bacteriuria in Schoolgirls on Renal Function at 18 Years and During Pregnancy
J.M. Davison, M.S. Sprott, and J.B. Selkon
Lancet 2:651–655, Sept. 22, 1984.   1–26

Over a 4-year period, 254 schoolgirls of a population of 13,462 (1.9%) were identified as having covert bacteriuria and 39 (15%) had renal scarring. Ureteric reflux was present in 15% of girls without renal scarring and 46% of those with scarring. The 39 subjects with renal scarring, the "obligatory chemotherapy group" (OCG), received chemotherapy for 2 years, whereas the remaining 215 subjects were randomized to either chemotherapy for 2 years (CG) or "no chemotherapy" (NCG).

At age 18 years, 52 girls of the original study population had satisfactory renal function tests: 10 had been classified as OCG, 20 as CG, and 22 as NCG. The index subjects and 9 controls had negative urine cultures at the time of renal function testing. Fractional reabsorption of glucose (tubular reabsorption divided by filtered load), T/F glucose, was significantly reduced in OCG and NCG girls when compared with controls, whereas other values showed no such difference. There was no time relation between the detection of covert bacteriuria and subsequent development of urinary tract infection (UTI). Occasionally UTI developed without preceding covert bacteriuria having been detected. During pregnancy, 57% of index patients had covert bacteriuria compared with 7% of the control group (C1) and 8% of the entire hospital population (5,450 maternity admissions per year).

The average interval between testing at age 18 years and conception was 3.8 years across the three index groups. All patients showed a rise in glomerular filtration rate during pregnancy. There were no differences between the groups in the prepregnancy and postpartum values for insulin and 24-hour creatinine clearance. All groups had greater 24-hour glucose excretion during pregnancy. During pregnancy T/F glucose decreased in all index groups and in the C1 group but decreased significantly only in OCG and NCG subjects. The T/F glucose values in OCG and NCG subjects were significantly lower than in the C1 group, whereas during nonpregnant states these values were significantly lower only in OCG subjects.

There was no significant difference in the frequency of pregnancy-induced hypertension between index pregnancies and control pregnancies.

Infants of index cases did not differ significantly from those of controls in mean gestational age at delivery, mean birth weight, and incidence of preterm birth.

Five-year follow-up of schoolgirls indicated that covert bacteriuria did not lead to progressive renal damage even in the absence of prophylactic chemotherapy. Continued follow-up showed that these subjects are more likely to have covert bacteriuria during pregnancy whether or not chemotherapy had been given when they were schoolgirls. Untreated patients had smaller increments in glomerular filtration rate, reduced fractional reabsorption of glucose, and had more than the usual degree of glycosuria during pregnancy. It is concluded that a 2-year course of prophylactic chemotherapy given to bacteriuric schoolgirls may allow the kidneys to develop the capacity to cope with the enhanced demands of pregnancy and may prevent subclinical renal damage. However, this advantage of prophylactic chemotherapy is only unmasked by the physiologic demands of pregnancy, and the incidence of UTI during pregnancy is unaltered.

▶ The long-term follow-up of young girls with covert bacteriuria continues to demonstrate that renal function is only minimally different between those receiving long-term (2-year) prophylactic antibiotics and those receiving no prophylaxis. However, the propensity of girls with a history of covert bacteriuria to develop bacteriuria during pregnancy remains high and warrants close monitoring of this population.—M.K.

Virulence-Associated Traits in *Escherichia coli* Causing First and Recurrent Episodes of Urinary Tract Infection in Children With or Without Vesicoureteral Reflux
Helena Lomberg, Mikael Hellström, Ulf Jodal, Hakon Leffler, Knut Lincoln, and Catharina Svanborg Edén (Univ. of Göteborg)
J. Infect. Dis. 150:561–569, October 1984   1–27

Vesicoureteral reflux is among the host factors that predispose to recurrent pyelonephritis in children, but reflux appears to compensate for virulence of *Escherichia coli* in these patients. Virulence-associated properties of 606 urinary isolates from 174 children who had urinary tract infection were related to grade II or more severe reflux and to the P_1 blood group phenotype, a marker of host susceptibility. The study group included 68 girls with at least two episodes of acute pyelonephritis and 19 patients with recurrent cystitis. Other girls had a history of asymptomatic bacteriuria without symptomatic infections. Eighty-four healthy girls with no history of urinary tract infection were also studied.

The frequencies of reflux were 47% in patients with recurrent pyelonephritis, 21% in those with recurrent cystitis, and 14% in girls with asymptomatic bacteriuria. The P_1 blood group phenotype was prevalent in all groups, including the healthy controls. A high proportion of *E. coli* strains causing acute pyelonephritis in children without reflux expressed resistance to serum killing, hemolysin production, and adhesive capacity. These traits were significantly less frequent in isolates from children who had both pyelonephritis and reflux, and non-*E. coli* isolates were more frequent in this group. The same findings were obtained in the groups with cystitis and asymptomatic bacteriuria. The distribution of virulence factors could not be related to the P blood group phenotype.

Vesicoureteral reflux is a determinant of the level of infection and of the bacterial properties required for pyelonephritis to occur. Attempts to prevent or treat urinary tract infection by interfering with "virulent" organisms may be less helpful in patients with recurrent pyelonephritis and reflux, who are most likely to develop renal scarring. Data on patient populations are essential for a meaningful approach to pathogenic mechanisms in urinary tract infection.

▶ Urinary tract infection represents a triad of factors: individual host susceptibility, availability of bacteria for retrograde contamination, and virulence properties of the invading microorganism. In normal individuals, the latter two factors predominate. Children with vesicoureteral reflux clearly shift the balance to host factors. The implication is that successful management of the underlying host problem may be the only way to improve the outlook for these children.—S.G.

Role of Fimbriated *Escherichia coli* in Urinary Tract Infections in Adult Women: Correlation With Localization Studies
Robert H. Latham and Walter E. Stamm (Univ. of Washington)
J. Infect. Dis. 149:835–840, June 1984   1–28

A population of 179 adult women with urinary tract infections (UTIs) due to *Escherichia coli* was studied. Twenty-three women with lower urinary tract symptoms were thought to have acute pyelonephritis on the basis of clinical symptoms, 116 were judged to have infection limited to the lower urinary tract, and 40 with documented recurrent infections were asymptomatic at ureteral catheterization.

Escherichia coli strains bearing type 1 fimbriae were encountered in 60% to 70% of patients with pyelonephritis, cystitis, and asymptomatic bacteriuria; there was no significant difference in the proportions of patients in each group. However, 14 (61%) of 23 strains of *E. coli* from patients with pyelonephritis agglutinated human type O erythrocytes in the presence of mannose (MRHA), compared with 27 (23%) of 116 strains from cystitis patients and 8 (20%) of 40 from asymptomatic patients. The MRHA was attributed to the presence of p fimbriae in 41 (84%) of the 49 strains of *E. coli* showing this hemagglutination reaction. Strains of *E. coli* with both type 1 and p fimbriae were recovered from 10 of 22 patients with pyelonephritis, compared with 9 of 111 strains from patients with cystitis and 4 of 38 from patients with asymptomatic bacteriuria.

Of the 23 pyelonephritis infections due to *E. coli*, 17 (74%) were localized to the upper part of the urinary tract, as determined by antibody-coated bacteria (ACB) testing, whereas only 29 (25%) of the 116 strains from cystitis patients were ACB positive. *Escherichia coli* strains from 13 of 46 patients with positive ACB tests possessed p fimbriae, compared with 22 of 93 from patients with ACB-negative infections. Twenty-two of the 40 asymptomatic infections were localized to the upper part of the urinary tract. Two (9%) of the 22 upper UTIs and 4 (22%) of the 18 lower UTIs were caused by p-fimbriated *E. coli.*

Among all patient groups, infection with type 1 fimbriated *E. coli* was unrelated to age or history of previous UTI; these factors were also unrelated to infection with p-fimbriated *E. coli* among patients with acute pyelonephritis and asymptomatic bacteriuria. Among 105 patients with acute lower UTI, the 20 with p-fimbriated *E. coli* were significantly older than the 85 not so infected.

Although p fimbriation appears to be an important virulence factor associated with acute pyelonephritis in adult women, its detection does not seem to be a useful localization test per se. Efforts to prevent these infections should not be directed against this factor alone.

The Diaphragm: An Accomplice in Recurrent Urinary Tract Infections
Larrian Gillespie (Univ. of California, Irvine)
Urology 24:25–30, July 1984   1–29

One hundred-fifty nonparous women, aged 16 to 35 years, referred for culture-proved recurrent urinary tract infections (UTI), were studied. Patients who had had previous vaginal or bladder operations or a history of childhood infections were excluded. Urodynamic evaluation included a water cytometrogram, uroflow determination, residual urine check, and cystoscopy. Patients using a diaphragm were asked to return for a uroflow determination and residual urine check with their diaphragms. To control the somewhat subjective choice of diaphragm fitting by various physicians, the author was fitted by all referring physicians and nurse practitioners whose patients were studied.

Ten physicians and 4 nurse practitioners fitted the author for a diaphragm. Thirteen participants concurred with an 80-mm size, whereas 1 prescribed a 75-mm diaphragm. It was therefore assumed that practitioners were consistent in diaphragm fittings. In 87% of the patients, UTI developed only after they became sexually active; 94% had culture-proved infections within 48 hours after intercourse. The most common method of contraception used by 69% of women was the diaphragm. Birth control pills and intrauterine devices were the other choices. Uroflow studies that used the Endotek voiding-initiating system were performed on all patients as a screening process once they were free from infection. Normal average flow rates of 18 to 20 ml/second were found in all but 4 patients.

The effect of a "properly fitted" diaphragm and a smaller diaphragm on flow rates showed that although flow remained the same, times to peak and average flow were greatly affected. To overcome the obstruction caused by the diaphragm, the bladder must generate a higher pressure before voiding can be initiated, thereby shortening time to peak flow. A diaphragm two sizes smaller does not significantly improve the flow rate nor the time to reach peak flow. Some patients were able to empty to completion. However, this required abdominal strain and double voiding, which they did spontaneously when using the diaphragm. Among 81 women followed for 1 year, the diaphragm was still the method of choice for 74%. Recurrent infections after completion of a urologic evaluation showed 85% of patients to be infection free. Twelve women returned with one or more recurrent culture-proved infections over the year; 3 were aware of breaks in hygiene and prevented further infections.

Changes in both the fitting of diaphragms and their construction could alter the obstruction to the bladder neck. A proposed diaphragm would be U-shaped with a soft anterior Seldinger wire. The stronger coils would fix in position periurethrally; the soft, flexible Seldinger wire portion would not obstruct the bladder neck during voiding. Gynecologists have argued that a smaller diaphragm is less effective. However, the vagina becomes engorged during intercourse so that the penis, which also comes in various sizes, can be snugly fitted against the cervix and the anterior vaginal stimulating zones, such as the Graffenberg spot. More often, the pregnancy rate seen with diaphragms is the result of the "diaphragm in the drawer" syndrome rather than inadequate coverage of the cervix.

Single-Day Treatment With Trimethoprim for Asymptomatic Bacteriuria in the Elderly Patient
Jan Renneberg and Anders Paerregaard (Copenhagen)
J. Urol. 132:934–935, November 1984   1–30

The presumed benign nature of asymptomatic bacteriuria in elderly patients recently has been questioned. A double-blind trial was undertaken to ascertain the value of one-day trimethoprim therapy in elderly hospitalized patients with asymptomatic bacteriuria. Trimethoprim is an inexpensive antimicrobial agent that causes few side effects and has little acquired resistance. Forty consecutive patients, aged 60 years and older, who were asymptomatic for urinary tract infection and had counts of at least 10^5 colonies/ml of urine were entered into the study. Tablets of 100 mg of trimethoprim or a placebo were given twice on one day.

The 20 treated and 20 control patients were comparable demographically and with regard to infecting organisms. No trimethoprim-treated patient had a positive urine culture at 3 days, whereas all placebo-treated patients remained bacteriuric. Seven trimethoprim-treated patients had recurrent bacteriuria after 2 weeks, and 14 had it after 6 weeks. No side effects were noted, and no resistance was observed.

Asymptomatic bacteriuria in elderly persons can be eliminated by single-day treatment with trimethoprim, but relapse is frequent. Long-term clearance of bacteriuria in these patients will require other regimens, possibly continuous low-dose antibiotic therapy or intermittent single-day treatment at 2-week intervals. Further knowledge of the relation between asymptomatic bacteriuria and excess mortality in the elderly patient is needed before rational treatment decisions can be made.

Single-dose Therapy for Cystitis in Women: Comparison of Trimethoprim-Sulfamethoxazole, Amoxicillin, and Cyclacillin

Thomas M. Hooton, Kate Running, and Walter E. Stamm
JAMA 253:387–390, Jan. 18, 1985   1–31

Single-dose treatment of cystitis in nonpregnant women has many advantages including ensured compliance, fewer adverse effects, and lower cost, but few studies have compared the efficacy of different antimicrobials in this setting. A randomized, investigator-blinded comparison of single-dose regimens of trimethoprim-sulfamethoxazole (TMP-SMX), amoxicillin, and cyclacillin was performed in ambulatory nonpregnant women, aged 18 years and older, who presented with symptoms suggestive of acute cystitis but no fever or costovertebral angle tenderness. All had pyuria but no history of urinary tract anomaly. Treatment was with 320 mg of TMP and 1,600 mg of SMX, 3 gm of amoxicillin, or 3 gm of cyclacillin as a single dose. Fifteen subjects were enrolled in each treatment group, and a total of 38 subjects were evaluable.

The outcome of treatment is shown in the table. The cure rate was highest with TMP-SMX therapy when persistent bacteriuria at 2 days and relapse at 2 weeks were taken as evidence of failure. Reinfection was more frequent in the TMP-SMX group. All but 2 of 15 single-dose failure or reinfections were cured by conventional treatment with TMP-SMX or ampicillin. Resistant organisms did not emerge in any group. Two patients had symptomatic evidence of upper tract infection after single-dose therapy. Adverse effects generally were mild and of short duration.

Single-dose treatment of cystitis in unselected women using amoxicillin

OUTCOME OF TREATMENT FOR CYSTITIS WITH SINGLE-DOSE REGIMENS OF TRIMETHOPRIM-SULFAMETHOXAZOLE, AMOXICILLIN, OR CYCLACILLIN

Outcome	Single-Dose Regimens			All Patients n (%)
	TMP-SMZ n (%)	Amoxicillin n (%)	Cyclacillin n(%)	
Initial cure	13 of 13 (100)*	9 of 13 (69)	8 of 12 (67)	30 of 38 (79)
Relapse	2 of 13 (15)	2 of 12 (17)	3 of 10 (30)	7 of 35 (20)
Overall Cure Rate	11 of 13 (85)	6 of 12 (50)	3 of 10 (30)	20 of 35 (57)

*$P = .04$ v cyclacillin
†Patients were not included in the denominator if they were initially cured but missed the second follow-up visit.
‡$P = .01$ v cyclacillin.
(Courtesy of Hooton, T.M., et al.: JAMA 253:387–390, Jan. 18, 1985; copyright 1985, American Medical Association.)

or cyclacillin may result in low cure rates, and ineffective treatment can be followed by acute pyelonephritis. Further studies of single-dose treatment are needed before this approach can be generally adopted.

Aztreonam Compared With Gentamicin for Treatment of Serious Urinary Tract Infections
Fred R. Sattler, James E. Moyer, Margaret Schramm, Jeffrey S. Lombard, and Peter C. Appelbaum (Pennsylvania State Univ.)
Lancet 1:1315–1317, June 16, 1984   1–32

Aztreonam is one of the new class of monobactam antibiotics which inhibits the growth of most Enterobacteriaceae and *Pseudomonas aeruginosa* isolates in vitro, and has the potential to replace aminoglycosides in the treatment of gram-negative infections. Aztreonam and gentamicin were compared in a series of 52 adults with a presumptive diagnosis of urinary tract infection necessitating systemic antibiotic therapy. Thirty-five patients received aztreonam in a dose of 1 gm every 8 hours, whereas 17 received 1 mg/kg gentamicin every 8 hours. If bacteremia was suspected, the doses were raised to 2 gm and 1.7 mg/kg, respectively. Both drugs were given by infusion over 20–30 minutes, or intramuscularly if venous access was inadequate. Treatment was continued for 5–10 days in uncomplicated cases. An open study was conducted in patients with gentamicin-resistant organisms and in those with renal failure.

The 2 treatment groups were comparable in nearly all respects. All aztreonam-treated patients and 82% of the gentamicin group had a favorable microbiologic response. Signs and symptoms cleared in all cases. However, 6 patients treated with aztreonam relapsed after an initial microbiologic response and another 6 cases developed reinfection. In comparison, 1 patient in the gentamicin group relapsed, 4 were reinfected, and 3 failed therapy. Among patients with treatment failure, relapse, or reinfection, 11 of the 12 given aztreonam and 7 of the 8 given gentamicin had anatomical or physiologic urinary tract abnormality. All 11 elderly patients given aztreonam in the open trial were cured. Aztreonam-related toxicity included single cases of phlebitis at the infusion site and *Candida* vaginitis. Seven patients in the aztreonam group and 2 in the gentamicin group had liver function abnormalities. Renal function deteriorated in 4 gentamicin-treated patients. Several aztreonam-treated patients were colonized by group D streptococci, but only 1 required treatment.

Aztreonam was highly effective in the treatment of serious urinary tract infections in this study. The drug is unlikely to be nephrotoxic. Many gentamicin-resistant nosocomial gram-negative bacilli are susceptible to aztreonam. Furthermore, unlike aminoglycosides, the drug remains bactericidal under anaerobic conditions. Superinfection by group D streptococci may be a problem. Theoretic considerations may favor aztreonam over the newer broad-spectrum cephalosporins.

▶ Aztreonam may have several potential advantages over the newer broad spectrum cephalosporins. It lacks cross reactivity to human IgE antibodies against penicillin determinants and should be useful in penicillin-allergic patients. In addition, aztreonam has no significant activity against anaerobic bacteria and should maintain gastrointestinal tract colonization. Moreover, aztreonam is very resistant to plasmid and chromosomially-mediated β-lactamase. Finally, the agent is more active in vitro against *Pseudomonas aeruginosa* than are most third generation cephalosporins.—D.S.

Bacterial Adherence in the Human Ileal Conduit: A Morphological and Bacteriologic Study
Andrew W. Bruce, Gregor Reid, Raphael C. Y. Chan, and J. William Costerton
J. Urol. 132:184–188, July 1984   1–33

Most patients who undergo urinary diversion are reported to have bacteriuria from uropathogens, and a significant number of patients develop renal deterioration that may be indirectly due to infecting bacteria. Review was made of the data on 50 patients who underwent ileal conduit diversion in a 5-year period. All received antibiotics before and for a variable time after the operation. Four patients were studied serially after urinary diversion, and 13 others were studied prospectively to determine the long-term effects of urine flow on bacterial adherence in the ileal conduit. The latter patients had had diversion in the previous 16 years. Twenty-three pathogenic strains isolated from the ileal conduits of 7 patients were examined.

In 84% of the 50 study patients, bacteriuria from a variety of pathogenic organisms developed. Fourteen percent of the patients had clinical evidence of pyelonephritis. Several different pathogens were isolated from the urine. Ultrastructural study of cup biopsy specimens from conduits showed virtually no bacteria adhering to the columnar cells, although gram-positive cocci adhered to keratinized cells from the mucocutaneous junction. The conduit mucus was, however, heavily colonized, eventually with gram-negative bacteria. Large numbers of uropathogens were present long after urinary diversion. Nine of the 23 conduit isolates studied possessed hemagglutinins. All 18 strains attached to uroepithelial cells in vitro, and all 6 *Escherichia coli* strains studied attached to ureteral transitional epithelial cells in vitro.

Upper tract involvement is not infrequent in patients who undergo ileal conduit urinary diversion. Many different pathogens are isolated from conduit urine in these cases. In a number of patients, a nonpathogenic flora develops, and it may be possible to use indigenous bacteria to colonize the mucus biofilm of the ileal conduit, preventing uropathogenic colonization.

▶ The normal intestinal tract apparently has developed protective mechanisms be which its indigenous microflora colonize the mucosal surface, thereby preventing introduction of potential pathogens. This study shows that a similar protective mechanism may exist in an ileal conduit constructed for urinary diversion. The electron micrographs are outstanding. Whether the protective mechanism of mucosal colonization can be artificially manipulated, as suggested by the authors, is another matter. It is certainly worth investigating, but it is not answered in the present study.—S.G.

Clinical and Microbiologic Characterization of Patients With Nonspecific Vaginosis Associated With Motile, Curved Anaerobic Rods

J. L. Thomason, P. C. Schreckenberger, W. N. Spellacy, L. J. Riff, and L. J. LeBeau (Univ. of Illinois, Chicago)
J. Infect. Dis. 149:801–809, May 1984

Mobiluncus
1–34

The role of anaerobic bacteria in patients with nonspecific vaginosis (NSV) has recently been investigated. The authors undertook a study to establish the history, clinical characteristics, and bacteriologic findings of patients with highly motile, curved rods in their vaginal secretions. The vaginal secretions of 20 nonpregnant controls and 21 nonpregnant patients with motile, curved anaerobic rods were cultured for aerobic and nonaero-

CLINICAL CHARACTERISTICS OF PATIENTS WITH AND WITHOUT MOTILE, CURVED ANAEROBIC RODS

Features	Control group ($n = 20$)	CARS* group ($n = 21$)
Clinical history		
Mean age	28.3	30.8
Unmarried	17	18
One sex partner	19	16
Use of contraception	16	14
Previous vaginal infection	11	17
Douche	5	9
Abnormal Pap smear history	1	4
Past history UTI[†]	12	9
Symptoms		
None	20	3[‡]
Length of complaint		
Weeks	0	3
Months	0	6
Years	0	9[‡]
Vulvar pruritis	0	10[‡]
Stains clothing	0	7[‡]
Odor	0	17[‡]
Complaint of discharge		
related to menstrual cycle		
Follicular	0	1
Mid-cycle	0	3
Secretory	0	5
None noted	0	10[‡]
Signs		
Discharge at introitus	4	15[‡]
White discharge	18	5[‡]
Homogenous secretions	1	21[‡]
Foul odor at direct exam	0	20[‡]
Succinate: lactate ratio ≥ 0.4	0	21[‡]
pH > 4.5	0	21[‡]

*Curved anaerobic rods.
†Urinary tract infection.
‡$P < .001$ (probabilities for fourfold contingency table).
(Courtesy of Thomason, J.L., et al.: J. Infect. Dis. 149:801–809, May 1984.)

bic bacteria, *Chlamydia trachomatis,* herpes simplex virus, and *Trichomonas vaginalis.* Extensive histories and physical examinations and microscopic appearances and gas-liquid chromatography patterns of vaginal secretions were compared in the two groups.

The curved, anaerobic, rod-shaped bacteria (CARS) group had constant foul odor associated with discharge. Characteristic physical examination showed homogeneous vaginal secretions at the introitus, a foul odor, pH of higher than 4.5, and a succinate-lactate ratio of at least 0.4 (table). The secretions were characterized by an absence of lactobacilli, numerous highly motile, curved, rod-shaped bacilli, and a greater number of background bacteria than in those of controls. Although lactobacilli were not seen under the microscope, 15 (71%) of the 21 CARS patients were found on culture to be colonized with aerobic lactobacilli. The fourfold greater number of facultative gram-negative bacteria isolated from CARS patients were mostly attributable to *Gardnerella vaginalis.* Anaerobic bacteria were isolated more often from the CARS group ($P < .001$), with increased numbers of *peptococcus, Peptostreptococcus, Propionibacterium,* and *Bacteroides* species.

All patients with motile, curved rods in their vaginal secretions met the clinical criteria of NSV as defined by Pheifer et al., and all had abnormal succinic acid-lactic acid ratios, as defined by Spiegel et al. The high incidence of *G. vaginalis* in this study may be due to use of more selective and differential mediums (HBT agar) for isolation of this bacterium. The characteristic pattern of motility of the organisms, the absence of lactobacilli, and the increased number of background bacteria are pathognomonic microscopic appearances of NSV patients with CARS.

▶ It may be that the etiologic agent of nonspecific vaginosis, or vaginitis depending on your prejudice, may have been found at last. Several authors have noted a highly significant correlation between the presence of this organism and active disease, and it has not been found in healthy women. The story is certainly more attractive than that implicating *G. vaginalis,* the "traditional" pathogen. Many studies have failed to find a difference between isolation of *Gardnerella* from healthy women and those with NSV. In addition, the response to metronidazole speaks more in favor of an obligate anaerobe than *Gardnerella.* Yet, the vaginal flora in these patients is extremely complex, and the burden of proof remains on the adherents of this organism to prove its pathogenicity. Unfortunately, the organism is extremely difficult to isolate from vaginal discharge, as positive cultures can be as low as 20% among specimens in which the organism is observed under the microscope. We are still left with a clinical condition diagnosed by nonspecific criteria and treated with an empiric drug, metronidazole, which seems to be highly effective.—S.G.

Skin and Soft Tissue

Pyomyositis: Report of 18 Cases in Hawaii

Joel D. Brown and Bruce Wheeler (Tripler Army Med. Center, Honolulu)
Arch. Intern. Med. 144:1749–1751, September 1984   1–35

Pyomyositis is rare in temperate climates. The authors describe 18 cases of tropical pyomyositis seen in Honolulu, in the past 10 years. Most patients were young men or boys, although the age range was 5–51 years. Ten patients were natives; 8 had never traveled abroad. Onset of symptoms was acute or subacute (range, 1–42 days). Muscle pain and swelling were present in all cases. A history of recent muscle injury and pyoderma was obtained in 12 (67%) and 13 (72%) patients, respectively. Fever was present in all cases. Tender, swollen muscle was evident; 9 patients had woody hard induration of a muscle or muscle group. A single muscle was infected in 14 (78%) patients. Leukocytosis was common. Pyomyositis mimicked cellulitis, muscle hematoma, appendicitis, thrombophlebitis, or rhabdomyosarcoma. *Staphylococcus aureus* was found in 13 cases and *Streptococcus pyogenes* in 2. Bacteremia occurred in 5 of 17 cases. Drainage and antimicrobial therapy for 1–6 weeks was usually effective; 1 patient died, and another had residual CNS damage.

The pathogenesis of pyomyositis is uncertain. However, nonpenetrating muscle injury and pyoderma are observed in most cases, suggesting that bacteria may invade muscle via the bloodstream or lymphatic system. Pain and swelling may be the only manifestations of early pyomyositis and may mimic a variety of diseases; however, fever, leukocytosis, muscle swelling, and typical woody induration eventually appear. Administration of antimicrobial drugs and drainage of pus are the mainstays of therapy.

Early Recognition of Potentially Fatal Necrotizing Fasciitis: Use of Frozen-Section Biopsy
Ivan Stamenkovic and P. Daniel Lew (Geneva)
N. Engl. J. Med. 310:1689–1693, June 28, 1984   1–36

Necrotizing fasciitis is a rare, often fatal soft tissue infection that may be difficult to recognize clinically at an early stage. Usually nonspecific findings are present after operation, minor trauma, or inadequate care of a cutaneous ulcer or perirectal abscess. A review was made of 19 cases of histologically proved necrotizing fasciitis seen between 1970 and 1983. Six other cases were clinically suspected, but histologic findings were normal. The 12 men and 7 women with a confirmed diagnosis had an average age of 56 years. Roentgenograms showed soft tissue gas in 2 of the 4 patients examined, both of whom had local crepitation. The initiating lesion was a minor cut or abrasion in most cases, usually on the extremity. A pure isolate of group A β-hemolytic streptococci was obtained in 14 cases.

Frozen-section soft tissue biopsy was performed in 14 cases, usually as an incisional biopsy with local anesthesia. Tissue samples at least $10 \times 7 \times 7$ mm were obtained. The diagnosis was made histologically in 8 patients who had immediate operation. In 6 other patients, necrotizing fasciitis was excluded by frozen-section biopsy, and conservative measures were adopted. Mortality from necrotizing fasciitis was 47% but only 1 of the 8 patients with a frozen-section biopsy diagnosis died. Requirements for resection were far greater in patients in whom frozen-section biopsy was not performed. An expectant approach was taken in 5 of these. All 3 patients initially seen with extensive lesions died despite radical surgical debridement.

The rapidity with which necrotizing fasciitis is recognized and treated appropriately is the major prognostic factor. Frozen-section soft tissue biopsy is recommended for early diagnosis. Incisional biopsy is preferable to punch biopsy. The superficial fascia and muscle tissue must be sampled. All lesions consistent with early necrotizing fasciitis should be evaluated in this way.

▶ I have some problems with this paper. No doubt, necrotizing fasciitis is a severe disease which, if unrecognized, can produce a high mortality. However, it is implied that a frozen section biopsy specimen is needed to diagnose it. Others have been able to make this diagnosis by direct inspection of the fascial planes which can be done by making a limited incision over the affected area. If the fascia dissects easily with an inserted finger or a blunt instrument, the diagnosis is established. The appearance of the fascia itself also is characteristic. I am somewhat skeptical of the necessity of including a frozen section beyond visual recognition by a skilled surgeon.

This report is somewhat unusual in that group A *Streptococcus pyogenes* was the pathogen in 14 of the 19 cases, an inordinately high incidence. Vascular disease, an important predisposing factor in most series, was apparently uncommon in their group of patients. Finally, they had a high mortality rate (73%) in the patients not subjected to biopsy and definitive surgical management. Overall, it would seem that a more urgent approach should be adopted in the management of this severe disease. In my view, early clinical recognition and aggressive surgical intervention is more important than concern about a frozen section biopsy.—S.G.

Pasteurella multocida Infections: Report of 34 Cases and Review of the Literature

David J. Weber, John S. Wolfson, Morton N. Swartz, and David C. Hooper (Massachusetts Gen. Hosp., Boston)
Medicine 63:133–154, March 1984   1–37

Pasteurella multocida, a small gram-negative coccobacillus that is part of the normal oral flora of many animals, including the cat and dog, is a major cause of wound infections secondary to animal bites. The findings in 17 cases seen in a 2-year period are summarized in the table. Infections most frequently follow cat bites or scratches and dog bites. Local wound infections from animal bites are the most common human infection caused by *P. multocida*. The most serious infections caused by *P. multocida* are septic arthritis and osteomyelitis. The latter can result from local extension of soft tissue infection or from direct inoculation of the organism into the periosteum. Bronchitis and pneumonia have been seen, as well as empyema. Bacteremia probably is more frequent than is recognized. Infection of the CNS can take the form of meningitis, brain abscess, or subdural empyema;

ALL ISOLATES OF *P. MULTOCIDA* AT MASSACHUSETTS GENERAL HOSPITAL FROM SEPTEMBER 1980 TO OCTOBER 1982

Case Number	Age Sex	Clinical Infection (site)	Animal Exposure	Culture Source	Associated Disease	Treatment	Outcome
1	9 M	Cellulitis (Hand)	Dog bite	Wound	None	Erythromycin, topical silver sulfadiazine	Recovered
2	34 F	Cellulitis, Abscess (Hand)	Cat bite	Wound	None	Oral pencillin/cefazolin/cephalexin	Recovered
3	84 F	Cellulitis, Gangrene (Leg)	Cat bite	Wound	Vascular disease	Clindamycin/gentamicin/cefoxitin/tobramycin, amputation	Died
4	4 M	Cellulitis (Leg)	Cat bite and scratch	Wound	Cerebral palsy	Oral penicillin	Recovered
5	52 F	Cellulitis (Hand)	Dog bite	Wound	Rheumatoid arthritis, SLE	Cephalexin/cephazolin/cefoxitin	Recovered
6	42 F	Cellulitis (Hand)	Cat Bite	Wound	None	Penicillin	Recovered
7	67 M	Cellulitis (Finger)	Dog Bite	Wound	Diabetes	Penicillin/cephalexin	Residual stiffness
8	38 M	Cellulitis (Finger)	Cat Bite	Wound	Not recorded	Oxacillin	Recovered
9	19 M	Cellulitis (Thumb)	Cat Bite	Wound	None	Ampicillin/penicillin	Recovered
10	74 F	Cellulitis, Osteomyelitis, Abscess (Leg)	Cat Bite	Wound, abscess	Diabetes	Cefazolin/chloramphenicol/cephalothin, penicillin	Slow healing
11	39 M	Septic arthritis, Osteomyelitis (Finger)	Cat Bite	Wound, joint	Poor dentition	Drainage, cephapirin/TMP-SMX/gentamicin/penicillin	Stiff joint
12	39 M	Decubitus ulcer	Not recorded	Wound	Paraplegia	Cefazolin, debridement/graft/femoral head resection	Slow healing
13	33 M	Chronic ulcer, Osteomyelitis (Foot)	Not recorded	Wound	Paraplegia	Cefazolin/cephalothin/ampicillin, below knee amputation	Recovered
14	64 M	Chronic ulcer, Osteomyelitis (Second toe)	Not recorded	Wound	Alcohol abuse	Cefazolin, amputation of second toe	Recovered
15	71 F	Tracheobronchitis	Not recorded	Sputum	COPD, CAD	Ampicillin	Recovered
16	78 F	Colonization (Tracheobronchial tree)	None	Sputum	COPD, CHF	Chest physical therapy	Recovered
17	69 F	Pneumonia	Not recorded	Sputum, Bronchial washings	COPD, s/p lobectomy for lung cancer	Cefazolin/tobramycin/cephalexin, bronchodilators	Recovered

COPD, chronic obstructive pulmonary disease; CAD, coronary artery disease; CHF, congestive heart failure; TMP-SMX, trimethoprim-sulfamethoxazole; SLE, systemic lupus erythematosus.
(Courtesy of Weber, D.J., et al.: Medicine 63:133–154, 1984.)

P. multocida can cause gastrointestinal and genitourinary tract infections and ocular infections, including endophthalmitis.

Local wound care is important, but the role of antibiotic prophylaxis for animal bites or scratches remains uncertain. Penicillin is the drug of choice for treating *P. multocida* infections, but susceptibility testing of isolates is indicated in cases of serious infection. Patients at high risk of complications from local wound infection should be treated with high doses of intravenously administered antibiotics in the hospital. Septic arthritis is similarly treated, as are serious lower respiratory tract infections. Penicillin is the best drug to use in treating meningitis due to *P. multocida*. Patients with *P. multocida* in the urine and systemic toxicity should be evaluated for pyelonephritis or renal abscess.

▶ The perils of too-close an encounter with some of man's best friends (cats and dogs) are highlighted in this comprehensive review of infections caused by *P. multocida*. While we usually think of this organism in the setting of postanimal bite cellulitis, this review also emphasizes the wide spectrum of *P. multocida* infections, including pneumonia, urinary tract infections, and meningitis.—M.K.

Cat-Scratch Disease: Bacteria in Skin at the Primary Inoculation Site
Andrew W. Margileth, Douglas J. Wear, Ted L. Hadfield, Charles J. Schlagel, G. Thomas Spigel, and Jan E. Muhlbauer
JAMA 252:928–931, Aug. 17, 1984   1–38

Cat-scratch disease is a zoonotic infection characterized by a skin papule at the site of the scratch followed by regional lymphadenitis. Recently, small gram-negative pleomorphic bacilli were demonstrated in sections of lymph node from patients with the disease. The authors now report identical bacteria in the primary inoculation site of 3 patients with cat-scratch disease. Lymph nodes from 2 of these patients also contained the same bacilli. Identical bacteria in both skin and lymph nodes from these patients are further evidence that the bacilli are the cause of cat-scratch disease.

Man, 40, had a nodule for 3 weeks on the proximal left index finger, which had been punctured by a cactus spine and scratched by a newly acquired cat. Two weeks later swelling in the left side of the neck, persistent fever, chills, malaise, and a dry cough developed. Physical examination showed a 1.5-cm erythematous nodule with central crusting on the left index finger. A 6-mm punch biopsy specimen showed ulceration and acanthosis of the epidermis. The Warthin-Starry silver impregnation stain demonstrated bacilli (Figure 1–2) that were gram-negative on the Brown-Hopps tissue Gram stain. Within 2–3 weeks the fever, cervical lymphadenopathy, and primary inoculation nodule resolved. About 2 months after the initial wound, 0.1 ml of cat-scratch antigen was injected intradermally, and a skin biopsy specimen showed a typical delayed-type hypersensitivity reaction.

In early infections, biopsy of the primary site of inoculation and demonstration of bacilli may replace excision and histologic examination of lymph node in establishing the diagnosis of cat-scratch disease. However,

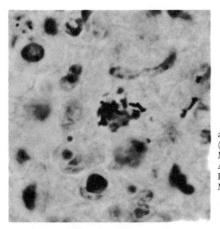

Fig 1–2.—Cat-scratch disease bacilli, alone and in macrophage, within area of dermal necrosis (Warthin Starry stain, ×1,000). (Courtesy of Margileth, A.W., et al.: JAMA 252:928–932, Aug. 17, 1984, and the Armed Forces Institute of Pathology; copyright 1984, by the American Medical Association.)

a skin or lymph node biopsy is not recommended in the typical patient with cat-scratch disease if the cat-scratch disease skin test antigen is available.

Central Nervous System

Shunt Fluid Examination: Risks and Benefits in the Evaluation of Shunt Malfunction and Infection
Michael J. Noetzel and Roy P. Baker
J. Neurosurg. 61:328–332, August 1984   1–39

Complication rates of up to 60% have been reported in association with cerebrospinal fluid (CSF) shunting. The efficacy of shunt fluid evaluation in detecting malfunction and infection was examined in 91 patients given shunts for treatment of hydrocephalus. A total of 209 diagnostic shunt "taps" were performed in these patients between 1972 and 1983. The children were followed prospectively for 18 months. Most of the children had ventriculoperitoneal shunts. The major symptoms leading to a shunt tap were emesis, headache, and lethargy. Irritability and fever were less frequent indications.

The presenting clinical features generally did not distinguish between a malfunctioning and a normally functioning shunt. All but 2 of 72 instances of mechanical obstruction that were documented at operation were correctly identified by abnormal CSF dynamics, either an opening pressure greater than expected valve pressure or absent flow of fluid. Slow but continuous flow with normal pressure was considered to be a normal finding. Roentgenograms confirmed suspected shunt malfunction in only about one third of cases in which revision was necessary. Computed tomography was not a reliable study for shunt malfunction. Shunt fluid cultures were positive in all cases of shunt-related infection. Lumbar or ventricular CSF, blood, and wound cultures were less reliable in isolating an organism. No patient had bleeding or CSF leakage from the puncture site, infection, or mechanical disruption of the system. Fifty-three patients were followed for an average of 26 months.

Shunt fluid examination is a safe and accurate means of diagnosing CSF shunt malfunction and shunt-related infection. No significant complications have resulted from the procedure.

▶ In one sense this paper documents the obvious, namely that the best way to make the diagnosis of CNS shunt infection is to examine shunt fluid. It also reminds us that this procedure can be done safely, and that sampling of other sites (blood, lumbar, or ventricular tap CSF) is inferior for identifying the etiologic organism. Valuable additional points are that a normal shunt fluid formula does not exclude the diagnosis of shunt infection (50% are abnormal) and that the presentation of shunt infections can be very subtle, ranging from a slight personality change to "shunt nephritis" (particularly with ventriculoatrial shunts), overwhelming ventriculitis, and meningitis.—M.K.

Neurologic Manifestations of Legionnaires' Disease
Judith D. Johnson, Martin J. Raff, and John A. Van Arsdall (Univ. of Louisville)
Medicine (Baltimore) 63:303–310, September 1984   1–40

Nine patients with neurologic sequelae of Legionnaires' disease were seen in 1978–1982. They were among a total of 21 patients seen with Legionnaires' disease in this period. All 9 patients had altered mentation, and 5 were deeply obtunded. Altered mentation sometimes preceded the appearance of pulmonary infiltrates. Hallucinations were not seen but have been described in previously reported cases. Two patients had a headache. Two patients had unclear or slurred speech but no other signs of cerebellar dysfunction. Focal signs of neurologic involvement are infrequent in reported cases. Other reported abnormalities include seizures, nystagmus, tremor, and papilledema. Four of the authors' 9 patients had dysrhythmias or generalized EEG slowing. No marked cerebrospinal fluid (CSF) abnormalities were observed. There are two autopsy reports of CNS invasion by *Legionella* organisms in normal and compromised hosts.

Encephalopathy is the most common neurologic manifestation of Legionnaires' disease, and it is apparently the only characteristic manifestation. A wide range of other neurologic disorders also can occur in association with Legionnaires' disease. Headache is a nonspecific symptom. Ataxia is infrequent, as is weakness or frank paresis. The cause of neurologic involvement in Legionnaires' disease is unknown. Isolation of the organism from the brain or CSF has been very infrequent, and *Legionella* organisms have not been cultured from the CSF. An immunologic reaction or toxin may be responsible. Patients with Legionnaires' disease and neurologic disorder must be thoroughly evaluated to rule out other entities.

Fever During Treatment for Bacterial Meningitis
Tzou-Yien Lin, John D. Nelson, and George H. McCracken, Jr. (Univ. of Texas at Dallas)
Pediatr. Infect. Dis. 3:319–322, July-Aug. 1984   1–41

The course of therapy for bacterial meningitis in children is often complicated by persistent fever or the development of secondary fever. A review was made of the patterns and etiologies of fever in 476 children aged 5 weeks to 11 years treated between 1979 and 1982 for bacterial meningitis. The bacterial etiology included *Hemophilus influenzae* in 335 instances, *Neisseria meningitidis* in 62, *Streptococcus pneumoniae* in 45, and other bacterial or unknown causes in 34. Before November 1981, ampicillin and chloramphenicol were given initially; after culture results were known treatment with a single drug was given. After November 1981, 48 patients received ceftriaxone and 48 received conventional therapy.

By the sixth hospital day, 90% of children with meningitis caused by *S. pneumoniae* or *N. meningitidis* were afebrile, as were 72% of those with *H. influenzae* meningitis ($P < .001$) (table). Secondary fever occurred within 4 days of the first afebrile day in 76% of the patients and then subsided in 74% within 4 days. The rates of prolonged fever for 10 days or more, persistent fever for 5–9 days, and secondary fever were 13%, 13%, and 16%, respectively. The rates of prolonged and secondary fever were not significantly different when evaluated by types of organism. The principal conditions associated with prolonged fever were subdural effusions (27%), drug fever (24%), arthritis (18%), and unknown cause (15%). The main conditions associated with persistent fever were other foci of disease (17%), nosocomial infection (16%), subdural effusions (14%), or drug fever (11%). The conditions associated with secondary fever were nosocomial infections (27%), subdural effusion (23%), and unknown cause (39%). There was no correlation between pattern of fever and neurologic status at discharge, including hearing deficit.

Prolonged, persistent, or secondary fevers occur frequently in infants and children treated for bacterial meningitis. Evaluation of these patients should include complete physical examination and appropriate laboratory evaluation for other foci of infection (e.g., arthritis and pneumonia), or for evidence of nosocomial infection, and a neurologic examination including computerized tomography for subdural effusions.

Physicians who see patients with meningitis are often faced with the problem of continuing fever in such patients (20 percent of patients in this series). As pointed out, many patients with persistent fever do not have continuing meningeal infection. However, such infections must first be ruled out before we search for other causes.

Prospective Evaluation of Hearing Impairment as a Sequela of Acute Bacterial Meningitis

Philip R. Dodge, Hallowell Davis, Ralph D. Feigin, Sandra J. Holmes, Sheldon L. Kaplan, David P. Jubelirer, Barbara W. Stechenberg, and Shirley K. Hirsh
N. Engl. J. Med. 311:869–874, Oct. 4, 1984   1–42

Up to 30% of infants and children with bacterial meningitis have been found to have some hearing impairment. Hearing was evaluated in a long-

FIRST AFEBRILE DAY IN 476 PATIENTS WITH BACTERIAL MENINGITIS BY ETIOLOGY

Hospital Day	Haemophilus influenzae		Neisseria meningitidis		Streptococcus pneumoniae		All Cases	
	No. of cases	Cumulative %	No. of cases	Cumulative %	No. of cases	Cumulative %	No. of cases	Cumulative %
1	30	9	14	23	10	22	58	12
2	39	21	17	50	8	40	80	29
3	71	42	10	66	5	51	92	48
4	49	56	7	77	8	69	66	62
5	38	68	6	87	9	89	58	74
6	13	72	2	90	1	91	16	78
7	12	75	0	90	0	91	12	80
8	13	79	1	92	0	91	14	83
9	8	82	1	94	0	91	9	85
10	11	85	0	94	0	91	11	87
11–14	42	97	3	98	4	100	50	98
>14	9	100	1	100	0	100	10	100

(Courtesy of Lin, T.-Y., et al.: Pediatr. Infect. Dis. 3:319–322, July–Aug. 1984.)

term, prospective study of 185 infants and children with acute bacterial meningitis seen between 1973 and 1977. Mean age was 20 months. The patients were followed for 5 years. Nearly two thirds of cases were caused by *Hemophilus influenzae.* Fifty-eight percent of the subjects were boys, and 43% were black. Sixty-six patients had otitis media at admission. One patient had tympanic membrane rupture, and another had mastoiditis. Otitis was associated with transient conductive hearing loss in 15 patients, and 11 others had a conductive loss. All had normal hearing at follow-up. Six patients with otitis had sensorineural hearing loss.

Sensorineural hearing loss was present at follow-up in 10.3% of patients. Ten of the 19 patients had bilateral impairment. Hearing loss was diagnosed by electric response audiometry and conventional testing in 31% of cases of *Streptococcus pneumoniae* meningitis, 10.5% of cases caused by *Neisseria meningitidis,* and 6% of cases of *H. influenzae* infection. None of the sensorineural deficits lessened over time. Sensorineural deafness could not be related to the duration of symptoms of meningitis before hospitalization and the start of antibacterial treatment. A relation with initial cerebrospinal fluid glucose concentrations of less than 20 mg/dl was apparent. Persistent, severe neurologic deficits were related to sensorineural deafness.

Early recognition of hearing impairment after bacterial meningitis permits timely institution of special education and hearing aid use. Audiometry should be performed in all infants and children recovering from acute bacterial meningitis. Bedside tests are not a substitute for formal audiometry in pediatric patients.

Pneumococcal Meningitis: Late Neurologic Sequelae and Features of Prognostic Impact
Vilhelm Bohr, Olaf B. Paulson, and Niels Rasmussen (Copenhagen)
Arch. Neurol. 41:1045–1049, October 1984   1–43

Ninety-four patients who survived pneumococcal meningitis in 1966 through 1976 had a follow-up examination at University Hospital in an attempt to determine which clinical factors at the time of acute illness are of prognostic significance. The sequelae of meningitis are listed in the table. The most frequent complaints were dizziness, fatigue, and memory deficiency. Hypersensitivity to noise, gait disturbance, and headache also were common findings. Seventeen patients had unsteadiness of gait on reexamination. Seven of the 17 had bilateral vestibular areflexia. In all, just over half of the patients had sequelae of meningitis.

Gait ataxia at follow-up was associated with agitation and confusion at admission for meningitis. Altered consciousness in the acute stage and a high number of white blood cells in the cerebral spinal fluid were associated with high sequelae ratings on follow-up. Patients with headache at follow-up often had had otitis media when admitted with pneumonia. Seizures in the hospital were a serious prognostic feature with regard to both sequelae of meningitis and death. The same was true for patients with respiratory problems who required artificial ventilation.

SEQUELAE OF PNEUMOCOCCAL
MENINGITIS IN 93 PATIENTS*

Symptom or Sign	Patients, No. (%)
Symptom	
Dizziness	22 (23.7)
Excessive fatigue	21 (22.6)
Memory deficiency†	20 (21.5)
Hypersensitivity to noise	14 (15.1)
Gait disturbances	13 (14.0)
Headache	10 (10.8)
Epilepsy	5 (5.4)
Paresis	3 (3.2)
Coordination disturbances	3 (3.2)
Sensory disturbances	2 (2.2)
Marked asthenopia‡	2 (2.2)
Involuntary movements and tremor	2 (2.2)
Sign	
Gait unsteady and ataxic	17 (18.3)
Coordination disturbances	3 (3.2)
Hemiparesis	3 (3.2)
Side differences of tendon reflexes	3 (3.2)
Hyperkinesia	2 (2.2)
Tremor	2 (2.2)

*Affected stereognosis, nystagmus, aphasia, positive Romberg's test, attacks with blurred consciousness, and alopecia were each found in 1 patient.

†Neuropsychologic examination revealed slight dementia in 13 patients (13.8%) and moderate to severe dementia in another 13.

‡Asthenopia indicates rapid fatigue of visual impression; on visual fixation picture initially appears to be sharp, but after few seconds or up to 1 minute it becomes blurred.

(Courtesy of Bohr, V., et al.: Arch. Neurol. 41:1045–1049, October 1984; copyright 1984, American Medical Association.)

Pneumococcal meningitis remains a serious disease with a high mortality and a substantial risk of sequelae in surviving patients, despite effective antibiotic therapy. Nearly one third of the present patients had sequelae that interfered with their daily life and work capacity. Memory and hearing deficiencies and fatigue were prominent findings. The postmeningitis syndrome in cases of pneumococcal meningitis should be expanded to include gait disturbances.

Trimethoprim-Sulfamethoxazole for Bacterial Meningitis

Robert E. Levitz and Richard Quintiliani (Hartford, Conn.)
Ann. Intern. Med. 100:881–890, June 1984

1–44

Although many cases of gram-negative bacillary meningitis are caused by cephalosporin-sensitive organisms, problems remain in treating cases caused by gram-negative organisms. Trimethoprim-sulfamethoxazole (TMP-SMX) has excellent activity against many gram-negative and gram-positive bacteria, and typically penetrates well into the cerebrospinal fluid. Trimethoprim-sulfamethoxazole has exhibited in vitro antimicrobial activity against most streptococci, *Staphylococcus aureus*, *Staphylococcus epidermidis*, *Listeria monocytogenes*, *Hemophilus influenzae*, and *Neisseria*. Among the Enterobacteriaceae, *Escherichia coli*, and most species of *Klebsiella*, *Enterobacter*, *Serratia*, and *Salmonella* are susceptible. Adults have most often been treated for gram-negative meningitis with 10 mg of TMP and 50 mg of SMX per kilogram body weight daily. Neonates have received about half these doses.

Trimethoprim-sulfamethoxazole has been quite effective in treating pneumococcal and meningococcal meningitis in developed countries. Patients with nonpneumococcal gram-positive meningitis have been bacteriologically cured. Bacteriologic cure has been achieved in most cases of gram-negative bacillary meningitis due to *E. coli* and other organisms. Adverse reactions were frequent but usually mild in the series of 33 treated patients. Only 1 of 14 neonates developed hyperbilirubinemia.

Trimethoprim-sulfamethoxazole may prove to be useful in the management of uncommon types of bacterial meningitis, especially those caused by organisms that are resistant or only moderately susceptible to β-lactam antibiotics. It is difficult to recommend TMP-SMX as initial treatment for pneumococcal and meningococcal meningitis because of the much greater experience gained with penicillin G and chloramphenicol in these cases.

Moxalactam Therapy for Neonatal Meningitis Due to Gram-Negative Enteric Bacilli: A Prospective Controlled Evaluation

George H. McCracken, Jr., Norma Threlkeld, Susan Mize, Carol J. Baker, Sheldon L. Kaplan, Idis Faingezicht, William E. Feldman, Urs Schaad, and the Neonatal Meningitis Cooperative Study Group
JAMA 252:1427–1432, Sept. 21, 1984   1–45

Preliminary reports have shown that concentrations of moxalactam, a β-lactam antibiotic with excellent in vitro activity against gram-negative bacteria, in the cerebrospinal fluid (CSF) of infants with meningitis were at least fiftyfold greater than the minimal bactericidal concentrations of most gram-negative enteric bacilli. The authors compared the efficacy of moxalactam and ampicillin sodium with amikacin sulfate and ampicillin for the treatment of neonatal meningitis due to gram-negative enteric bacilli. Sixty-three infants enrolled in the Third Neonatal Meningitis Cooperative Study were randomized into 2 treatment groups. Group A received ampicillin, 200–300 mg/kg per day intravenously, and moxalactam in an initial dose of 100 mg/kg intravenously and further doses of 100–300 mg/kg per day, with all doses depending on age. Group B received same dosage of ampicillin and amikacin sulfate, 15–30 mg/kg per day intravenously or intramuscularly, depending on age and birth weight. Amikacin was chosen because the study included infants who had meningitis due to gentamicin-resistant and tobramycin-resistant gram-negative enteric bacilli. Duration of treatment was a minimum of 21 days or 2 weeks after cultures of CSF were sterile. The population characteristics were comparable for both groups. Causative organisms included *Escherichia coli, Klebsiella-Enterobacter* and *Salmonella* species and *Citrobacter diversus.*

Cultures of CSF were positive for a mean of 2.9 days in each group. Case-fatality rates were 23.3% for the moxalactam and 15.2% for the amikacin groups. Developmental or neurologic abnormalities were found in about 40% of survivors, and the rates did not differ significantly between groups. Results of computed tomography, sonography, or both, among 44 infants were normal in 13 (30%). Hydrocephalus (20 infants), brain abscesses (8), and low-density areas (5) were the most frequent abnormalities. Mean concentrations of moxalactam in CSF, ventricular fluid, and cerebral abscess were 27.4, 26.4, and 20.9 mg/L, respectively, compared with 3.9, 6.3, and 2.2 mg/L, respectively, for amikacin. Therapy was well tolerated by all infants.

The superior CSF penetration and bactericidal activity of moxalactam do not equate with a superior outcome of neonatal meningitis, as case-fatality rates and duration of positive CSF cultures are similar in moxalactam- and amikacin-treated infants. However, moxalactam plus ampicillin is comparable with amikacin plus ampicillin for treatment of meningitis due to gram-negative enteric bacilli. Because of greater clinical experience with the combination of ampicillin and aminoglycoside, it is recommended for initial therapy of neonatal meningitis until results of culture and susceptibility tests are available.

Bacterial Vaccines

Prevention of *Hemophilus influenzae* Type B Bacteremic Infections With the Capsular Polysaccharide Vaccine
Heikki Peltola, Helena Käyhty, Marita Virtanen, and P. Helena Mäkelä (Helsinki)
N. Engl. J. Med. 310:1561–1566, June 14, 1984   1–46

The vaccine based on the capsular polysaccharide of *Hemophilus influenzae* type B (Hib) had shown good protective efficacy only among children vaccinated at 18 months or older. However, the highest incidence of *H. influenzae* meningitis occurs in children at about 12 months, thus placing a severe limitation on the use of the Hib vaccine. Also, meningitis occurs after age 18 months and the incidence of epiglottitis reaches a peak at 30–42 months of age. Knowing this, the authors analyzed the data collected in Finland on the long-term effect of the Hib vaccine given in 1974 to 48,977 children 3 months to 5 years of age. The dose was 12.7

NUMBERS OF BACTEREMIC *HEMOPHILUS INFLUENZAE*
INFECTIONS IN 2 AGE GROUPS OF CHILDREN GIVEN THE
H. *INFLUENZAE* TYPE B (HIB) POLYSACCHARIDE VACCINE OR
THE CONTROL, GROUP A MENINGOCOCCAL (MEN A)
VACCINE

YEAR AFTER VACCINATION	VACCINATED AT 18–71 MO		VACCINATED AT 3–17 MO	
	Hib GROUP (N = 37,393)	Men A GROUP (N = 38,431)	Hib GROUP (N = 11,584)	Men A GROUP (N = 10,864)
		no. of infections		
First *	0	11	7	1
Second *	2	• 5	1	3
Third	0	2	2	1
Fourth	0	2	0	0
Total	2 †	20 †	10 ‡	5 ‡

*Data from Peltola, H., et al.: Pediatrics 60:730–737, 1977.
†P of difference < .001.
‡P of difference not significant.
(Courtesy of Peltola, H., et al.: N. Engl. J. Med. 310:1561–1566, June 14,
1984. Reprinted by permission of *The New England Journal of Medicine*.)

μg. Infants aged 3–5 months received half this dose and children younger
than 18 months received a second dose of the same vaccine 3 months
later.

The table shows good protective efficacy (90%) of the vaccine in those
who received it at 18 months or older. Analyzing 956 cases of *H. influenzae*
infections over a period of 5 years, 94% of all cases occurred in children
younger than 10 years; of these, 40% occurred in children younger than
18 months and 60% in children between the ages of 19 months and 9
years. The suggested use of the Hib vaccine has the potential of preventing
invasive *H. influenzae* infections (Fig 1–3) that occur in the older group.
Analysis of the paired serum samples from 514 vaccinated children showed
that effective immunization with this vaccine could be performed after,
but not before, the age of 16–20 months. There were no adverse effects
observed from use of the vaccine.

The authors recommend a vaccination policy which includes vaccination
with the Hib vaccine at age 18 months with a second dose 1½ years later,
at the age of 3 years. This policy is recommended to most industrialized
countries.

► The *Hemophilus influenzae* type B vaccine was licensed in the United States in
1985 (*Morbid. Mortal. Week Rep.* 34:201–204, 1985). The Advisory Committee
on Immunization Practices recommends the Hib vaccine for all 2-year-old children. They also recommend immunization of children at 18 months of age if they
are among high-risk groups, such as those who attend day care centers or those
who are functionally or anatomically asplenic. There are insufficient data to make
a recommendation concerning older children or adults with chronic conditions
associated with an increased risk of *Hemophilus influenzae* disease.—D.S.

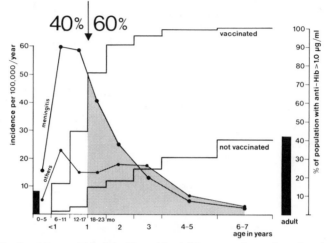

40% 60%

Fig 1–3.—Protective potential of the *Hemophilus influenzae* type b capsular polysaccharide (Hib) vaccine is shown as well as the age-specific incidence (left-hand scale) of invasive *H. influenzae* infections in children. *Arrow* indicates the suggested time of vaccination; 40% of infections occur before this age and 60% after it, the latter thus being preventable *(shaded area)*. Curves indicate the percentage of the population at each age who have at least 1 μg of anti-Hib/ml of serum before or after vaccination (right-hand scale). Black columns indicate the corresponding percentages among adults and newborns. (Courtesy of Peltola, H., et al.: N. Engl. J. Med. 310:1561–1566, June 14, 1984. Reprinted by permission of *The New England Journal of Medicine.*)

Response to Immunization With *Hemophilus influenzae* Type B Polysaccharide-Pertussis Vaccine and Risk of Hemophilus Meningitis in Children With the Km(1) Immunoglobulin Allotype

Dan M. Granoff, Janardan P. Pandey, Eyla Boies, Janet Squires, Robert S. Munson, Jr., and Brian Suarez
J. Clin. Invest. 74:1708–1714, November 1984   1–47

Antibody against *Hemophilus influenzae* type B capsule confers protection against invasive disease. It seemed possible that genes in linkage disequilibrium with those coding for Km(1) or Gm(23) allotypes might influence immunologic responses to the type B capsule, and thereby susceptibility to different manifestations of *Hemophilus* type B infection.

Sera were taken for study from 241 patients having *H. influenzae* type B meningitis or epiglottitis, confirmed by positive blood or CSF cultures or by detecting capsular antigen by countercurrent immunoelectrophoresis. Meningitis was present in 170 patients, and epiglottitis in 71. Sera also were obtained from 173 control children without a history of type B . disease. Seventy-four healthy children with a mean age of 19 months were given type B polysaccharide capsule-pertussis vaccine. A dose containing 10 μg of polysaccharide and 4 opacity units of pertussis vaccine was given intramuscularly.

The Km(1) allotype was less frequent in black children with meningitis than in those with epiglottitis or in control children. The relative risk of meningitis in these children was 3.2-fold lower than in those lacking the Km(1) allotype. The risk was not reduced in white chidren with the Km(1) allotype. No significant differences in Gm(23) were noted. Anticapsular antibody responses of black or white children with the Km(1) allotype were 4.6 to 9.5-fold greater than in children lacking the allotype. Antibody responses were unrelated to the Gm(23) determinant.

Genes associated with Km(1) may influence the immune response to a type B hemophilus vaccine in black children. The greater responses in these children may not be capsular antigen-specific, but rather may be modulated by different genetically regulated responses to the adjuvant. A given vaccine may be immunogenic in a majority of children, but have limited efficacy in the general population because of failure to protect a subpopulation at increased risk because of genetic factors.

A Controlled Evaluation of the Protective Efficacy of Pneumococcal Vaccine for Patients at High Risk of Serious Pneumococcal Infections
Eugene D. Shapiro and John D. Clemens (Yale Univ.)
Ann. Intern. Med. 101:325–330, September 1984   1–48

The use of pneumococcal vaccine in patients at risk of serious infection remains controversial, partly because efficacy trials have chiefly involved healthy young adults in epidemic circumstances. A case-control study has been done to evaluate pneumococcal vaccine in adults having current indications for vaccination. Cases with a first episode of documented systemic pneumococcal infection acquired in the community were compared with controls matched for age, date of hospitalization, and the duration of indications for vaccination before hospitalization. Nearly 90% of the 90 cases had bacteremic pneumonia.

Six of the 90 cases (7%) and 16 control subjects (18%) had received pneumococcal vaccine, for an odds ratio of 0.33. The protective efficacy of the vaccine was 67%, and this was virtually unchanged by adjusting for potential confounding variables. The vaccine was 77% effective for patients at a moderately increased risk of pneumococcal infection, but ineffective for severely immunocompromised patients. The overall protective efficacy of the vaccine for all patients aged 55 years and older, after controlling for other indications for vaccination, was 70%.

Pneumococcal vaccine appears to confer substantial protection against systemic pneumococcal infection in the elderly patient and in those patients having disorders associated with a moderately increased risk of pneumococcal infection. More and larger studies of the vaccine are needed. It would be helpbul to assess the efficacy of the vaccine against infections caused only by serotypes contained in the vaccine.

▶ The controversy about the actual efficacy of the pneumococcal vaccine in the populations for whom it is intended continues. Because of the low attack rate of pneumococcal disease, extremely large numbers of patients would be necessary to study the vaccine prospectively. The authors have made use of case-control methodology to demonstrate the 66% efficacy in patients who had an indication for vaccine.—D.S.

Immunity Against Tetanus and Effect of Revaccination 25–30 Years After Primary Vaccination
O. Simonsen, K. Kjeldsen, and I. Heron (Copenhagen)
Lancet 2:1240-1242, Dec. 1, 1984   1–49

Since 1950, children in Denmark have received 1 ml of tetanus toxoid (12 flocculation units/ml), adsorbed by aluminum hydroxide, along with inactivated polio and diphtheria vaccines at ages 5, 6, and 15 months. A further dose of subcutaneous tetanus vaccine is recommended for those wounded more than 2 years after primary vaccination or more than 10 years after revaccination. About 10 cases of tetanus have occurred each year in Denmark, some in vaccinated persons. The efficacy of the vaccination routine was examined in 500 randomly selected Danes aged 25–30 years. Blood samples were obtained from 418 subjects; nearly half had vaccination record cards.

Tetanus antitoxin levels were below the protective level of 0.01 IU/ml in 11% of subjects. Significantly more females than males were unprotected. Forty-nine percent of females and 79% of males had been revaccinated. Wide individual variation in immunity was seen in 91 subjects with documented complete primary vaccination who had never been revaccinated (Fig 1–4). Twenty-eight percent of those vaccinated more than

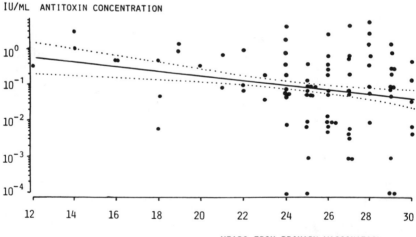

Fig 1–4.—Concentration of serum antitoxin measured by neutralization technique and its relation to interval since primary vaccination in 91 persons with documented complete primary vaccination and no subsequent revaccination (95% confidence limits for regression line are given). (Courtesy of Simonsen, O., et al.: Lancet 2:1240–1242, Dec. 1, 1984.)

25 years before and 10% of those vaccinated less than 20 years before were unprotected. All 61 persons given a single revaccination after a complete primary series were protected. Of the 220 persons revaccinated, 39.5% reported local reactions, and 2 noted fever and malaise.

A reinforcing dose of tetanus vaccine should be given before age 20 years in Denmark. The lack of serious side effects in the present series supports a recommendation for routine revaccination. Routine revaccination also seems wise in countries where vaccination in childhood is not routine, since a similar decline in immunity may be expected when primary vaccination is given later.

▶ Most adult patients receive booster injections for tetanus only when an injury occurs or they might be exposed to infection (i.e., travelers). This study confirms that a significant number of adults need revaccination within 20 years of the primary immunization.—S.G.

Antimicrobial Therapy

Clinical and Bacteriologic Efficacy of Ceftriaxone in the United States
Richard V. McCloskey (Hoffman-La Roche Inc., Nutley, N.J.)
Am. J. Med. 77:97–103, Oct. 19, 1984   1–50

Experience with ceftriaxone in 153 studies was reviewed in a total of 2,635 patients given the drug intramuscularly or intravenously, 930 patients given comparative antibiotics, and 81 placebo patients. Clinical response rates of 89% or above were obtained in 10 major categories of infection. Overall bacteriologic cure rates were 84% or greater, and 90% and above in 7 of the 10 categories of infections. Satisfactory clinical responses were obtained in from 89% to 99% of the treatment groups. The spectrum of susceptible organisms included most of the major bacterial pathogens encountered in hospital and in outpatient settings. More than 90% of strains of *S. aureus* and 95% of strains of *S. epidermidis* were eradicated, as were most strains of *Clostridium* and most *Bacteroides* species. Two thirds of strains of *P. aeruginosa* were eliminated. A wide spectrum of clinical significant aerobic gram-negative bacilli was eradicated from multiple major sites of infection.

Ceftriaxone was as effective as ampicillin-chloramphenicol therapy in the treatment of bacterial meningitis in infants and children. Doses as low as 125 mg eliminated *Nogonorrheae* from all sites, including the pharynx. Once-daily treatment with ceftriaxone was as effective as twice-daily treatment with various other antimicrobials. A single preoperative dose of ceftriaxone was as effective as cefazolin in preventing infections after coronary bypass surgery. Ceftriaxone was significantly more effective than placebo in patients having prostatic surgery.

Ceftriaxone is an effective antibiotic for use against most commonly encountered serious infections due to a broad range of organisms. Pediatric CNS infections due to gram-positive and gram-negative bacteria respond well to ceftriaxone. Low doses consistently cure gonorrhea, and a single dose of ceftriaxone can replace multiple doses of cefazolin in preventing postoperative infections. Clinical and bacteriologic response rates of about 90% have been obtained consistently.

Imipenem/Cilastatin Versus Gentamicin/Clindamycin for Treatment of Serious Bacterial Infections
Report From a Scandinavian Study Group
Lancet 1:868–871, Apr. 21, 1984   1–51

Imipenem is a carbapenem antibiotic with a wide antibacterial spectrum including most gram-negative and gram-positive anaerobes and aerobic species. Cilastatin increases its urinary excretion and has a probenecid-like effect on the plasma kinetics of imipenem. A multicenter trial of imipenem-cilastatin (I/C) therapy in comparison with gentamicin/clindamycin (G/C) was carried out in 163 patients with serious systemic infections. Patients with impaired renal function and those with CNS infections were not included. Seventy-seven patients received 500 mg imipenem and 500 mg cilastatin in saline over 20–30 minutes every 6 hours. Eighty-six patients received 1.5 mg/kg gentamicin at intervals of 8 to 24 hours to produce levels of 4 mg/L or below at 1 hour, and 600 mg clindamycin every 6 hours as a short intravenous infusion. Patients with resistant organisms received G/C therapy for at least 5 days.

Treatment failed in 4% of the I/C group and in 16% of the G/C group. Most of the latter failures were in cases of serious abdominal infection or deep soft tissue infection. Abdominal infections were more frequent in the G/C group. Failures in this group were not attributable to the use of inappropriately low doses. Bacteriologic efficacy tended to be superior in the I/C group. Side effects occurred in 6.5% of the I/C group and in 16% of the G/C group. Untoward microbiologic effects, usually colonization of wound secretion or sputum with *Candida,* staphylococci, or enterococci, occurred in 26 I/C cases and in 23 G/C cases. Thrombophlebitis was more frequent in the I/C group. No patient had treatment discontinued because of problems in tolerance.

The I/C regimen seemed more effective than G/C therapy in this study, possibly in part because of the occurrence of abdominal infection and septicemia in more of the G/C cases. Fewer adverse effects occurred with I/C therapy, although thrombophlebitis was more frequent in this group. The best overall results were obtained with I/C treatment in this series of patients with serious systemic infections.

Intravenous Antibiotic Therapy in Ambulatory Pediatric Patients
Robin I. Goldenberg, Donald M. Poretz, Lawrence J. Eron, James B. Rising, and Sarah B. Sparks (Falls Church, Va.)
Pediatr. Infect. Dis. 3:514–517, November 1984   1–52

Intravenous antibiotic therapy was evaluated in 89 pediatric patients with a variety of infections in a nonrandomized open study. A long in-patient stay sometimes was followed by home treatment, while other patients had a short hospitalization for teaching purposes only. Patients were discharged with a 20-gauge heparin lock in place and were given a 4-day supply of single-dose antibiotic solutions and minidrip infusion sets with in-line filters, heparin flush solution, and ancillary supplies. Bone and joint infections were the most frequent indication. The median patient age was 12 years.

The mean duration of outpatient intravenous therapy was 19 days. The most frequent causative organisms were *S. aureus, P. aeruginosa,* and *H. influenzae.* Sixty-four courses of cephalosporin therapy were administered. Aminoglycoside and clindamycin were used less frequently. A favorable outcome was documented in 95.5% of cases. Twenty children changed to oral treatment at home. Three of the 4 treatment failures were inpatients with *Pseudomonas mastoiditis.* Infections recurred in 2 patients. Two-thirds of the patients required cannula changes only at scheduled clinic visits. Five patients had allergic reactions. Only 1 patient had clinically significant phlebitis. Treatment was discontinued in 2 cases because of leukopenia, in 2 because of loss of intravenous access, and in 1 because of noncompliance.

Intravenous antibiotic treatment can be used by children and adolescents on an outpatient basis as a practical, safe, and cost-effective approach to selected infectious disorders. Careful patient screening and physician-centered follow-up are essential. A similar approach would be feasible for total parenteral nutrition, central venous catheter maintenance, transfusion of blood and blood products, and chemotherapy.

Prospective Controlled Evaluation of Auditory Function in Neonates Given Netilmicin or Amikacin
Terese Finitzo-Hieber, George H. McCracken, Jr., and Karen Clinton Brown (Univ. of Texas at Dallas)
J. Pediatr. 106:129–136, January 1985   1–53

It remains uncertain whether the aminoglycosides are a significant cause of early-onset hearing impairment in infants. Auditory function was evaluated longitudinally in 150 infants of gestational ages 27–42 weeks, using auditory brainstem response (ABR) recording, immittance measurement, and behavioral audiometry. Infants less than 1 week of age who were suspected of having systemic bacterial disease received 7.5 mg/kg amikacin or 3 mg/kg netilmicin twice daily in the first week of life, and 3 times daily at ages 2–4 weeks, intramuscularly or intravenously. Ampicillin also was given intravenously, in a dose of 50 mg/kg twice daily in the first week, and 3 times daily thereafter. Fifty infants received amikacin, 49 received netilmicin, and 51 healthy neonates were untreated. The 3 groups were demographically similar.

Bilateral sensorineural impairment was confirmed in 2% of all infants, 1 in each of the treated groups and 1 in the untreated control group.

Transient auditory abnormalities were prevalent in the population as a whole. Eighty percent of all infants were evaluated longitudinally, and comparison of ABR values at up to 18 months showed no significant group differences. No divergence in group performance was evident in outpatient assessments.

The risk of a neonate developing clinically significant hearing impairment from a 3 to 7 day course of aminoglycoside therapy appears to be small. Adverse effects can be minimized by monitoring serum drug levels and by keeping the total drug dose within the therapeutic range. Both drug and creatinine levels should be determined in the intensive-care-nursery infant early in the course of aminoglycoside therapy, and subsequently on a weekly basis. The ABR recording can be used to select those infants who require follow-up audiologic evaluation and management. The ABR recording should be repeated 6 weeks to 3 months after treatment, preferably after discharge.

Drug-Resistant Salmonella From Animals Fed Antimicrobials
Scott D. Holmberg, Michael T. Osterholm, Kenneth A. Senger, and Mitchell L. Cohen
N. Engl. J. Med. 311:617–622, Sept. 6, 1984   1–54

Multiple drug-resistant isolates have produced an increasing proportion of human salmonella infections, and it has been proposed that subtherapeutic amounts of antimicrobials in animal feed select for resistant bacteria that eventually infect humans. Eighteen persons in 4 Midwestern states were encountered in early 1983 who were infected by *Salmonella newport* resistant to ampicillin, carbenicillin, and tetracycline, and characterized by a 38-kilobase R plasmid. The outbreak cases were compared with other cases of *S. newport* infection seen in Minnesota and with cases of salmonellosis due to other serotypes.

Twelve of the 18 study patients had taken penicillin derivatives for medical problems other than diarrhea within 24–48 hours before the onset of salmonellosis. Eleven patients were hospitalized for salmonellosis for an average of 8 days. One had a fatal nosocomial infection following treatment with many antimicrobials. *Salmonella newport* resistant to ampicillin, carbenicillin, and tetracycline was isolated from the blood, sputum, and stool before the patient died. Epidemiologic investigation indicated that the patients had been infected before antimicrobials were taken by eating hamburger originating from beef cattle in South Dakota that had been subtherapeutic chlortetracycline for promotion of growth. Plasmid DNA from the epidermic strain hybridized with a labeled DNA probe containing a gene sequence coding for β-lactamase.

Antimicrobial-resistant organisms of animal origin can cause serious human illness, emphasizing the need for more cautious use of antimicrobials in animals as well as in humans. Persons taking antimicrobials are especially vulnerable to this form of infection.

▶ The main message from this article, despite the authors' intentions, is that antibiotic use in humans predisposes to *Salmonella* infection. Certainly, we all deplore the inclusion of antimicrobial agents in animal feed, and it would be better to eliminate this practice. This is assuming that we can afford the economic consequence of increased cost of beef production, estimated to be about 15% higher without antibiotics. Viewed on a medical level, the problem of resistant *Salmonella* is relatively minor, since most *Salmonella* infections are mild, don't require antibiotic therapy, and cure themselves regardless of the sensitivity of the infecting strain. As physicians, the major problems we face with resistant bacteria are caused by our own use of antibiotics, often injudiciously, especially in the hospital environment. One cannot blame animal feed for antibiotic resistance in *Pseudomonas, Serratia, Enterobacter,* and *Klebsiella.* Even in the present report, 12 of the 18 patients had taken antibiotics before the onset of *Salmonella* diarrhea, in most cases without an appropriate indication. Antibiotics generally are overused in our society, not only by farmers, but by doctors as well.—S.G.

Doxycycline Therapy for Leptospirosis
J. Bruce L. McClain, W. Ripley Ballou, Shannon M. Harrison, Donald L. Steinweg
Ann. Intern. Med. 100:696–698, May 1984   1–55

Several reports have questioned the efficacy of antibiotic therapy for leptospirosis. The authors present a randomized, double-blind study of 29 patients with anicteric leptospirosis, who were treated with doxycycline hyclate or placebo 100 mg orally twice a day for 7 days, to study the effects of antibiotics on the course of leptospirosis. Follow-up period was 3 weeks. Leptospiral culture for blood and urine were done during a 3-week period.

DURATION OF SIGNS AND SYMPTOMS OF LEPTOSPIROSIS
IN PATIENTS TREATED WITH DOXYCYCLINE OR
PLACEBO*

Symptom	Duration of Symptom		p Value
	Doxycycline Group	Placebo Group	
	←——— d ———→		
Illness	5.6 ± 0.4	7.7 ± 0.5	0.01
Fever	3.7 ± 0.3	5.4 ± 0.3	0.01
Fever-days	7.2 ± 0.8	9.3 ± 0.8	0.03
Headache	3.0 ± 0.4	4.0 ± 0.3	0.03
Myalgias	3.0 ± 0.3	3.9 ± 0.4	0.03
Malaise	3.5 ± 0.3	4.9 ± 0.6	0.02
Gastrointestinal symptoms	1.1 ± 0.3	2.1 ± 0.5	0.06
Conjunctival suffusion	4.1 ± 0.5	5.3 ± 0.6	0.07

*Values given are mean ± SE.
(Courtesy of McClain, J.B.L., et al.: Ann. Intern, Med. 100:696–698, May 1984.)

Fourteen patients received doxycycline and 15 received placebo. Duration of illness and severity of symptoms were the same in both groups. Doxycycline therapy reduced the duration of illness by 2 days and favorably affected every measurable aspect of the illness (table). Doxycycline therapy prevented leptospiruria and had no adverse side effects. Fourteen of 17 patients with adequate serologic tests done seroconverted to one or more of the following serovars: gorgas, alexi, gatuni, shermani, szwajizak, javanica, mankarso, pyrogene, borincana, chagres, kobbe, and bravo. Twenty-six patients had leptospiroses isolated from the blood, which became negative after 5 days in both groups.

The resolution of leptospiremia in both groups may represent antibody-mediated clearing of leptospiroses rather than antibiotic effects. The study shows that doxycycline therapy is effective when begun early in an anicteric leptospirosis. The effectiveness of doxycycline or other antibiotics in modifying illness in the patient with Weil's syndrome is unknown.

Miscellaneous

Microbial Causes of Neonatal Conjunctivitis

K. Inger Sandström, Thomas A. Bell, John W. Chandler, Cho-Chou Kuo, San-Pin Wang, J. Thomas Grayston, Hjordis M. Foy, Walter E. Stamm, Marion K. Cooney, Arnold L. Smith, and King K. Holmes
J. Pediatr. 105:706–711, November 1984   1–56

Purulent conjunctivitis is the most common infection in the first month of life. Earlier studies have shown *Staphylococcus aureus* and *Streptococcus pneumoniae* to be associated with neonatal conjunctivitis, while more recent British studies have implicated *S. aureus, E. coli,* and *S. viridans.* A case-control study was carried out in 61 infants seen in 1980–1981 with purulent conjunctivitis starting before age 1 month, and 60 healthy infants of similar age who had received 1% silver nitrate drops at birth, but no subsequent antimicrobial therapy. Nineteen of the 55 neonates with confirmed conjunctivitis had received antimicrobials other than silver nitrate drops.

Chlamydia trachomatis was isolated from the eye in 5 of 19 affected neonates who had received antimicrobials. Pathogens were isolated from 4 other infants in this group. The isolates from untreated infants are shown in the table. Pathogens associated with conjunctivitis were isolated from 58% of 36 untreated infants with conjunctivitis and from 5% of control infants (Fig 1–5). The presence of gram-negative coccobacilli in smears correlated with the isolation of *Hemophilus* species. Both unilateral and bilateral infections were seen with most pathogens. Chlamydial inclusions were seen on Giemsa staining in 5 of 8 conjunctival scrapings from infants harboring *C. trachomatis.* Eight infants had evidence of dacryostenosis as the conjunctivitis resolved.

Neonatal conjunctivitis in this series was associated with *C. trachomatis, Hemophilus* species, *S. aureus,* enterococci, and *S. pneumoniae.* The initial clinical features usually were not indicative of specific pathogens, but the

MICROBIAL CAUSES OF NEONATAL CONJUNCTIVITIS: MICROORGANISMS ISOLATED MORE OFTEN FROM INFANTS WITH UNTREATED CONJUNCTIVITIS

Organisms isolated	Infants with conjunctivitis (n = 36) Culture positive		Controls (n = 60) Culture positive		P*
	n	%	n	%	
Haemophilus spp.	6	17	1	2	0.01
Staphylococcus aureus	6	17	1	2	0.01
Chlamydia trachomatis	5	14	0	0	0.01
Streptococcus pneumoniae	4	11	1	2	0.06
Enterococci	3	8	0	0	0.05
Total infants with one or more of above	21	58	3	5	<0.01
Other organisms†	29	81	42	70	0.34
No growth	2	6	16	27	0.01

*Fisher exact test.
†Staphylococcus epidermidis, α- and γ-hemolytic streptococci, diphtheroids, Escherichia coli, Acinetobacter calcoaceticus, and nonpathogenic Neisseria sp.
(Courtesy of Sandström, K.I., et al.: J. Pediatr. 105:706–711, November 1984.)

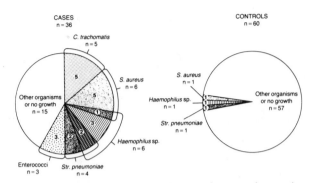

CASES
n = 36

CONTROLS
n = 60

C. trachomatis
n = 5

S. aureus
n = 6

Other organisms
or no growth
n = 15

Enterococci
n = 3

Str. pneumoniae
n = 4

Haemophilus sp.
n = 6

S. aureus
n = 1

Haemophilus sp.
n = 1

Str. pneumoniae
n = 1

Other organisms
or no growth
n = 57

Fig 1–5.—Prevalence of pathogens in 36 infants with previously untreated neonatal conjunctivitis and 60 neonates without conjunctivitis. (Courtesy of Sandström, K.I., et al.: J. Pediatr. 105:706–711, November 1984.)

presence of more than 5 white blood cells per oil immersion field on a Gram-stained smear of conjunctival exudate correlates well with clinical purulent conjunctivitis. Gram-stained smears should be routinely obtained to exclude *Neisseria gonorrheae*. Cultures for bacterial pathogens and C. *trachomatis* are indicated.

▶ There are a wide range of pathogens that may cause neonatal conjunctivitis. Clinical findings are not useful in distinguishing among the different pathogens.—D.S.

Clinical Features and an Epidemiologic Study of *Vibrio vulnificus* Infections
Carol O. Tacket, Frances Brenner, and Paul A. Blake (Centers for Disease Control)
J. Infect. Dis. 149:558–561, April 1984   1–57

Vibrio vulnificus is a halophilic *Vibrio* species isolated from the blood, wounds, and other skin lesions of patients with wound infection or primary sepsis. A case-control study was conducted in 30 patients from whom isolates recently were submitted to the Centers for Disease Control. Eighteen patients had primary sepsis, 9 had wound infections, and 3 had cellulitis with no history of wound or puncture. The organism was isolated from blood in all patients with primary sepsis and in 7 of the 9 with wound infections. Illnesses were most frequent in the late summer. The mean follow-up was 4½ months.

Patients were primarily in their early fifties. Underlying chronic illness was identified in 89% of patients with primary sepsis; liver disease was most common. Sixty-one percent of patients with primary sepsis died. The skin lesions began as large hemorrhagic bullae on the limbs or trunk and developed into necrotic ulcers. Patients with wound infections also had fever and chills, but gastrointestinal symptoms were less frequent in this group. About half these patients had underlying chronic illnesses. Two patients, 1 a diabetic, required amputations. The mortality was 22%. One of the 3 patients with cellulitis died. Patients with primary sepsis were more likely than controls to have recently eaten raw oysters, and also to have a history of liver disease. Those with wound infection were more likely than controls to have recently had skin exposure to salt water or shellfish.

Infections by *V. vulnificus* often are life-threatening, but the organism usually is sensitive to all antimicrobials commonly used in the initial empiric treatment of sepsis or severe wound infection. Persons with liver disease should avoid eating raw oysters. The *V. vulnificus* infection should be considered in the differential diagnosis of severe wound infection when there is a history of exposure of the skin to salt water or to shellfish harvested from coastal waters.

▶ Shellfish are able to filter and apparently concentrate several human pathogens, including viruses (hepatitis and Norwalk agent) and bacteria, especially vibrios, as shown in this report. The prescription against eating raw shellfish for patients with liver disease that these authors offer might even be reasonably applied to healthy individuals. Such dietary proclivities represent a form of microbial roulette, similar to that practiced by advocates of raw meat.—S.G.

Incidence and Cumulative Frequency of Endemic Lyme Disease in a Community

John P. Hanrahan, Jorge L. Benach, James L. Coleman, Edward B. Bosler, Dale L. Morse, Donald J. Cameron, Robert Edelman, and Richard A. Kaslow
J. Infect. Dis. 150:489–496, October 1984   1–58

Lyme disease is a tick-borne disorder whose distribution closely parallels that of certain *Ixodides* ticks. Most of the cases in the United States have been reported from the northeastern seaboard, but major and minor foci have occurred in other parts of the country. A prospective population-based study of Lyme disease was undertaken in a focal endemic area, a residential-vacation community on Fire Island, New York. Fourteen cases had been reported in residents of the study site in 1979–1981. The area consists of 135 single-family dwellings and 12 public-use structures.

A history of erythema chronicum migrams (ECM), with or without other features of Lyme disease, was reported by 15 (7.5%0 of the 200 participants in the study; 5 subjects had joint involvement, 5 had other associated symptoms such as headache and myalgia, and 5 had ECM alone. Indirect immunofluorescence antibody assays showed that 9.7% of 176 subjects had serologic evidence of exposure to the Lyme spirochete, including 6 of the 15 with a history of Lyme disease. The overall rate of symptoms and serologic findings of Lyme disease in the community was 0.7%–1.2%. Three percent of 129 subjects having sera collected before and after the summer season showed a four-fold or greater risk in IgG antibody to the Lyme spirochete, including 1.6% of persons without symptoms of Lyme disease.

Lyme disease can be significantly more frequent in endemic regions than has been recognized. Subclinical or inapparent seroconversion may follow infection by the Lyme spirochete. Endemic areas are likely to continue to expand as the disease is better recognized, and also with the spread of spirochete-infected *Ixodes* ticks or the involvement of other ticks in transmission of the disease. Awareness of the features of Lyme disease will help ensure prompt treatment and minimize long-term morbidity.

Diagnosing Early Lyme Disease

Mahesh Shrestha, Robert L. Grodzicki, and Allen C. Steere (Yale Univ.)
Am. J. Med. 78:235–240, February 1985   1–59

An early diagnosis of Lyme disease is important, since appropriate treatment prevents subsequent manifestations, but viral infection may be diagnosed if erythema chronicum migrans is atyical or absent. The diagnostic value of various findings was examined in a prospective series of 41 patients with a recent onset of Lyme disease. The 21 males and 20 females had a median age of 42 years. Adult patients were treated with tetracycline in a dose of 250 mg 4 times daily for 10–20 days, while children received phenoxymethyl penicillin in a daily dose of 50 mg/kg for the same period.

All patients but 1 had erythema chronicum migrans. Fifteen patients seen a median of 7 days after the onset of symptoms had evidence of infection localized to this lesion or to the regional nodes. Twenty-six patients seen after a median of 9 days had clinical evidence of disseminated infection. Nervous system involvement was evident in 21 of these patients, secondary annular lesions in 14, and arthralgia or arthritis in 8. Five patients had respiratory symptoms, and 1 had signs of liver involvement. Five patients with disseminated infection required another 10 days of treatment. No patients had subsequent manifestations of the illness. Only 1 of 40 blood cultures yielded spirochetes. One of 10 evaluable patients with localized infection had a specific IgM response in the acute phase. Eight of 22 patients with disseminated disease, including the one without erythema chronicum migrans, had elevated specific IgM levels, and 5 had increased specific IgG levels in the acute phase. Eight of the 22 patients had a four-fold or greater rise in antibody titer between acute and convalescent samples.

Recognition of characteristic clinical features of Lyme disease, especially erythema chronicum migrans, in the summer in a person from an endemic area remains very important in promptly diagnosing and treating the disease at an early stage. Serologic studies may be helpful in cases of disseminated infection and where the clinical findings are confusing.

► This study underscores the lack of utility of Lyme serologic tests (antibody to *Boreelia burgdorferi*) in the diagnosis of early Lyme disease. The serologic tests have been most useful in sorting out the cause of late complications (Russell, H., et al.: *J. Infect. Dis.* 149:465–470, 1984. Craft, J.E., et al.: *J. Infect. Dis.* 149:789–795, 1984).—D.S.

Diagnostic Bias and Toxic Shock Syndrome
Mary Harvey, Ralph I. Horwitz, and Alvan R. Feinstein (Yale Univ.)
Am. J. Med. 76:351–360, March 1984   1–60

Epidemiologic findings in toxic shock syndrome may have become biased during decisions made when practitioners diagnosed the syndrome, and when investigators chose to retain or reject a reported case as fulfilling the diagnostic criteria. The diagnosis is exclusively a clinical one. An attempt was made to determine whether diagnostic bias can occur in this way by preparing a set of descriptive vignettes for 6 cases having varying resemblances to toxic shock syndrome or Kawasaki disease. A paired case in a complementary series was identically described except for different information about gender, menstrual history, or tampon use. Either series was sent to a random sample of internists, family practitioners, and infectious disease specialists, and they were asked 6 weeks later to provide diagnoses for the complementary series of cases. A total of 368 physicians, 26% of those included, completed at least one set of case histories, and 218 completed both sets.

The respondents were more likely to diagnose toxic shock in menstruating tampon users or menstruating women than in nonmenstruating women or men, regardless of medical specialty or which series was received first. Toxic shock was diagnosed in 85% of instances where the case was described in a menstruating tampon user, and in 23% when the same case was described in a man; the odds ratio was about 19.

Diagnostic bias is likely when candidates for the diagnosis of toxic shock syndrome are menstruating tampon users, or menstruating women for whom no data on tampon use are given. A substantial degree of bias can occur in this relationship, raising serious doubt about current epidemiologic evidence for a relation between tampons and toxic shock syndrome. Objective studies of this purported relationship are needed.

▶ This paper presents a clear demonstraiton that the widespread publicity regarding the possible relationship of tampon use to toxic shock syndrome (TSS) could have led to diagnostic bias and, hence, a spurious relationship between tampons and TSS. Others (Davis, J. P., and Vergeront, J. M.: *J. Infect. Dis.* 145:449–457, 1982) have shown how the massive publicity in 1980 that was given to TSS influenced reporting of this disease. Although diagnostic bias may have influenced the results, the large odds ratios reported in a number of studies suggest a real relationship between tampon use and TSS.—S.G.

Detection of Teichoic Acid Antibodies in Children With Staphylococcal Infections
Usa Thisyakorn, Sharon Shelton, Tzou-Yien Lin, George H. McCracken, Jr., and John D. Nelson (Univ. of Texas Health Science Center)
Pediatr. Infect. Dis. 3:222–225, May 1984   1–61

Recent reports have shown that enzyme-linked immunosorbent assay

(ELISA) was a sensitive, specific, and rapid method of quantifying antibody to *Staphylococcus aureus* teichoic acid in adults with staphylococcal infections. The authors compared the sensitivity and specificity of the gel diffusion and ELISA assays for detection of teichoic acid antibodies in serum of children with staphylococcal infections. The study consisted of 14 children with deep-seated staphylococcal infections, 5 children with superficial staphylococcal infections, 10 children with deep-seated infections due to gram-positive organisms other than *S. aureus,* and 12 uninfected children of the same age.

Teichoic acid antibodies were detected by gel diffusion in 5 of 14 children (35.7%) with deep-seated staphylococcal infections, 1 of 10 patients with gram-positive infection other than *S. aureus,* and in none of the other patients. The largest titers of antibody developed within the first 2 weeks of illness. Teichoic acid antibody was detected by ELISA in all patients with deep-seated staphylococcal infections and in 5 patients with superficial staphylococcal infections (Fig 1–6). However, the titers of teichoic acid antibodies found in patients with deep-seated staphylococcal infections were significantly larger than those in other groups of patients. Antibody was detected by ELISA as early as the first week of illness. The gel diffusion method had a specificity of 95% but poor sensitivity of only 36% for deep-seated infections and 26% for all staphylococcal infections. Using a titer of 1:3,200 or greater as a diagnostic level in children, the ELISA method had a sensitivity of 93% and specificity of 89% for deep-seated staphylococcal infections, and a sensitivity of 79% and specificity of 95% for all staphylococcal infections.

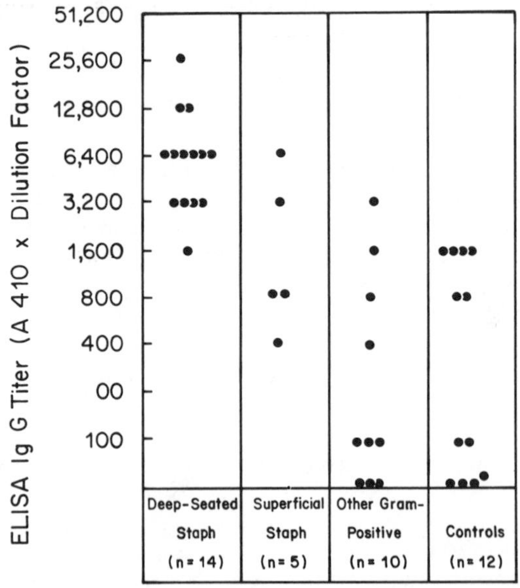

Fig 1–6.—Maximal IgG antibodies against teichoic acid in staphylococcal infections, other gram-positive deep-seated infections, and age-matched controls. (Courtesy of Thisyakorn, U., et al.: Pediatr. Infect. Dis. 3:222–225, May 1984.)

The low sensitivity and prolonged time required before results are available limit the usefulness of the gel diffusion test. All patients with positive gel diffusion tests had higher titers of antibody as assessed by ELISA tests than did patients who had negative gel diffusion tests. The authors conclude that detection of teichoic acid antibody by ELISA method is a sensitive and specific test for rapid diagnosis of staphylococcal infection in children.

▶ Teichoic acid antibodies are considered to represent a response to a prolonged systemic *S. aureus* infection such as endocarditis or osteomyelitis. This study is a favorable report of the use of an ELISA method to demonstrate antibody in infected children. Both sensitivity and specificity appear to be good and could be correlated with the presence of deep infections in these patients. However, the small number of subjects involved makes it difficult to recommend routine use of the test at this time. Larger prospective studies are needed to validate its use.—G.K.

Acute Renal Failure Due to Leptospirosis: Clinical Features and Outcome in Six Cases
C. G. Winearls, L. Chan, Joyce D. Coghlan, J. G. G. Ledingham, and D. O. Oliver (London)
Q. J. Med. (New Series) 53:487–495, August 1984   1–62

Acute renal failure is a recognized complication of leptospirosis and a common cause of death in this otherwise self-limited infection. Six cases of severe acute renal failure were encountered in 1978–1981. All patients had high-risk occupations or had been exposed to water that was probably polluted by the urine of rats or other animals. All patients had severe myalgia, fever, and jaundice, and 3 had headache. All patients were jaundiced at presentation, but only 2 were febrile. Petechial hemorrhages were noted in 4 cases. Only 2 patients exhibited meningism. Five patients had a palpable, tender liver.

Five patients had oliguric renal failure, but all had a diuretic phase and 4 patients required intravenous fluid supplements. All patients had substantial recovery of renal function within 2 months. All patients but 1 required dialysis for 1 to 3 weeks. Both renal ultrasound studies showed enlarged kidneys. Only 2 patients had significant leukocytosis, but 5 had an increased proportion of polymorphs. Five patients were thrombocytopenic. Bilirubin levels usually were high, but aspartate aminotransferase and alkaline phosphatase values were only minimally elevated. Muscle biopsy in 2 cases showed segmental necrosis and mild inflammatory-cell infiltration. Leptospires were not found in the urine in the 5 patients examined, but all patients had a diagnostic rise in leptospira complement fixation test titer after 5–8 days. Three of 5 patients given penicillin had a Jarisch-Herxheimer reaction. Five patients had gastrointestinal blood loss. Three developed atrial fibrillation, and 2 of these were hypotensive.

All these patients were severely ill, but none died. Early diagnosis is important. Treatment is essentially supportive. Liver failure is not a major threat. Leptospirosis is preventable where the risk is recognized in occupational and recreational settings.

Pasteurized Milk as a Vehicle of Infection in an Outbreak of Listeriosis

David W. Fleming, Stephen L. Cochi, Kristine L. MacDonald, Jack Brondum, Peggy S. Hayes, Brian D. Plikaytis, Marion B. Holmes, A. Audurier, Claire V. Broome, and Arthur L. Reingold
N. Engl. J. Med. 312:404–407, Feb. 14, 1985   1–63

The epidemiology of listeriosis remains poorly defined. Both sporadic and epidemic cases are recognized. Forty-nine patients acquired listeriosis in Massachusetts in a 2-month period in the summer of 1983. The attack rate was 4 to 5 times higher than in previous summers. Forty-two adults and 7 mother-infant pairs were affected. All adults had preexisting illnesses or conditions causing immunosuppression. One nosocomial case was included in the series. No obvious geographic clustering of cases within the state was evident. Thirty-two of 40 cases serotyped were serotype 4b, subsequently defined as the epidemic strain. The mortality was 29%. Case-control studies involved matching for neighborhood of residence and for underlying disease.

The illness appeared to be closely associated with drinking a specific brand of pasteurized whole or 2% milk. The odds ratio was 9 in the neighborhood-matched study and 11.5 in the illness-matched study. A dose-response effect was demonstrated, as well as a protective effect of skim milk. Cases were associated with the same product in Connecticut. A specific phage type was associated with the milk, which came from a group of farms where listeriosis was known to have occurred in dairy cows at the time of the outbreak. Multiple serotypes of *Listeria monocytogenes* were isolated from raw milk taken from the farms following the outbreak. There was no evidence of improper pasteurization of the milk.

These findings support the view that *L. monocytogenes* is a pathogen transmitted to humans via infected animals or their byproducts, and that ingestion of the organism can cause infection. Milk should be considered a possible vehicle of infection in sporadic cases of listeriosis. Pasteurization, though a highly effective means of eliminating bacterial pathogens from milk, is not always totally effective.

▶ *Listeria* is becoming recognized as a foodborne pathogen. Several other recent outbreaks (Schlech, W. F., III, et al.: *N. Engl. J. Med.* 308:203–306, 1983; *Morbid. Mortal. Week. Rep.* 34:357–359, 1985) have been associated with cabbage and pasteurized cheese. Common among all these epidemics is the high attack rate of disease among pregnant women, neonates, and other immunosuppressed individuals. The source of sporadic *Listeria* infection remains largely unknown.—D.S.

2 Viral Infections

Hepatitis Viruses

Hepatitis B Virus DNA in Patients With Chronic Liver Disease and Negative Tests for Hepatitis B Surface Antigen

Christian Bréchot, Françoise Degos, Claire Lugassy, Valérie Thiers, Serge Zafrani, Dominique Franco, Henri Bismuth, Christian Trépo, Jean-Pierre Benhamou, Jack Wands, Kurt Isselbacher, Pierre Tiollais, and Pierre Berthelot
N. Engl. J. Med. 312;270–276, Jan. 31, 1984   2–1

It has been proposed that some HBsAg-negative chronic liver diseases, including hepatocellular carcinoma, may be related to HBV infection. The presence of HBV DNA in liver and serum was examined in 134 patients with HBsAg-negative chronic liver disease, including 20 having hepatocellular carcinoma. The patients included 105 with chronic active hepatitis, 8 with chronic persistent hepatitis, and 1 with chronic lobular hepatitis. All but 1 of the patients with cancer had cirrhosis. Liver samples from 88 patients and sera from 105 were available for the HBV DNA hybridization assay. Fifteen renal transplant recipients and 8 other patients had received immunosuppressive therapy. The control group included 100 healthy HBsAg-negative subjects and 49 patients with various liver diseases.

The HBV DNA sequences were detected in 59% of liver samples from the study group and in 17 of 20 samples from patients with hepatocellular cancer. Presumably "replicative" forms of HBV DNA were found in 5 patients, including 3 without serologic markers of HBV. The presence of HBV DNA sequences was confirmed in 9.5% of sera from the study group; 6 of these patients had no HBV serologic markers. Five of 17 patients who were positive for HBV DNA and none of 14 negative patients had HBsAg-associated determinants.

These findings show that HBsAg-negative, HBV DNA-positive viral infection of the liver is not infrequent, and suggest that multiplication of HBV may occur in the absence of conventional serologic markers of the virus. The virus involved appears to be the same as that in "classical" HBsAg-positive HBV-induced liver disease, but it remains possible that some patients are infected by a different HBV strain.

Hepatitis B Vaccine in Patients Receiving Hemodialysis: Immunogenicity and Efficacy

Cladd E. Stevens, Harvey J. Alter, Patricia E. Taylor, Edith A. Zang, Edward J. Harley, Wolf Szmuness, and the Dialysis Vaccine Study Group
N. Engl. J. Med. 311:496–501, Aug. 23, 1984   2–2

Many hemodialysis patients who are infected with hepatitis B become chronic carriers, and most remain highly infectious. A multicenter double-blind, placebo-controlled trial of hepatitis B vaccine has been completed in 1,311 patients on hemodialysis. Patients were recruited at 41 dialysis units having chronic HBsAg carriers or recent cases of acute hepatitis B viral infection. Criteria for inclusion included negative studies for all markers of hepatitis B virus or low levels of anti-HBs only; an alanine aminotransferase level of 100 IU/L or below; and expected survival of at least 2 years. Three vaccine injections were administered; the first 2 were given a month apart and the third at 6 months. Vaccine was given to 660 patients and placebo to 651.

No major side effects were observed. Anti-HBs was found in 55.5% of vaccine recipients after the first 2 doses and in 63% after the booster dose (Fig 2–1). The response rate at 2 years was 49%. Attack rates of hepatitis B viral infection did not differ significantly (table). Eight vaccine recipients and 14 placebo subjects developed chronic hepatitis B viral infection. Four cases of hepatitis B occurred in patients having an apparent antibody response to vaccine, but low or undetectable levels of antibody were present in each instance, or immunosuppressive therapy had been given. Rates of non-A, non-B hepatitis also were similar in the vaccine and placebo groups.

No protective efficacy from vaccination against hepatitis B was found in this study of hemodialysis patients. Anti-HBs may not be the critical protective factor; some other antibody or cell-mediated immune response may be necessary for protection against hepatitis B viral infection. Current control measures, such as isolation of infected patients, the use of disposable equipment, and hepatitis B immune globulin remain necessary for controlling hepatitis in dialysis units.

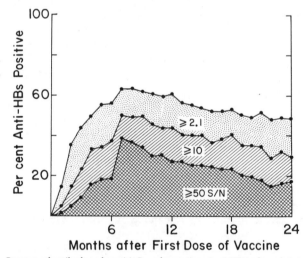

Fig 2–1.—Presence of antibody to hepatitis B surface antigen (anti-HBs) after administration of hepatitis B vaccine in patients treated with dialysis. The S/N is the ratio of counts per minute in the sample to the mean value in negative controls by radioimmunoassay. (Courtesy of Stevens, C.E., et al.: N. Engl. J. Med. 311:496–501, Aug. 23, 1984. Reprinted by permission of *The New England Journal of Medicine*.)

LIFE-TABLE ATTACK RATES DURING 25 MONTHS OF
STUDY FOR HEPATITIS B VIRAL EVENTS IN PATIENTS
RECEIVING DIALYSIS*

VIRAL EVENT	STUDY GROUP	
	PLACEBO	VACCINE
	no. of cases (%)	*no. of cases (%)*
Hepatitis B	20 (3.3)	16 (3.1)
Any ALT elevation (including hepatitis B)	24 (4.0)	24 (4.7)
All HBsAg+ (including above cases)	30 (5.1)	31 (6.0)
All events	31 (5.4)	34 (6.4)

*One viral event in each group was excluded from the life-table analysis because it occurred after 25 months when too few patients were being followed to make reliable estimates of attack rates. Log-rank chi-square values were all <1.0 and P values were >.30. ALT = alanine aminotransferase. HBsAg+ = a positive response for hepatitis B surface antigen.
(Courtesy of Stevens, C.E., et al.: N. Engl. J. Med. 311:496–501, Aug. 23, 1984. Reprinted by permission of *The New England Journal of Medicine*.)

▶ Although the demonstration of hepatitis B vaccine efficacy in hemodialysis patients is lacking, the Advisory Committee on Immunization Practices recommends the use of hepatitis B vaccine in seronegative hemodialysis patients (*Morb. Mortal. Week. Rep.* 34:313–315, 1985). The lack of efficacy demonstration in this population is in contrast to two other studies (Desmyter, J., et al.: *Lancet* 2:1323–1327, 1983; Crosnier, J., et al.: *Lancet* 1:797–780, 1981) performed in dialysis patients and may reflect a type II error due to a lower than expected overall attack rate.—D.S.

Hepatitis B Vaccine in Health Care Personnel: Safety, Immunogenicity, and Indicators of Efficacy

Jules L. Dienstag, Barbara G. Werner, B. Frank Polk, David R. Snydman, Donald E. Craven, Richard Platt, Clyde S. Crumpacker, Rita Ouellet-Hellstrom, and George F. Grady (Boston)

Ann. Intern. Med. 101:34–40, July 1984   2–3

Clinical hepatitis B infection continues to occur in health care workers, usually without an identifiable or recalled source of infection, and only active immunization before exposure is likely to be effective. An effective and safe vaccine prepared from HBsAg particles has been used in populations at risk such as homosexual and hemodialysis staff. A double-blind, placebo-controlled trial of hepatitis B vaccine was undertaken to evaluate the current 20-μg preparation in hospital workers at several institutions in Boston. A total of 1,330 high-risk subjects were assigned to receive either three 20-μg doses of vaccine or placebo.

Nearly 80% of vaccine recipients achieved peak levels above 1,000 estimated radioimmunoassay units. Only 1 of 6 hepatitis B virus infections

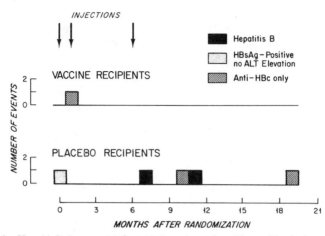

Fig 2–2.—Hepatitis B virus events in hepatitis B vaccine trial participants. The third consecutive case in the placebo group (at 10 months) followed an accidental HBsAg-positive inoculation and passive immunoprophylaxis with hepatitis B immune globulin. The first case in the placebo group, an asymptomatic HBsAg seroconversion, occurred on the day of randomization but was not detected until that day's serum sample was tested retrospectively. Because eligibility for entry into the study was determined on the basis of a serum sample drawn within 2 weeks before randomization, and not on the basis of the randomization-day sample, this participant was not excluded. The last case in the placebo group was identified 1 month after the code was broken. (Courtesy of Dienstag, J.L., et al.: Ann. Intern. Med. 101:34–40, July 1984.)

identified was in a vaccine recipient (Fig 2–2). Seroconverison to anti-HBc occurred in this subject, an anesthesiologist, one month after entry to the study. The difference in attack rates tended toward significance. None of 8 vaccine recipients who were exposed accidentally became infected with hepatitis B virus, but all 10 exposed placebo recipients required hepatitis B immune globulin prophylaxis, and one of them still became infected. Three cases of non-B hepatitis occurred, 2 in vaccine recipients and 1 in a placebo recipient. Adverse effects occurred in about one fourth of each group, and no serious effects were noted.

Hepatitis vaccine appeared to be effective in this study of health care workers other than hemodialysis staff. No cases of clinical hepatitis B or hepatitis B surface antigenemia were seen in vaccine recipients, and no recipient who acquired anti-HBs following vaccination later became infected with hepatitis B virus. The vaccine is expensive, but much less so than hepatitis B immune globulin, and vaccination is more likely to prevent hepatitis B virus infection than is postexposure prophylaxis with immune globulin.

Live Recombinant Vaccinia Virus Protects Chimpanzees Against Hepatitis B

Bernard Moss, Geoffrey L. Smith, John L. Gerin, and Robert H. Purcell
Nature 311:67–68, Sept. 6, 1984

2–4

Hepatitis B virus (HBV) is responsible for more than 200 million cases of chronic infection, many of which progress to hepatocellular carcinoma. Subunit vaccines made from plasma of chronically infected patients are safe, but are expensive and limited in quantity, and therefore unavailable to most developing countries. A novel candidate vaccine hs been prepared from an infectious vaccinia virus recombinant that expresses hepatitis B surface antigen in animal cells, and stimulates the production of antibody to HBsAg in rabbits. Chimpanzees now have been protected against HBV challenge by vaccination with live recombinant vaccinia virus.

The recombinant vaccinia virus was made by fusing a DNA fragment of HBV strain adw, containing the entire gene coding for HBsAg, to an early vaccinia virus promoter and inserting it into the coding sequence of the vaccinia virus thymidine kinase gene by homologous recombination in vivo. Two chimpanzees were given 10^8 plaque forming units of the recombinant virus intradermally, while a third animal was vaccinated with the same amount of wild-type vaccinia virus. All 3 animals developed primary vaccinia lesions, but these lesions were less extensive in those given the recombinant virus. Challenge with live HBV 14 weeks after vaccination was followed by typical hepatitis B in the control chimpanzee. The 2 study animals had no detectable HBsAg or biochemical evidence of hepatitis. Anti-HBs appeared 4–7 weeks after challenge and rapidly rose to high levels. Both animals developed low levels of anti-HBc. Liver biopsies obtained 11 months after HBV challenge showed no acute or chronic hepatitis.

A live recombinant vaccinia virus expressing HBsAg can protect chimpanzees against hepatitis B. Current work is directed at increasing HBsAg expression by the use of stronger vaccinia virus promoters. Vaccinia virus recombinant expressing herpesvirus glycoprotein and malaria sporozoite antigen also have been prepared.

Fulminant B Viral Hepatitis: Role of Delta Agent

Sugantha Govindarajan, Kenneth P. Chin, Allan G. Redeker, and Robert L. Peters (Rancho Los Amigos Hosp., Downey, CA)
Gastroenterology 86:1417–1420, June 1984   2–5

The clinical importance of delta-agent infection superimposed on chronic hepatitis B virus (HBV) carriers and coincident with acute hepatitis B has been reported. Recent studies revealed a much higher prevalence (39%) of delta markers among patients with fulminant hepatitis B (FHB) than among patients with ordinary acute viral hepatitis B (AVHB) (19%). Forty-two percent of patients with delta markers among the FHB group were asymptomatic carriers of HBV presenting a fulminant course associated with acute superinfection with delta agent. It appears that more severe liver necrosis occurs when acute delta infection is superimposed on preexisting HBV infection than occurs with the simultaneous acute infections of the delta agent and HBV.

The authors reviewed 71 hepatitis B surface antigen (HBsAg)-positive patients with the diagnosis of fulminant hepatitis (FH) and studied the serologic markers that reflected whether the hepatitis B or the delta infection was acute or chronic. Sera from 118 patients with acute icteric HBsAg-positive viral hepatitis, whose clinical course was not associated with hepatic failure, were also studied for delta markers and HBV markers. This group included patients with epidemiologic background similar to the FH group.

The prevalence of delta markers among the 71 patients with fulminant B viral hepatitis was found to be 33.8%. Most patients with delta markers showed serologic evidence of simultaneous acute delta infection and B viral infection. Only 5 of the 24 patients with serologic markers of acute delta infection in this fulminant group were presumably infected chronically with HBV as shown by the absence of immunoglobulin M antibody to hepatitis B core antigen. The serologic markers of acute delta infection among the 118 patients with nonfulminant acute B viral hepatitis, in contrast, revealed only 4.2% incidence. When the fulminant group was divided into AVHB without delta markers (subgroup 1), simultaneous acute B and delta infections (subgroup 2), and chronic asymptomatic B with acute delta infections (subgroup 3), for comparison of survival data, the mortality was not significantly different in the first 2 groups when the patients were age-matched.

Increased morbidity appears to be associated with delta infection when it occurs simultaneously with HBV or when it develops as a superinfection on chronic HBV infection. In cases of FHB with a short clinical course and fatal outcome, patients with acute delta infection may not survive long enough to develop IgG anti-delta; 11 of 24 patients in this series had IgM anti-delta alone detected without IgG antibody. These patients will be typed as delta-negative cases if the IgM anti-delta is not determined or if there are not adequate serial serum samples following the acute episode to detect the appearance of IgG anti-delta. Although blocking solid-phase radioimmunoassay (RIA) for total anti-delta should detect both IgM and IgG anti-delta in the early stages if IgM anti-delta alone is present, the total anti-delta is often negative. This is probably due to that fact that blocking RIA is less sensitive than the IgM capture solid-phase RIA for IgM anti-delta. This might have accounted for the finding of serum delta antigen without anti-delta in 1 of the 6 patients with FHB reported by Tabor et al. The present data indicate that delta infection in the Los Angeles area has been an important factor in FHB.

▶ Delta virus infection is caused by a defective RNA virus that requires hepatitis B for replication. The delta agent has been found in 20%–30% of patients with chronic hepatitis B infection and has been recently linked to an epidemic of fulminant hepatitis among drug addicts. *Morbid. Mortal. Week. Rep.* 33:493–494, 1984).—D.S.

Chronic Delta Infection and Liver Biopsy Changes in Chronic Active Hepatitis B

Gary C. Kanel, Sugantha Govindarajan, and Robert L. Peters (Univ. of Southern California)
Ann. Intern. Med. 101:51–54, July 1984   2–6

The delta agent is a defective RNA virus dependent on hepatitis B virus that has been associated with severe clinical forms of chronic B viral liver disease. It is not clear whether infection with the combination of hepatitis B virus and delta agent has a morphological pattern distinct from infection by hepatitis B virus alone. Review was made of the liver biopsy or autopsy findings in 57 patients with chronic active hepatitis B in an attempt to distinguish delta-positive and delta-negative cases. Eighteen patients had serologic evidence of chronic delta infection, with high titers of IgG anti-delta and low titers of IgM anti-delta.

Livers with chronic infection had a more predominantly mononuclear infiltrate in the portal and septal regions. More parenchymal necrosis was evident in delta-positive patients. The inflammatory infiltrate was mainly lymphocytic, and often present in a periseptal or periportal pattern. Eosinophilic granular cells were not commonly seen in biopsies in both delta-positive and negative cases. Delta-positive patients had greater degrees of hepatic nuclear polyploidy and dysplasia. Cirrhosis was a nearly constant finding at autopsy. Fourteen of 16 evaluable patients had delta antigen within hepatocyte nuclei. In only one biopsy was HBcAg found in the liver.

Chronic delta infection with ongoing replication may increase the degree of liver damage in patients with chronic active hepatitis B, and possibly may hasten the progression of liver disease. Further studies are needed to identify any contribution the delta agent may have in the development of hepatocellular carcinoma in patients with B-viral chronic liver disease.

Delta Virus Infection and Severe Hepatitis: An Epidemic in the Yucpa Indians of Venezuela
Stephen C. Hadler, Maria de Monzon, Antonio Ponzetto, Elias Anzola, Dalia Rivero, Alejandro Mondolfi, Ana Bracho, Donald P. Francis, Michael A. Gerber, Swan Thung, John Gerin, James E. Maynard, Hans Popper, and Robert H. Purcell
Ann. Intern. Med. 100:339–344, March 1984   2–7

Unusual large outbreaks of acute hepatitis recently have been reported in Asia, and attributed to a non-A, non-B agent presumably spread through water. The delta agent is a defective virus requiring hepatitis B virus as a helper for replication. Coinfection with hepatitis B usually causes acute hepatitis which resolves, but superinfection of a hepatitis B carrier usually leads to persistent delta infection that can progress to chronic active hepatitis and cirrhosis. Fulminant hepatitis has ben associated with both types of delta infection. An epidemic of severe hepatitis resulted from spread of the delta agent in a rural Venezuelan Indian population in which hepatitis B infection was endemic. A

CHRONIC HEPATITIS AMONG HEPATITIS B CARRIERS WITH OR WITHOUT
DELTA INFECTION

	Total Patients	Patients Followed	Disease Severity			
			Severe*	Moderate†	Mild‡	None
			n			
With delta infection	35	31	10	11	6	4
Without delta infection	21	21	0	0	2	19

*Severe: transaminase activity of more than 100 U/ml and liver or spleen more than 3 cm enlarged.
†Moderate: transaminase activity of more than 100 U/ml with normal liver and spleen; or alanine transaminase (ALT) activity of 46 to 100 U/ml and liver or spleen more than 3 cm enlarged.
‡Mild: transaminase activity of 46 to 100 U/ml and liver or spleen more than 3 cm enlarged; or normal ALT activity and liver or spleen more than 3 cm enlarged.
(Courtesy of Hadler, S.C., et al.: Ann. Intern. Med. 100:339–344, March 1984.)

total of 149 Yucpa Indians developed hepatitis in a 3-year period. Thirty-four of them died, and at least 22 others developed chronic hepatitis.

Three communities were severely affected during the epidemic. Children and young adults were primarily affected. Active hepatitis B viral infection was a significant factor, but was not the cause of the epidemic. All but 7 of 50 HBsAg-positive patients tested for anti-delta were positive, compared with 4 of 33 HBsAg-positive subjects without illness. More than two thirds of 81 patients tested serologically had delta infection, most were hepatitis B carriers with superinfection by delta agent. Twenty-five deaths occurred within a month of the onset of illness. Chronic hepatitis was found in neary 90% of persons with both hepatitis B and delta infections, and in 10% of those with hepatitis B infection alone (table). No subject with hepatitis B infection alone had moderate or severe liver disease.

Fulminant hepatitis may be a common consequence of delta virus infection. The source of delta virus in this population is uncertain; it has not previously been reported in South America. Prevention of hepatitis B infection is the best means of controlling delta infection over the long term. An effective program of vaccinating persons at high risk eventually could eliminate the population susceptible to delta infection.

Detection of Reverse Transcriptase Activity in Association With the Non-A, Non-B Hepatitis Agent(s)
Belinda Seto, William G. Coleman, Jr., Sten Iwarson, and Robert J. Gerety
Lancet 2:941–943, Oct. 27, 1984   2–8

The diagnosis of non-A, non-B hepatitis (NANBH) continues to be one of exclusion. The activities of DNA-polymerase, protein kinase, and reverse transcriptase (RT) have been associated with HBV, and an HBV-like NANBH hepatitis agent has been proposed. Particle-associated RT activity was sought in sera from 12 patients with histologically confirmed NANBH and in sera from 49 healthy control subjects. Three of the patients were blood recipients, 4 were intravenous drug users, and 5 had sporadic disease. Reverse transcriptase activity also was determined in infectious serum inocula used in previous transmission studies of NANBH and in 2 infectious plasma-derived products.

Particle-associated RT activity was detected in all sera from patients with NANBH and in 2 of 49 control sera. The latter were considered low-positives. Particle-associated RT activity was detected in all 6 infectious NANBH materials tested, 4 human serum specimens, and 2 plasma-derived products. Sucrose density gradient fractions of 2 of the infectious human sera transmitted NANBH to chimpanzees. The RT activity banded at a discrete density and was associated with viral particles.

The NANBH agent appears to be a retrovirus or a retrovirus-like agent. Inactivation of NANBH agents by formalin, heat, and chloroform is consistent with their being retroviruses. Whether antibodies neutralize retroviruses is not known but, if NANBH is caused by a retrovirus, it may not readily be neutralized by antibodies.

Hepatitis B Virus Antibody in Blood Donors and the Occurrence of Non-A, Non-B Hepatitis in Transfusion Recipients: An Analysis of the Transfusion-Transmitted Viruses Study

Cladd E. Stevens, Richard D. Aach, F. Blaine Hollinger, James W. Mosley, Wolf Szmuness, Richard Kahn, Jochewed Werch, and Virginia Edwards
Ann. Intern. Med. 101:733–738, December 1984   2–9

A correlation has been found between donor serum alanine aminotransferase (ALT) levels and the incidence of non-A, non-BN hepatitis in transfusion recipients. Epidemiologic circumstances predisposing donor populations to hepatitis B virus infection also may favor exposure to non-A, non-B hepatitis agents. Data from the Transfusion-Transmitted Viruses Study were analyzed to test this hypothesis. The study, done in 1974–1979, was designed to determine the risk of posttransfusion hepatitis in transfusion recipients in four regions of the United States. Data were available from 1,151 recipients and their 4,304 donors. The total prevalence of HBV antibody in donors was 7.6%. Antibody to HBsAg only was present in 2.5% of donors; anti-HBc in 1.1%; and both anti-HBs and anti-HBc in 4.0%.

Anti-HBc-positive donors were associated twice as often with the development of non-A, non-B hepatitis in recipients than negative donors, regardless of whether or not anti-HBs was also present. The prevalence of anti-HBc increased with the donor serum ALT level, although only 8.6% of anti-HBc-positive donors had an ALT of 45 IU/L or more. The risk was greatest in recipients of blood from donors who both were anti-HBc-positive and had an elevated ALT level. Both parameters were related to the severity of non-A, non-B hepatitis as well as to the risk of disease. More than 60% of recipients given blood with both risk factors had severe hepatitis.

The risk of non-A, non-B hepatitis is increased in recipients of anti-HBc-positive blood, especially when a serum ALT above 45 IU/L also is present. The high prevalence of anti-HBc in donor populations impedes its use as a screening measure. It appears that ALT screening remains preferable to anti-HBc screening to prevent the occurrence of a non-A, non-B hepatitis in transfusion recipients.

Herpes Viruses

Double-Blind Placebo-Controlled Trial of Oral Acyclovir in First-Episode Genital Herpes Simplex Virus Infection

Gregory J. Mertz, Cathy W. Critchlow, Jacqueline Benedetti, Richard C. Reichman, Raphael Dolin, James Connor, David C. Redfield, Maria C. Savoia, Douglas D. Richman, David L. Tyrrell, Lilian Miedzinski, Joseph Portnoy, Ronald E. Keeney, and Lawrence Corey
JAMA 252:1147–1151, Sept. 7, 1984   2–10

Both topical and intravenous acyclovir effectively shorten the course of primary first episodes of genital herpes infection. A multicenter double-blind, placebo-controlled trial of oral acyclovir was undertaken in patients with first episodes of genital herpes who were seen in 1980–1982 within 6 days of the onset of lesions. The age range was 18–50 years. The dose of acyclovir was 200 mg 5 times daily for 10 days.

A total of 119 patients with primary, and 31 with nonprimary first episodes of genital herpes participated in the study. Acyclovir was given to 61 and 12 patients, respectively. The overall mean age was 26 years, and the mean interval from the onset of lesions to initial treatment was 3½ days. Cases of herpesvirus type 2 infection predominated. The median duration of viral shedding from genital lesions in patients with primary genital herpes was 2 days in the acyclovir-treated group and 9 days in the placebo group. A similar difference was seen in patients with nonprimary genital herpes. The median times to complete healing of all genital lesions was shorter in acyclovir-treated patients with primary episodes. The period of symptoms was somewhat shorter in actively treated patients. No patient withdrew because of adverse side effects. The rate of recurrences was similar in acyclovir- and placebo-treated patients. Patients with first-episode HSV 2 infection had more recurrences than those with first-episode HSV 1 infection.

Oral acyclovir has significant beneficial effects in patients with primary first-episode genital herpes. It is not curative, but it is a safe and convenient means of treating a disease that can produce significant morbidity. Patients with first-episode infection, especially caused by HSV 2, should be advised about the risk of recurrences and of the increased chance of transmitting disease during recurrences.

▶ The results of this study agree with two previously published studies on the efficacy of oral acyclovir in first-episode genital herpes infection (Nilsen, A. E., et al.: *Lancet* 2:571–573, 1982; Bryson, Y. J., et al.: *N. Engl. J. Med.*

308:916–921, 1983). Although a great advance over previous therapies, a major goal now is to find an agent that will prevent recurrences in the chronically injected patient.—G.K.

Suppression of Frequently Recurring Genital Herpes: A Placebo-Controlled Double-Blind Trial of Oral Acyclovir
Stephen E. Straus, Howard E. Takiff, Mindell Seidlin, Susan Bachrach, Lloyd Lininger, John J. DiGiovanna, Karl A. Western, Holly A. Smith, Sandra Nusinoff Lehrman, Teresa Creagh-Kirk, and David W. Alling
N. Engl. J. Med. 310:1545–1550, June 14, 1984   2–11

Thirty-five adults with frequently recurring genital herpes were studied in a double-blind trial comparing the efficiency of oral acyclovir with placebo in the suppression of recurrent infection. Patients were given 200 mg capsules 5 times daily for the first 5 days and one capsule 3 times daily thereafter until 385 capsules had ben dispensed or unless the infection recurred. On confirmation of recurrence, the patient was treated in an open-study phase with acylovir given the same way as in the blind phase.

Among 32 patients who completed their treatment course, there were significantly fewer recurrences during acyclovir treatment (4 of 16) than during placebo treatment (16 of 16). Four patients from the acyclovir group and 15 of 16 patients from the placebo group entered the open phase, in which all 4 from the acyclovir group and 13 patients from the placebo group were succesfully treated with acyclovir. Only 2 of 19 patients had recurrences in the open phase. The mean duration of therapy was significantly longer for patients receiving acyclovir than for those receiving placebo (114.9 vs. 24.8 days). The mean duration between occurrences was significantly longer in the acyclovir group. All patients had recurrences after completing acyclovir treatment. Acyclovir was well tolerated, with minimal gastrointestinal upset and one hypersensitivity reaction. Viral isolates from the study group showed a wide range of sensitivity including resistant strains from 2 patients who had not received acyclovir treatment. Studies of the viral isolates demonstrated that lesions developing in patients receiving acyclovir contained drug-resistant virus. Later recurrences in these patients were associated with drug-sensitive virus.

The authors conclude that in adults with frequently recurring genital herpes, oral acyclovir significantly reduces the recurrence during treatment. Because of the possibility of long-term hazards of continuous treatment, oral acyclovir is best for reliable patients who have well-established patterns of frequent or complicated herpetic recurrences and treatment should be of limited duration. Suppressive acyclovir treatment is associated with shedding of resistant virus and may pose a risk for uninfected sexual partners of treated patients.

▶ Oral acyclovir may be used to prevent recurrent genital herpes simplex. Two other studies published in 1984 support the data presented here (Douglas, J. M., et al.: *N. Engl. J. Med.* 310:1551–1556, 1984; Mindel, A., et al.: *Lancet*

2:57–59, 1984). All 3 studies confirm that the risk of recurrence returns to the baseline rate once the drug is discontinued. The study mentioned above by Douglas does demonstrate that 200-mg capsules given orally twice a day is equal to 200-mg capsules given five times per day. Considering the expense of acyclovir, the lower prophylactic dose should be kept in mind.

Most studies on intravenous acyclovir were published prior to 1984. One study worthy of note in 1984 was a comparison trial of intravenous acyclovir vidarabine for herpes simplex encephalitis (Skoldenberg, B., et al.; *Lancet* 2:707–711, 1984). Acyclovir in a dose of 10 mg/kg IV every 8 hours lowers the mortality to 19% compared with a rate of 50% using vidarabine. The Swedish investigators did not use brain biopsy documentation of herpes simplex encephalitis as a requirement for all cases. They also relied upon CSF/serum herpes simplex titers to make the diagnosis. The reliance on these ratios and the high mortality in the vidarabine group together raise some questions about this study. A group of investigators from the United States are completing a similar comparative study in which brain biopsy is used to make the diagnosis. Results should be available in 1985.—G.K.

Detection of Herpes Simplex Viral Antigen in Skin Lesions of Erythema Multiforme
Paul W. Orton, J. Clark Huff, Marcia G. Tonnesen, and William L. Weston (Denver)
Ann. Intern. Med. 101:48–50, July 1984   2–12

Recurrent herpes simplex virus infection has been the most common factor precipitating erythema multiforme. To better understand the immunopathogenesis of herpes-associated erythema multiforme, the authors examined skin biopsy specimens for the presence of herpes simplex viral antigen by a low background, indirect immunofluorescence technique with a murine monoclonal antibody to a major type-common glycoprotein antigen, gB. The study included specimens from 16 patients with herpes-associated disease, skin biopsies from 20 patients with other skin diseases which served as controls, and 4 skin biopsies from patients with lesions of recurrent herpes simplex virus infections which served as positive control specimens.

Twelve of the 16 biopsy sections from herpes-associated erythema multiforme skin lesions stained positively for gB. The staining was similar to, but less intense than that seen in biopsy samples of lesions of recurrent herpes simplex virus infections. A positive stain showed a slightly granular fluorescence of keratinocyte cytoplasm and membranes adjacent to focal areas of epidermal damage which corresponded in specimens of erythema multiforme to the central areas of papules or the erythematous borders of target lesions adjacent to the central epidermal necrosis. The control monoclonal antibody stain was negative in all specimens. Staining for gB was negative in the control specimens and in uninvolved skin from patients with herpes-associated erythema multiforme.

These findings suggest that the immune reaction and prominent epidermal necrosis of herpes-associated erythema multiforme are due to the presence of herpes antigens in the skin.

▶ This is an interesting and provocative study. As the authors suggest, their findings must be confirmed. If they are, then similar studies looking for other antigens will undoubtedly be done in the large number of patients who have erythema multiforme in the absence of a herpes simplex infection.—S.G.

Live Attenuated Varicella Virus Vaccine: Efficacy Trial in Healthy Children
Robert E. Weibel, Beverly J. Neff, Barbara J. Kuter, Harry A. Guess, Carol A. Rothenberger, Alison J. Fitzgerald, Karen A. Connor, Arlene A. McLean, Maurice R. Hilleman, Eugene B. Buynak, and Edward M. Scolnick
N. Engl. J. Med. 310:1409–1415, May 31, 1981   2–13

The Oka strain of the live attenuated varicella virus vaccine has been successfully used to prevent disease in both children and adults after exposure to the virus. However, it has not been shown to be efficacious in protecting against natural disease when administered to children before exposure. The authors conducted a double-blind, placebo-controlled efficacy trial of the live attenuated Oka/Merck varicella vaccine among 956 children between the ages of 1 and 14 years with a negative history of varicella. Of the 914 children who were originally seronegative, 468 received the 1 ml of the vaccine subcutaneously while 446 received placebo. There were few clinical reactions noted, i.e., pain and redness at the injection site. Antibody to varicella developed in 432 of 461 vaccine recipients giving a seroconversion rate of 94% (Table 1). During the 9–month surveillance period, 39 clinically diagnosed cases of varicella occurred in placebo recipients, 38 of which were confirmed by laboratory tests; none occurred in children who received the vaccine (Table 2). The vaccine has a protective efficacy of 100% in these seronegative children. The attack rate was analyzed in 27 families in which a laboratory-

TABLE 1.—SEROCONVERSION RATES AND GEOMETRIC MEAN TITERS AMONG INITIALLY SERONEGATIVE VACCINE RECIPIENTS, ACCORDING TO AGE

AGE	NO. OF CHILDREN VACCINATED	SEROCONVERSION RATE no. of children	SEROCONVERSION RATE per cent	GEOMETRIC MEAN TITER
12–14 mo	16	15/15	100	13.9
15–17 mo	16	14/15	93	11.6
18–23 mo	26	24/25	96	11.5
2–4 yr	199	189/195	97	13.4
5–14 yr	211	190/211	90	10.4
Total	468	*432/461*	*94*	*12.1*

(Courtesy of Weibel, R.E., et al.: N. Engl. J. Med. 310:1409–1415, May 31, 1984. Reprinted by permission of *The New England Journal of Medicine*.)

TABLE 2.—ATTACK RATE AND PROTECTIVE EFFICACY ON THE BASIS OF LABORATORY-CONFIRMED CASES AMONG INITIALLY SERONEGATIVE VACCINE AND PLACEBO RECIPIENTS DURING THE 9-MONTH SURVEILLANCE PERIOD

GROUP	ALL PARTICIPANTS			27 HOUSEHOLDS WITH ≥1 VACCINE RECIPIENT EXPOSED TO ≥1 SIBLING WITH VARICELLA					
	NO. OF CHILDREN	CASES OF VARICELLA	ATTACK RATE	NO. OF CHILDREN	PRIMARY CASES OF VARICELLA	NO. OF CHILDREN EXPOSED TO VARICELLA	SECONDARY CASES OF VARICELLA	SECONDARY ATTACK RATE	PROTECTIVE EFFICACY
Placebo	446	38	8.5% (38/446)	36	27	9	4 *	44% (4/9)	
Vaccine	468	0	0% (0/468)	33	0	33	0	0% (0/33)	100%

*A fifth infection occurred 1 week after the study was ended, increasing the secondary attack rate to 56% (5 of 9 patients).
(Courtesy of Weibel, R.E., et al.: N. Engl. J. Med. 310:1409–1415, May 31, 1984. Reprinted by permission of The New England Journal of Medicine.)

confirmed case of natural varicella occurred and placed an initially sero-negative vaccine recipient at risk. Varicella developed in 4 of 9 placebo recipients (44%) and in none of 33 vaccine recipients exposed to a sibling with varicella. An analysis of the data based on household exposure showed that the protective efficacy of the vaccine was 100%.

This study shows that the live attenuated Oka/Merck varicella virus vaccine is safe, highly immunogenic, and protective in healthy children before exposure to natural varicella. Further studies are needed to determine the long-term safety of the vaccine, the incidence of zoster in recipients, and the duration of immunity provided by the vaccine in comparison to immunity from natural disease.

▶ The studies of the live attenuated varicella vaccine reported here are very promising. This clinical trial is extremely well-designed and well-executed, and it should serve as a classic example of a well conducted, randomized, placebo-controlled, double-blind trial.—G.K.

Live Attenuated Varicella Vaccine: Efficacy for Children With Leukemia in Remission
Anne A. Gershon, Sharon Projansky Steinberg, Lawrence Gelb, George Galasso, William Borkowsky, Philip LaRussa, Angelo Ferrara, and The National Institute of Allergy and Infectious Diseases Varicella Vaccine Collaborative Study Group
JAMA 252:355–362, July 20, 1984   2–14

No studies have been reported regarding the protective efficacy of live attenuated varicella vaccine in immunocompromised children. The authors began a collaborative investigation of varicella vaccine in 191 varicella-susceptible children with acute lymphocytic leukemia (ALL) in remission to determine whether these high-risk patients could be protected from severe varicella by immunization. Children were given approximately 1,000 plaque-forming units of live attenuated varicella vaccine virus subcutaneously initially as one dose; however, 79 vaccinees received two doses at least 3 months apart. Chemotherapy was suspended for one week before and after immunization. For the second dose of the vaccine, chemotherapy was not suspended in 18 children who had experienced seroconversion after the first dose. Fifty-one matched control patients with ALL and prior natural varicella served as control group.

There was serologic evidence of immune response in approximately 80% of patients after one dose and in more than 90% of patients after two doses. Of 69 children who received a second dose, 63 (93%) cases showed improvement in antibody response to varicella zoster (VZ) virus (Table 1). The major side effect was a mild to moderate rash which was more common in children on maintenance chemotherapy (36% and 14% after the first and second vaccine dose, respectively) than in those whose chemotherapy has been completed (7% each after first and second dose). Children with rash had higher antibody titers than those without rash, but those with rash were also at risk (10%) to transmit vaccine virus to others. Seven (4%) of the 191 vaccines had clinical varicella between 2 and 10 months after the first dose of vaccine (Table 2). Four of 22 children with household exposures to VZ virus developed mild clinical varicella, an attack rate of 18%. The mild character of varicella in recipients of the vaccine was clearly different than varicella in unimmunized children re-

TABLE 1.—SEROLOGIC DATA FROM 69 CHILDREN WITH LEUKEMIA
WHO WERE REVACCINATED

	No. (%) Receiving Chemotherapy (N=25)	No. (%) Not Receiving Chemotherapy (N=44)	Total No. (%) (N=69)
Seroconversion	19/19 (100)	33/37 (89)	52/56 (93)
Persistence of antibody for longer interval than after first injection	7/11 (64)	16/28 (57)	23/39 (59)
Booster response*	17/25 (68)	34/44 (77)	51/69 (74)

*Titer is two dilutions higher than previously achieved or presence of varicella zoster fluorescent antibody to membrane antigen 3 wks or sooner after second dose, or both. Second dose of vaccine was often associated with booster response to varicella zoster virus.
(Courtesy of Gershon, A.A., et al.: JAMA 252:355–362, July 20, 1984; copyright 1984, American Medical Association.)

ceiving chemotherapy for leukemia. By standard calculation for vaccine efficacy, the vaccine was approximately 80% effective in preventing clinical varicella in children with ALL in remission and 100% effective in preventing severe varicella in this high-risk group.

The results indicate that live attenuated varicella vaccine is effective in preventing severe varicella in children with ALL in remission. The illness in the immunocompromised vaccinated children is clearly milder than varicella in normal children. Vaccination decreases the attack rate of clinical varicella in vaccines; 18% in those with household exposures as compared with a rate of 87% in varicella-susceptible persons with household exposures. Used carefully, varicella vaccine should provide relief from fear of severe chickenpox in children with leukemia.

▶ It is important to note that all the study subjects were in remission from ALL for at least 1 year. Whether the varicella vaccine will be safe and effective when given to children earlier in this therapy of ALL remains to be determined. Children with a vaccine-associated rash can transmit their infection to susceptible-household contacts; therefore, those with rash who are vaccinated may need to be isolated as one would isolate a child with varicella.—D.S.

Oral Acyclovir for Prevention of Herpes Simplex Virus Reactivation After Marrow Transplantation
James C. Wade, Barbara Newton, Nancy Fluornoy, and Joel D. Meyers (Seattle)
Ann. Intern. Med. 100:823–828, June 1984   2–15

Prolonged use of intravenous acyclovir for prevention of herpes simplex virus reactivation after marrow transplantation is limited by the need for venous access and inpatient care. The authors report a prospective, randomized, double-blind, placebo-controlled trial of oral acyclovir for prophylaxis of herpes simplex virus infection after marrow transplantation. Acyclovir was given at a dose of 400 mg every 4 hours 5 times daily to 24 patients. Placebo was given to 25 patients. Prophylaxis was given for

TABLE 2.—VARICELLA IN RECIPIENTS OF VARICELLA VACCINE

Patient No.	Type of Exposure	Before Illness		Incubation Period, Days	No. of Lesions	Quality of Illness	Varicella Zoster Virus Isolate
		FAMA*	CMI*				
1†	Sibling	16	6	22	58	Mild	Wild
2†	Sibling	4	32	29	30	Mild	Wild
3†	Sibling	8	1	13	46	Mild	Wild
4†	Sibling (varicella zoster immunoglobulin)	<2	45	16	Unknown	Mild	None
5†	School	8	59	Unknown	50	Mild	Wild (brother)
6	Friend	8	2	Unknown	20	Mild	None
7	Unknown	8	7	Unknown	70	Mild	Wild

*FAMA: fluorescent antibody to membrane antigen; CMI: cell-mediated immunity.
†Patients 1, 2, 3, and 4 had fever 1 to 3 days; Patients 1, 2, 3, 4, and 5 received chemotherapy until onset of rash; Patients 1, 2, and 3 received two injections of vaccine; Patient 4 was given antiviral chemotherapy for 3 days until it was realized that the disease was mild.
(Courtesy of Gershon, A.A., et al.: JAMA 252:355–362, July 20, 1984; copyright 1984, American Medical Association.)

5 weeks beginning 1 week before transplantation. All patients received cyclophosphamide and total body irradiation before marrow transfusion and either methotrexate or cyclosporine after transplantation.

Five of 24 patients receiving oral acyclovir developed first reactivation of herpes simplex virus infection during prophylaxis, compared to 17 of 25 patients receiving placebo ($P < .01$). The median time to first virus reactivation was significantly longer among patients receiving oral acyclovir (78 days versus 9 days after transplant, $P = .006$) (Fig 2–4, top). Drug compliance was very erratic because of severe oropharyngeal mucositis due to radiation chemotherapy and herpes simplex virus infection. Hence, when the analysis was adjusted for drug compliance, among patients taking a minimum of 40% of their prescribed drug, the median time to first virus reactivation among patients receiving acyclovir was 84 days after transplantation compared to 9 days among patients receiving placebo ($P<.0002$) (Fig 2–4, bottom). With this adjustment for drug compliance, acyclovir prophylaxis was 96% virologically effective and 100% clinically effective during the period of administration. Patients receiving methotrexate showed a significantly more rapid marrow engraftment than patients on placebo. No virus resistant to acyclovir was isolated. The use of oral acyclovir was not associated with any hepatic, renal, or neurologic toxicity and, except for periods of severe oropharyngeal mucositis, it was well tolerated.

This study shows that oral acyclovir at a dose of 400 mg every 4 hours

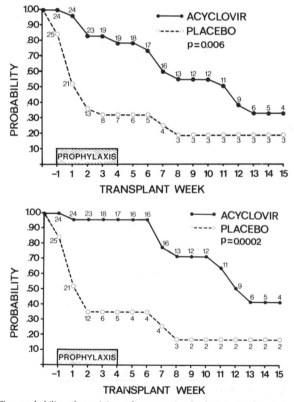

Fig 2–4.—*Top*, probability of remaining culture negative for herpes simplex virus among patients receiving acyclovir *(solid circles)* and patients receiving placebo *(open circles)* by week before or after marrow transplant. Numbers above or below curves refer to number of culture-negative patients eligible for analysis for each week. Probability of remaining culture negative was different at $P < .006$ by Mantel-Cox test for the two patient groups. *Bottom*, probability of remaining culture negative for herpes simplex virus among patients taking 40% or more of their prescribed drug during each week of prophylaxis. Solid circles represent patients receiving acyclovir and open circles, those receiving placebo. Numbers above or below curves refer to number of culture-negative patients eligible for analysis each week. Probability of remaining culture negative was different at $P = .0002$ by Mantel-Cox test for the two patient groups. (Courtesy of Wade, J.C., et al.: Ann. Intern. Med. 100:823–828, June 1984.)

five times daily was safe, well-tolerated, and highly effective for the prevention of herpes simplex virus reactivation in immunosuppressed patients receiving marrow transplants. Based on adjustments for drug compliance, the data suggest that dosage schedules that use either lower doses or less frequent administration may also be effective, especially among patients with better absorption of orally administered acyclovir. Acyclovir prophylaxis was associated with a longer interval to reactivation after prophylaxis was stopped (median of 8 weeks) than would have been predicted from previous studies. It appears that this longer period of prophylaxis delayed virus reactivation until a period of relative immunocompetence resulting in slightly lower overall rate of virus positivity, a prolonged interval to first recurrence and less severe disease.

▶ Although this study was performed in bone marrow transplant recipients, it is reasonable to assume that oral therapy would also be effective for severe oral HSV type 1 recurrence in the nonimmunocompromised patient. It is encouraging that acyclovir resistance was not noted in any study patient.—G.K.

Persisting Illness and Fatigue in Adult With Evidence of Epstein-Barr Virus Infection
Stephen E. Straus, Giovanna Tosato, Gary Armstrong, Thomas Lawley, Olivia T. Preble, Werner Henle, Richard Davey, Gary Pearson, Jay Epstein, Irene Brus, and R. Michael Blaese
Ann. Intern. Med. 102:7–16, January 1985   2–16

A lifelong latent infection of B-lymphocytes by Epstein-Barr virus (EBV) follows primary infection, and apparently is subject to reactivation in association with recurrent or chronic disease. Thirty-one patients older than 16 years of age were seen in a 4-year period with chronic illness and fatigue following infectious mononucleosis. Twenty-three of them had serologic or immunologic evidence of chronic EBV infection. All patients had been chronically ill for more than a year and had easy fatigability. Other chronic infectious and immune-impairing disorders were excluded.

The patients were Caucasian adults, mostly older than age 30 years. Thirteen patients had the onset of chronic illness within a year of a mononucleosis-like disorder, and 6 others more than a year after a mononucleosis-like illness. Most patients described a chronic or relapsing "flu-like" syndrome with unusual fatigue. There were one to six exacerbations a year, with less marked fatigue continuing in the intervals. Little fever was present. Most patients had considerable psychosocial problems. Ten were unable to work. The serologic findings are given in the table. Circulating immune complexes were found in 11 of the 15 patients tested. Circulating interferon was not identified, but 5 patients had increased activity of the interferon-induced enzyme 2-5 oligoadenylate synthetase. All but 1 of 19 patients had persistent suppressor T cell activity.

It appears that EBV may be associated with chronic illness in adults. If it is shown that EBV causes the syndrome or has an ongoing role in its

Patients and Matched Controls With Selected Serologic Titers Specific for Epstein-Barr Virus on 1 or More Occasions*

Antibody	Titer	Patients	Controls	p Value
		n		
VCA-IgM	$\geq 1{:}10$	5	0	< 0.05
VCA-IgG	$\geq 1{:}320$	19	3	< 0.001
	$\geq 1{:}640$	14	1	< 0.001
EA-D	$\geq 1{:}10$	9	1	< 0.005
EA-R	$\geq 1{:}10$	18	5	< 0.005
EA (D or R)	$\geq 1{:}10$	19	6	< 0.005
	$\geq 1{:}20$	16	2	< 0.005
EBNA	$< 1{:}5$	7	0	< 0.001
ADCC	$\leq 1{:}240$	4†	Not done	...

*VCA-IgM, IgM antibodies to viral capsid antigen; VCA-IgG, IgG antibodies to viral capsid antigen; EA-D, antibodies to the diffuse components of early antigen; EA-R, antibodies to the restricted components of early antigen; EBNA, antibody to the Epstein-Barr nuclear antigen; ADCC, antibodies to Epstein-Barr virus membrane antigens detected by an antibody-dependent cellular cytotoxicity assay. Statistical comparisons by Fisher's exact test.
†Based on 11 patients tested.
(Courtesy of Straus, S.E., et al.: Ann. Intern. Med. 102:7–16, January 1985.)

chronic persistence, antiviral agents might prove helpful. Interferon or other lymphokines could be beneficial if EBV infection induces or augments an immunoregulatory disorder in these patients. Mere documentation of an organic cause of the symptoms is very helpful.

Evidence for Active Epstein-Barr Virus Infection in Patients With Persistent, Unexplained Illnesses: Elevated Anti-Early Antigen Antibodies

James F. Jones, C. George Ray, Linda L. Minnich, Mary Jane Hicks, Ruthann Kibler, and David O. Lucas (Univ. of Arizona)

Ann. Intern. Med. 102:1–7, January 1985
2–17

High titers to "early" antigen are thought to occur only during initial Epstein-Barr virus (EBV) infection. Forty-four patients, including 18 children, had recurrent or persistent illness and pharyngitis, lymphadenopathy, fever, headache, arthralgia, fatigue, depression, and myalgia. All but 5 had EBV antibody. No other cause of infection was found in these patients. The 39 with EBV antibody had detectable anti-early antigen antibody for at least 1 year while under observation. None of the 44 patients had evidence of underlying or previous disease or had received immunosuppressive therapy.

The study patients had significantly higher antiviral capsid antigen and anti-early antigen titers than found in age-matched controls. Patterns of illness could not be related to changes in specific antibody titers or clinical findings. No consistent abnormalities in lymphocyte phenotype or function were found in the 11 patients studied. Only 1 of 32 patients had circulating interferon, which was present in all 7 patients who had acute infectious mononucleosis. Ten of the 39 patients who were seropositive for EBV had a positive result on the heterophil antibody test at onset of symptoms, but none had detectable antibody during follow-up.

The data suggest that EBV infection may not be self-limited, and that the virus may be associated with clinical illness other than infectious mononucleosis in both children and adults. The findings are not conclusive, but they provide a useful basis for future prospective case-control studies. Many patients have had certain difficulties (e.g., self-doubt and family-social conflicts) that could at least be alleviated by a better understanding of the underlying disease process.

► For years many of us saw patients with persistent lethargy and easy fatigability. We were loath to call such symptoms "chronic mononucleosis" and often resorted to such terms as "postinfectious asthenia." The two papers abstracted above now provide a strong basis on which to support a persistent illness associated with EBV infection. Using serologic tests, these authors have shown that changes, once thought to be characteristic of only acute infection, can occur in chronic illness as well. Since it has been known for some time that infectious mononucleosis is associated with a variety of immunologic abnormalities, and that lymphocytes are chronically infected with EBV, in the future such patients may be amenable to therapy with antiviral agents.—S.M.W.

Cytomegalovirus Infection in the Normal Host

Jeffrey I. Cohen and G. Ralph Corey (Duke Univ.)
Medicine 64:100–114, March 1985   2–18

The clinical presentation of cytomegalovirus (CMV) infection is ex-

---

TABLE 1.—SIGNS AND SYMPTOMS IN PATIENTS WITH CYTOMEGALOVIRUS
MONONUCLEOSIS, TAKEN FROM THE LITERATURE

N=62
Age: mean, 27.5 years
(range, 2–66 years)

		Number	%
Symptoms:	myalgias	28/46	61
	malaise	16/29	55
	sore throat	11/29	38
	headache	10/29	34
	rash	11/36	31
	abdominal pain	4/41	10
Signs:	fever	53/54	98
	T maximum	mean, 39.3 C	(range, 38.0–41.0 C)
	T duration	mean, 18 d	(range, 3–35 days)
	3 weeks	11/42	26
	splenomegaly	17/45	38
	pharyngeal erythema	10/26	38
	adenopathy	15/53	28
	hepatomegaly	8/32	25
	exudative		
	tonsillitis	3/46	6
	jaundice	1/35	3

(Courtesy of Cohen, J.I., and Corey, G.R.: Medicine 64:100–114, February 1984.)

TABLE 2.—LABORATORY DATA AND COMPLICATIONS IN PATIENTS WITH
CYTOMEGALOVIRUS MONONUCLEOSIS, TAKEN FROM THE LITERATURE

N=62

Laboratory data:	Number	%
anemia	4/32	13
WBC count	mean, 12.650/mm^3 (range, 5,500-37.900 mm^3)	
lymphocytes %	mean, 52.4% lymphocytes	
45% present	26/36	72
atypical lymphocytes %	mean, 21% atypical lymphocytes	
present	42/48	88
SGOT elevated	39/43	91
3-fold elevation	7/43	16
SGPT elevated	21/23	91
alkaline phosphatase elevated	9/23	39
3-fold elevation	2/23	9
bilirubin elevated	4/26	15
3-fold elevation	1/26	4
ESR	mean, 31 mm/hr (range, 8-126 mm/hr)	
rheumatoid factor positive	4/11	36
ANA positive	2/11	18
Complications:		
pneumonia	4/62	6
myocarditis	4/62	6
CNS*	3/62	5
jaundice	1/62	2

*One case each: encephalitis, Landry-Guillain-Barre syndrome, VIII cranial nerve palsy.
Abbreviations: WBC = white blood cell; SGOT = serum glutamic oxalocetic transaminase; SGPT = serum glutamic pyruvic transaminase; ESR = erythrocyte sedimentation rate; ANA = antinuclear antibody; CNS = central nervous system.
(Courtesy of Cohn, J.I., and Corey, G.R.: Medicine 64:100–114, February 1984.)

tremely variable. The findings in 62 reported nonimmunocompromised patients with spontaneous CMV infection are reviewed in Tables 1 and 2. The average patient age was 28 years. The mean duration of fever exceeded 2 weeks. Splenomegaly, pharyngeal erythema, and adenopathy all were present in about one third of patients. Most of the authors' 10 patients had leukocytosis, and all had atypical lymphocytes at some point. Serum transaminase elevations also were universal. Only 2 of the 10 patients had an elevated serum bilirubin. Two of 5 patients were anergic. The liver biopsy appearances in 1 case are shown in Figure 2–5.

Cytomegalovirus infection is the most frequent cause of heterophile-negative mononucleosis in adults. Icteric hepatitis is an infrequent finding, but several cases of granulomatous hepatitis have been reported. Landry-Guillain-Barré syndrome has often been associated with CMV infection. Several cases of encephalitis have occurred in nonimmunocompromised hosts. Myocarditis has been described in 6% of cases of CMV mononucleosis, and pneumonia has occurred in 6% of cases. Retinal involvement is less prevalent in nonimmunocompromised hosts than in immunosuppressed patients. Most cases of presumed gastrointestinal involvement have been in patients given steroids or multiple transfusions.

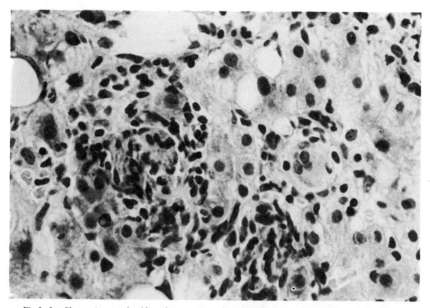

Fig 2–5.—Photomicrograph of liver biopsy. Granulomatous hepatitis is present with giant cells; original magnification, ×400. (Courtesy of Cohn, J.I., and Corey, G.R.: Medicine 64:100–114, February 1984.)

Cytomegalovirus mononucleosis usually is a self limited disorder, but laboratory changes can persist for years after clinical recovery. Potentially dangerous tests can be avoided where CMV infection is suspected early in the course of illness. All 10 of the authors' patients recovered.

▶ Since cytomegalovirus (CMV) infection is considered in the differential diagnosis of febrile patients with acquired immunodeficiency syndrome, febrile patients after organ transplantation, or febrile neutropenic patients who have received cytotoxic chemotherapy, we often overlook this virus as a cause of fever of unknown origin in normal hosts. This review describes the clinical findings in normals infected with CMV and makes the point that this virus must be considered in the work-up of patients with fever of unknown origin. Although rare, it is also noteworthy that CMV is also a cause of granulomatous hepatitis.—S.G.

Other Viruses

Rotavirus Carriage, Asymptomatic Infection and Disease in the First Two Years of Life: Serologic Response
H. Champsaur, M. Henry-Amar, D. Goldszmidt, J. Prevot, M. Bourjouane, E. Questiaux, and C. Bach
J. Infect. Dis. 149:675–682, May 1984   2–19

Serologic response to rotavirus and virus shedding were prospectively studied in 179 children (neonates to 24 months) upon hospital admission during September 1, 1979 to August 1, 1980. Analysis of the evolution of IgG and IgM enzyme-linked immunosorbent assay (ELISA) titers revealed 24 cases of rotaviral disease (serologic response and diarrhea), 13 cases of asymptomatic infection (serologic response and no diarrhea), 36 cases of virus carriage (absence of a serologic response), 3 cases of past infection, and 6 possible cases of nosocomial infection. Rotaviral disease was encountered 2 of 3 times and was characterized by diarrhea associated with fever and vomiting. Asymptomatic rotaviral infection and disease, observed from the neonatal period onwards, affected 2% of neonates, 20% of children aged 1–6 months, and 37% of children aged 7–24 months. In contrast, virus carriage occurred, in 27%, 19%, and 14% of those children, respectively. Altogether, these results indicate that during the period of age 1–24 months, when asymptomatic rotaviral infection and disease were prevalent, about 2 of 10 children had rotaviral disease, 1 of 10 had asymptomatic infection, 2 of 10 were virus carriers, and 5 of 10 were not infected with rotavirus.

Yolken et al. and Ghose et al. demonstrated that ELISA is a sensitive and efficient tool in the evaluation of the immunologic response to rotaviral infection. About 50% of the 179 children in this prospective study were infected by rotavirus at any age. However, they constituted a heterogeneous population with regard to the exact association with rotavirus, since five states were evident: asymptomatic infection, disease, carriage, convalescence, and nosocomial infection. The demonstration of a high proportion of carriers of virus emphasizes the value of serologic data, since apart from children with asymptomatic infection and children with disease, another group of children who were simply carriers were seen to constitute about 50% of all children infected. In those cases virus was excreted, but a serologic response did not develop. The possibility that the test used was unable to detect every serologic response cannot be discounted. However, it is unlikely that 1 IgG and 2 IgM ELISAs would fail to detect any serologic response in as many as 100 of the 142 children. Furthermore, the frequency of occurrence of diarrhea in those children who were carrying virus and in those with no rotavirus infection was not different, and neither was the occurrence of a variety of other symptoms. In contrast, when these frequencies are compared with those of children with illness associated with rotavirus, the frequencies of the same symptoms were totally different. Finally, while the proportion of such carriers decreased with age, the proportion of children with asymptomatic infection and disease increased with age, an observation that confirms that the two populations are indeed different. Consequently, they may be regarded as asymptomatic virus carriers, probably even when diarrheic.

Therefore, infection of a child with rotavirus does not necessarily result in disease. The outcome depends on age, state of immunity, and possibly maturity of the gastrointestinal tract. These factors contribute to a state of transient virus-host equilibrium, which results in carriage, asymptomatic infection, or disease.

▶ This study distinguishes rotavirus carriage from infection. Carriage was more frequent than acute infection in younger infants and the ratio was reversed in the second year of life, suggesting that age-specific host factors may modify the response of the organism. Since diarrhea occurred in noninfected subjects as often as in carriers, defined by the presence of the virus in stool with no serologic response, it suggests that diagnosis of rotavirus by stool ELISA for virus antigen may overestimate the incidence of rotavirus-associated diarrhea.—G.K.

Protection of Infants Against Rotavirus Diarrhea by RIT 4237 Attenuated Bovine Rotavirus Strain Vaccine
Timo Vesikari, Erika Isolauri, Eric D'Hondt, Andrée Delem, Francis E. André, and Georges Zissis
Lancet 1:977–981, May 5, 1984   2–20

Previous reports have shown that RIT 4237 live attenuated bovine rotavirus vaccine stimulates an immune response in children; however, the reports did not show whether the vaccine-induced immunity would protect against human rotavirus infection. A randomized double-blind, placebo-controlled trial was conducted to evaluate the ability of RIT 4237 (subgroup I) vaccine strain to protect against natural rotavirus infection in children. A total of 178 infants aged 8 to 11 months received a single oral dose of RIT 4237 vaccine (86 patients) or placebo (92 patients) and were followed up serologically and clinically during a subgroup 2 rotavirus epidemic.

Initially, 113 children were seronegative for rotavirus and 65 were seropositive. Four weeks after vaccination, 50% of the seronegative recipients and 7% of the initially seronegative placebo recipients had seroconverted. There were no side effects noted from the use of the vaccine. During the 5-month follow-up period after vaccination, 2 of 86 vaccine recipients and 18 of 92 placebo recipents had rotavirus diarrhea lasting more than 24 hours ($P<.001$) giving a vaccine-protection rate of 88% (table). The 2 vaccine recipients with rotavirus diarrhea were regarded as primary vaccine failures since they had no detectable serum antibody after vaccination. There were 2 days of confirmed rotavirus diarrhea in the vaccine group as compared to 58 days in the placebo group with mean duration of rotavirus diarrhea 0.2 ± 0.4 days and 3.2 ± 1.4 days ($P<.001$), respectively. Analyzing the protection offered by vaccination or naturally acquired immunity, patients given the RIT 4237 vaccine who did not seroconvert had less diarrheal days per child than the placebo group ($P<.001$) and clinical outcome was better among all those given the RIT vaccines. Strains of rotaviruses found in 20 stool specimens were of subgroup 2 (19) and subgroup I (1).

This study shows that RIT 4237 live attenuated bovine rotavirus vaccine protects against rotavirus diarrhea in man. When all cases of frank diarrhea were considered, the protection rate was 70%, indicating that 70% of all cases of infantile winter diarrhea might be prevented by the RIT 4237

EPISODES OF DIARRHEA DURING 5 MONTHS'
FOLLOW-UP OF 178 VACCINEES DURING A ROTAVIRUS
EPIDEMIC SEASON

No of episodes

	RIT 4237 (n = 86)	Placebo (n = 92)	p	Protection rate
Any diarrhoea or loose stools	15 (*17·4*%)	28 (*30·4*%)	NS	47%
Clinically significant diarrhoea over 24 h	8 (*9·3*%)	28 (*30·4*%)	<0·01	70%
Any diarrhoea or loose stools with rotavirus	9 (*10·5*%)	18 (*19·6*%)	NS	50%
Clinically significant diarrhoea over 24 h with rotavirus in stools	2 (*2·3*%)	18 (*19·6*%)	<0·001	88%

(Courtesy of Vesikari, T., et al.: Lancet 1:977–981, May 5, 1984.

vaccine. The duration of vaccine-induced protection is not known but it may be sufficient to afford clinical protection against rotavirus diarrhea until the child is 3 years old, at which time attacks of acute diarrhea are rare. It has not been shown yet whether the immunity induced by the RIT 4237 vaccine will confer protection against all subgroups of human rotavirus; this study shows that RIT 4237 vaccine is effective only for diarrhea caused by subgroup 2 rotaviruses.

▶ Rotavirus is the most common cause of infantile diarrhea. This paper presents the first evidence that cross-reacting antigens in a bovine rotavirus isolate that grows well in vitro can confer protection against a human strain. While work continues on development of primate and human rotavirus-derived vaccines, the present paper offers considerable hope that an effective vaccine will be forthcoming in the not too distant future. Field trials of the bovine vaccine are proceeding, and more information about its efficacy will become available soon.—G.K.

Intranasal Interferon-α2 for Prevention of Natural Rhinovirus Colds
Barry M. Earr, Jack M. Gwaltney, Jr., Katherine F. Adams, and Frederick G. Hayden (Univ. of Virginia)
Antimicrob. Agents Chemother. 26:31–34, July 1984   2–21

Experimental rhinovirus infections in susceptible subjects have been prevented by the intranasal administration of either leukocyte-derived human interferon (HuIFN) or recombinant DNA-produced HuIFN-α2. A placebo-controlled, double-blind study of HuIFN-α2 was carried out in 304 adult insurance company employees. Most were women younger than 35 years of age. Study patients received intranasal instillations of HuIFN-α2 in a dose of 10^7 IU daily or placebo sprays. Two sprays per nostril were

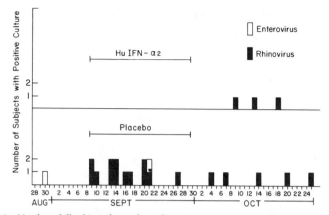

Fig 2–6.—Number of ill subjects from whom rhinovirus or enterovirus was isolated, shown by date of isolation. The 22-day treatment period is indicated by the horizontal bar above each graph. The enterovirus isolated during the treatment period was identified as echovirus type 24 by neutralization testing. (Courtesy of Farr, B.M., et al.: Antimicrob. Agents Chemother. 26:31–34, July 1984.)

used each day for 4 weeks. During the week they were self-administered under supervision by a nurse.

The number of rhinoviruses isolated from subjects with upper respiratory illness was significantly reduced by HuIFN-α2 prophylaxis (Fig 2–6). No rhinovirus was isolated from a study subject during treatment. When enterovirus and possible picornavirus isolated were included, 12% of placebo recipients and 2% of the study group had positive picornavirus cultures. The overall number of upper respiratory illnesses was not reduced by interferon administration, but episodes with at least 3 days of rhinorrhea were less frequent. Nasal obstruction was more frequent in recipients in weeks 2 and 3. Significantly more interferon recipients developed leukopenia during the study, but all counts were normal 2 months later.

Intranasal HuIFN-α2 was effective in preventing rhinovirus colds under natural conditions in this study, although the results were somewhat confounded by nasal side effects from prolonged topical administration. Further study of the practical use of interferon to control the spread of colds appears to be warranted. Long-term prophylaxis as used in the present study may not be feasible because of local side effects, but short-term use just after exposure to a cold may be useful. Different preservatives or methods of administrations also may be worth exploring.

▶ Although there was a marked antiviral effect from intranasal HuIFN-α2, the frequent local side effects documented by the investigators demonstrate that long-term intranasal prophylaxis at this dosage is not feasible.—D.S.

Safety of Prolonged Administration of Rimantadine Hydrochloride in the Prophylaxis of Influenza A Virus Infections in Nursing Homes

Peter A. Patriarca, Nancy A. Kater, Alan P. Kendal, Dennis J. Bregman, John D. Smith, and R. Keith Sikes (CDC)

Antimicrob. Agents Chemother. 26:101–103, July 1984   2–22

   Amantadine prevents most influenza type A infections, but its effects on the central nervous system raises concern over its use in elderly subjects. Rimantadine is an analogue that is effective in preventing infections in young, healthy subjects and has fewer side effects than amantadine. Its safety of elderly, chronically ill persons was examined in a double-blind, placebo-controlled study in 3 nursing homes during the time of a community influenza A (H3N2) epidemic. Thirty-five residents who were not at particular risk from treatment were assigned to receive either 100 mg rimantadine HCl twice daily or placebo. The 2 groups were demographically and clinically comparable. The mean duration of chemoprophylaxis was 80 days.

   Clinical evidence suggesting toxicity was obtained in 78% of the study group and in 76% of placebo recipients (Fig 2–7). There was no definite temporal relation between any sign or symptom and the duration of prophylaxis. Significantly more study patients had anxiety or nausea, or both,

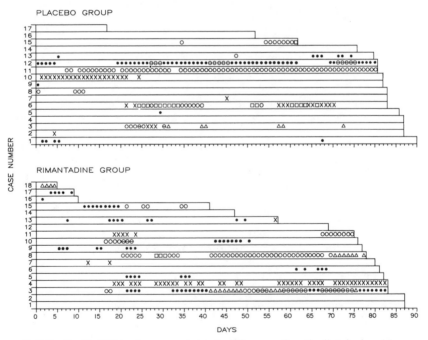

Fig 2–7.—Possible CNS involvement, gastrointestinal illness, or other side effects by day of therapy. Symbols: ●, CNS; X, gastrointestinal illness; O, other; ⊖, CNS plus other; □, gastrointestinal illness plus other; △, CNS, gastrointestinal, plus other. (Courtesy of Patriarca, P.A., et al.: Antimicrob. Agents Chemother. 26:101–103, July 1984.)

but no effects interfered substantially with daily activities or with patient care. Two rimantadine patients withdrew because of insomnia, nausea, or both. Another subject with a seizure disorder had a seizure after 10 days of prophylaxis. Serum drug levels were higher than in young adults on the same regimen, but could not be related to the presence or duration of side effects or to the type of underlying illness present.

Rimantadine prophylaxis of influenza A virus infection is associated with nausea and anxiety in some elderly subjects. Side effects are, however, transient and seldom functionally significant. Further pharmacokinetic studies are needed to determine whether lower doses of rimantadine would be appropriate for older subjects. Further study also is needed to determine how safe rimantadine is in patients with various medical disorders.

Human Papillomavirus Infection and Cervical Neoplasia: New Perspectives
Christopher P. Crum and Richard U. Levine (Columbia Univ.)
Int. J. Gynecol. Pathol. 3:376–388, 1984   2–23

Human papillomavirus (HPV) infection of the lower female genital tract now is recognized as a prevalent sexually transmitted disease. The cervix frequently is involved, and this site accounts for more than half of all genital condylomas. Koilocytotic atypia is the most distinctive feature of cervical HPV infection. Evidence has accumulated that HPV may cause squamous neoplasia in the lower female genital tract. The spectra of both cervical HPV infection and intraepithelial neoplasia are determined in part by the maturational characteristics of the involved transformation-zone epithelium. Lesions of atypical immature metaplasia usually do not contain HPV antigens, but the epithelium nevertheless appears to respond to the presence of the virus. Human papillomavirus usually does not replicate and assemble in immature epithelium. Neoplastic change in well-differentiated epithelium will result in cervical intradermal nevus 1 with maturation and koilocytosis, while in a poorly differentiated, or metaplastic epithelium a higher-grade lesion will be found. It remains uncertain whether benign-appearing warts evolve into cervical intradermal nevus lesions, or whether cervical intradermal nevus lesions begin as neoplastic lesions indistinguishable from warts.

In most cases, it is not critical to distinguish between condyloma and cervical intraepithelial neoplasia. Where extensive cervical or vaginal involvement is present, however, the distinction may influence the short-term therapeutic approach. Some small vulvar or vaginal lesions in young patients will regress spontaneously. Immunosuppressed patients probably are at an increased risk of developing neoplasia. Lesions with extensive canal involvement may resemble condyloma while actually containing invasive carcinoma. The chief distinction for treatment purposes is between reactive change and HPV-related change: the former is managed medically or followed; and the latter, either infectious or neoplastic, should be removed. Typing of viral strains now is feasible, but there is no assurance that a given strain correlates consistently with progression. It is not clear whether treatment of male partners with external condylomas will reduce the incidence of disease. It is possible that some of them carry oncogenic viruses, suggesting the need for further study of this population.

▶ It would be fair to say that most infectious disease specialists rarely think about the lowly genital wart virus, human papilloma virus (HPV). Yet this virus may be sexually transmitted and some strains may be oncogenic. As further studies are performed on the molecular biology of this organism, we may be called upon to make the distinction between HPV and other genital infections, or to interpret DNA hybridization data to distinguish HPV strains. There's a lot more to HPV than warts.—D.S.

Expression of Rabies Virus Glycoprotein From a Recombinant Vaccinia Virus
M. P. Kieny, R. Lathe, R. Drillien, D. Spehner, S. Skory, D. Schmitt, T. Wiktor, H. Koprowski, and J. P. Lecocq
Nature 312:163–166, Nov. 8, 1984   2–24

Effective rabies vaccines of tissue culture origin have been developed but are expensive. Live vaccinia virus (VV) recombinants expressing influenza or hepatitis B antigens recently have been used to immunize against these diseases, and this approach now has been used to produce a novel rabies vaccine. The recombinant virus used to produce virus-neutralizing antibodies harbored the rabies glycoprotein cDNA. The glycoprotein spike is the only viral component capable of reacting with virus-neutralizing antibodies and eliciting their production.

The rabies glycoprotein cDNA first was altered by site-directed mutagenesis, and the poly(dG) tail removed. The modified cDNA then was aligned with an early VV promoter sequence inserted within a cloned copy of the vaccina thymidine kinase gene, and this plasmid was transfected into VV-infected cells. Recombination of the virus and plasmid led to a virus harboring the rabies glycoprotein cDNA. Inoculation of rabbits with

RESISTANCE OF IMMUNIZED MICE TO RABIES VIRUS

Immunizing agent	% Protection
None	0
Vaccinia wild-type virus	0
Recombinant virus VVTGgRAB-26D3	100

Female mice were infected intradermally by scarification with ~5 × 10^7 PFU of VVTGgRAB-26D3 or wild-type VV. Four skin scratches were made on base of tail by using hypodermic needle and virus suspension rubbed over abrasion. On day 15 all vaccinated and control animals were infected by intracerebral inoculation with CDC strain tissue-culture-adapted street virus (2,400 mouse LD$_{50}$ units.) Test animals were monitored for 2 months after challenge; unprotected mice died after 8 to 10 days.

(Courtesy of Kieny, M.P., et al.: Nature 312:163–166, Nov. 8, 1984. Reprinted by permission of *Nature*, MacMillan Journals Ltd.)

live recombinant virus induced high titers of rabies virus-neutralizing antibody. Scarification with the recombinant VV protected mice against challenge with street rabies virus in large dosage, while mice immunized with wild-type VV alone were not protected (table). Study of reactivity with monoclonal antibodies showed the binding activity of the recombinant glycoprotein to be nearly identical to that observed with purified ERA rabies virus.

Live VV expressing rabies glycoprotein can confer protection against experimental rabies infection. The preparation and administration of attenuated viruses such as VV is an inexpensive alternative to procedures involving propagation of the pathogen on cultured mammalian cells and subsequent toxicity testing.

► Vaccinia virus has not retired from the world but instead is being retread. In this instance, a recombinant vaccinia virus expressing a rabies glycoprotein antigen has been constructed. Vaccinia may no longer be needed for immunization against smallpox, but as a vehicle to deliver immunizing antigens from one or more other organisms, vaccinia clearly has a future.—G.K.

Poliomyelitis in the USA: Virtual Elimination of Disease Caused by Wild Virus

Robert J. Kim-Farley, Kenneth J. Bart, Lawrence B. Schonberger, Walter A. Orenstein, Benjamin M. Nkowane, Alan R. Hinman, Olen M. Kew, Milford H. Hatch, and Jonathan E. Kaplan (Centers for Disease Control)
Lancet 2:1315–1317, Dec. 8, 1984   2–25

An average of 16,000 cases of paralytic poliomyelitis were reported each year in the United States in the early 1950s, when it became a noticeable disease. The annual average number of cases reported has declined to only 12 in 1978–1982. Eighteen of the 69 cases (26%) reported in this 6-year period were not vaccine-associated. The van Wezel antigenic differentiation test and oligonucleotide fingerprinting provide a basis for definitively characterizing wild and vaccine-like poliovirus strains. Isolates from 42 cases were analyzed; 31 were found to be vaccine-like poliovirus, and 11, wild poliovirus. Seven wild isolates were from cases in a 1979 outbreak caused by virus imported from the Netherlands through Canada. Another isolate was from a single importation, and 3 isolates were from isolated cases without an identified source. No indigenous wild strain has been isolated from reported cases of poliomyelitis since 1981, when an isolate was obtained from an immunodeficient subject.

Although poliovaccines are safe and effective, this is not the case with all vaccines. The poliovirus isolated from a patient with paralytic disease may not always be the virus causing the patient's disease. The absence of reported cases of indigenous wild paralytic poliomyelitis does not necessarily indicate an absence of transmission of wild polioviruses, but it seems likely that few wild polioviruses have circulated in the United States in recent years. The absolute number of vaccine-associated cases has remained constant in recent years, and the increase in the relative proportion of all cases that are vaccine-associated indicates the rarity of wild paralytic poliomyelitis. Wild poliovirus will continue to be introduced into the United States, and high levels of poliomyelitis vaccination must be maintained. It continues to be necessary to attempt to reach populations that have tended to refuse immunization or that have been missed by immunization programs.

▶ In 1982–1983 virtually all cases of paralytic poliomyelitis in the United States have been associated with vaccine use. The Advisory Committee on Immunization Practices (ACIP) continues to recommend the use of oral poliovaccine for routine immunization of children. However, with improved inactivated poliovaccine and the continued rare oral-vaccine associated paralysis, this position should be reexamined periodically (McBean, A.M., et al.: *Rev. Infect. Dis.* 6:S552–S555, 1984).—G.K.

3 Fungal Infections

Fungal and Yeast Infections of the Central Nervous System: A Clinical Review
John S. Salaki, Donald B. Louria, and Herman Chmel (Univ. of Medicine and Dentistry of New Jersey)
Medicine 63:108–132, March 1984   3-1

The types of CNS involvement associated with various fungi and yeasts are listed in Table 1. All the major fungi and yeasts can produce generalized meningitis and focal CNS mass lesions. Infection by *Blastomyces dermatitidis, Histoplasma capsulatum, Coccidioides immitis, Cryptococcus neoformans,* and *Candida albicans* most often presents as meningitis, while the aspergilli and zygomycetes generally produce focal lesions. Headache is the most prominent symptom in all reported types of CNS fungal or yeast infection. The dematiaceous fungi, aspergilli, zygomycetes, and *Paracoccidioides brasiliensis* are manifested as brain abscess, infarction, and granuloma formation. There are few pathognomonic CSF findings associated with any of the organisms. Most of the fungi and yeasts causing CNS infection have been cultured from the CSF, either via lumbar punc-

TABLE 1.—Types of CNS Infections Caused by Fungi and Yeasts

Meningitis	Brain Abscess or Granuloma	Spinal Cord Lesion
Alternaria sp.	Aspergillus sp.	Aspergillus sp.
Aspergillus sp.	*Blastomyces dermatitidis*	*Blastomyces dermatitidis*
Blastomyces dermatitidis	Candida sp.	Candida sp.
Candida sp.	*Cladosporium trichoides*	*Coccidioides immitis*
Cephalosporium sp.	*Coccidioides immitis*	*Cryptococcus neoformans*
Cladosporium trichoides	*Cryptococcus neoformans*	*Petriellidium boydii*
Coccidioides immitis	Curvularia sp.	
Cryptococcus neoformans	*Drechslera spicifera*	
Drechslera hawaiiensis	Fusarium sp.	
Histoplasma capsulatum	*Histoplasma capsulatum*	
Paracoccidioides brasiliensis	*Paracoccidioides brasiliensis*	
Petriellidium boydii	Penicillium sp.	
Sporotrichum schenckii	*Petriellidium boydii*	
Ustilago sp.	Rhinosporidium sp.	
Zygomycete sp.	Sepedonium sp.	
	Sporotrichum schenckii	
	Streptomyces griseus	
	Torulopsis glabrata	
	Trichophyton rubrum	
	Zygomycete sp.	

(Courtesy of Salaki, J.S., et al.: Medicine 63:108–132, February 1985.)

TABLE 2.—Treatment of Yeast and Fungal CNS Infections

Organism	Amphotericin (AMB)	Miconazole	5 Fluoro-cytosine (5 FC)	Other
Aspergillus sp.	++, IV		only with AMB	surgery for mass lesions
Blastomyces dermatitidis	++, IV			surgery for mass lesions
Candida sp.	+++, IV alone or w/5-FC	may be useful	must do sensitivity testing	
Coccidioides immitis	+++, IV and IT	++, IV	(−)	surgery for hydroceph.
Cryptococcus neoformans	+++, IV alone or w/5-FC;	+, IV and IT	with AMB	surgery for mass lesions
Dematiaceous fungi	(−)	no data	no data	occas. surgery for mass lesions
Histoplasma capsulatum	+++, IV			occas. surgery for mass lesions
Zygomycetes	+++, IV, usually with surgery			surgery almost always needed
Paracoccidioides brasiliensis	+, combined with surgery			
Petriellidium boydii	insufficient data	no data	no data	surgery for mass lesions
Sporotrichum schenckii	++, insufficient data	no data	no data	

- = ineffective; + = rarely useful; ++ = Probably beneficial; +++ = drug of choice.
IV = intravenously; IT = intrathecal, intraventricularly, or through Ommaya reservoir.
(Courtesy of Salaki, J.S., et al.: Medicine 63:108–132, February 1985.)

ture or at the time a cerebral granuloma is excised or an abscess drained.

Amphotericin B remains the most effective antimycotic agent for use in treating CNS fungal and yeast infections (Table 2). The other most frequently used drugs are 5-fluorocytosine and the imidazoles miconazole and ketoconazole. Amphotericin B has the broadest antifungal and anti-yeast spectrum of the available drugs, accounting for its frequent use despite the risks of nephrotoxicity, hypokalemia, and phlebitis. Chemotherapy is indicated in postoperative patients because of the possibility of multiple lesions and the risk of accidental spillage. The smear and CSF culture can be negative despite continued cryptococcal CNS infection.

▶ This is a timely and comprehensive review (there are 369 references!) of the ever-increasing problem of fungal infections of the central nervous system. In addition to an appropriate emphasis on the host populations which acquire the various fungal infections, the authors have pointed out where noncultural methods of diagnosis (CSF or serum serology, skin tests) may be useful or where they may obscure the diagnosis. They have also mentioned and referenced some of the very unusual fungal pathogens. I'll leave it to the better punsters than I how to deal with Ustilagomycosis (or Istilayours)!—M.K.

Aspergillomas Complicating Sarcoidosis: A Prospective Study in 100 Patients
Christine Wollschlager and Faroque Khan (State Univ. of New York at Stony Brook)
Chest 86:585–588, October 1984   3-2

Aspergillomas caused life-threatening hemoptysis in 2 patients with chronic sarcoidosis, leading to a prospective study of the prevalence of aspergilloma in 100 patients with histologically-proved sarcoidosis, seen consecutively in 1971–1981. Serum precipitins against Aspergillus antigen were used to screen all patients, and the 12 patients with precipitins underwent serial serum testing and tomography.

Ten of the 12 patients with serum precipitins against Aspergillus were found to have aspergillomas. All patients with aspergilloma had stage III sarcoid, for an incidence of 53% in this group. The incidence of aspergilloma was much higher in men than in women (table). None of the 88 patients without serum precipitins developed aspergilloma during the 10-year study period. One patient with aspergilloma died of massive hemoptysis before tomography could be done. Another who was diagnosed by chest roentgenography had complete clearing of the lesion and disappearance of serum precipitins, suggesting spontaneous lysis of the aspergilloma.

Aspergilloma is quite common in patients with stage III cystic sarcoidosis, especially men. Steroid use has not been associated with aspergilloma formation. It is important to identify patients who have or are developing an aspergilloma, so that appropriate treatment can be promptly given if hemoptysis occurs. Chest roentgenograms of patients with cystic sarcoid should be periodically reviewed for changes of early aspergilloma. Serial

DISTRIBUTION OF SARCOID STUDY POPULATION AND ASPERGILLOMAS ACCORDING TO SEX AND CHEST ROENTGENOGRAPHIC STATE

Roentgenographic Stage	Study Population			Documented Aspergillomas		
	No. Men	No. Women	Total	No. Men	No. Women	Total
I. Hilar adenopathy (No. = 36)	3	33	36	0	0	0
II. Adenopathy and parenchymal disease (No. = 32)	4	28	32	0	0	0
III. Parenchymal disease only (No. = 32)						
CxR (−) for cystic spaces*	0	13	13	0	0	0
CxR (+) for cystic spaces	10	9	19	7	3	10
Totals	17	83	100	7	3	10

*C×R, chest roentgenogram.
(Courtesy of Wollschlager, C., and Khan, F.: Chest 86:585–588, October 1984.)

screening for serum precipitins against various Aspergillus antigens is appropriate in this patient population.

▶ This paper calls attention to the important association between pulmonary aspergilloma and sarcoidosis. The fact that aspergillomas occurred in more than 10% of sarcoidosis patients is noteworthy. However, the authors' suggestion, that a useful screening method for aspergillus infection would be testing sarcoidosis patients' serums for precipitins to *Aspergillus* antigens, might be challenged by most authors who have found serum precipitins to the aspergillus organism to be of little value.—S.M.W.

Focal Hepatic Candidiasis: A Distinct Clinical Variant of Candidiasis in Immunocompromised Patients
Louise S. Tashjian, Jon S. Abramson, and James E. Peacock, Jr. (Bowman Gray School of Medicine)
Rev. Infect. Dis. 6:689–703, Sept.–Oct. 1984   3-3

Hepatic involvement by *Candida* infection appears to be occurring increasingly often in immunocompromised patients. Five pediatric and adult patients were seen in a 15-month period with an antemortem diagnosis of focal hepatic candidiasis. All the patients had an underlying hematologic disorder, but 4 were in remission at the time candidal infection was diagnosed. Only 1 patient had a total neutrophil count below 1,000/cu mm at diagnosis. All patients had received broad-spectrum antibiotics, and 4 had received cytotoxic chemotherapy, usually high-dose cytosine arabinoside. Patients generally presented with fever, dysphagia, nausea, abdominal pain, or diarrhea, and with abdominal distention and hepato-

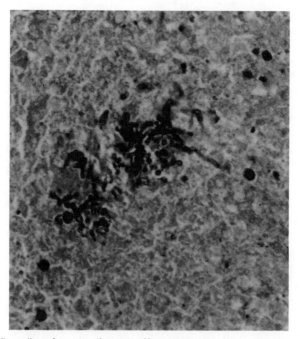

Fig 3–1.—Gomori's methenamine-silver stain of liver (100 ×) with yeast and pseudohyphae indicative of *Candida* species. (Courtesy of Tashjian, L.S., et al.: Rev. Infect. Dis. 6:689–703, Sept.–Oct. 1984.)

megaly on examination. All patients had evidence of oral candidiasis. The rise in alkaline phosphatase was disproportionate to other enzyme changes. Fungemia was documented in only 1 case. Only 1 liver culture was positive, but yeast or pseudohyphae usually were evident microscopically (Fig 3–1). Three patients died with progressive candidal infection despite aggressive amphotericin B therapy. One patient responded to ketoconazole, and 1 to amphotericin B and 5-flucytosine.

Twenty immunocompromised patients with an antemortem diagnosis of focal hepatic or hepatosplenic candidiasis have been reported in the world literature. All but 2 of them had acute leukemia, and most had received broad-spectrum antibiotics and cytotoxic chemotherapy. Candidemia was documented in only 4 cases. Computed tomography usually showed lesions suggestive of microabscesses. Macroscopic liver nodules were evident at biopsy or autopsy in most cases. Five of 10 patients treated with amphotericin B alone died, while 5 of 7 also given 5-flucytosine were improved.

Risk factors in focal hepatic candidiasis may include prolonged neutropenia, broad-spectrum antibiotic therapy, gastrointestinal colonization with Candida, and cytotoxic chemotherapy. The optimal treatment remains uncertain, but aggressive parenteral amphotericin B therapy remains the basic measure. Many believe that the addition of 5-flucytosine is helpful. The role of ketoconazole is unclear. Better means of preventing visceral candidiasis in immunocompromised patients are needed.

Combined Therapy With Amphotericin B and 5-Fluorocytosine for *Candida* Meningitis

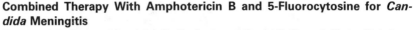

Raymond A. Smego, Jr., John R. Perfect, and David T. Durack (Duke Univ.)
Rev. Infect. Dis. 6:791–801, Nov.–Dec. 1984   3–4

Meningitis is an infrequent manifestation of systemic *Candida* infection. It usually is seen as a nosocomial infection in seriously ill hospitalized patients. Amphotericin B generally is used, but it can cause serious toxicity and it penetrates poorly into the cerebrospinal fluid. The value of combining amphotericin B and 5-fluorocytosine, which has excellent penetration into cerebrospinal fluid, was examined in 17 cases of culture-proved *Candida* meningitis seen in 1970–1983. Eleven patients were less than 1 year of age, and 7 of these were neonates. Thirteen cases were due to *Candida albicans*. All but 2 patients had risk factors for systemic *Candida* infection, most frequently systemic antibiotic therapy and prematurity.

Primary resistance to 5-fluorocytosine was noted in isolates from 4 of 11 patients, but 3 of these did well on combined treatment. A patient whose isolate became resistant during 5-fluorocytosine therapy alone did well when amphotericin B was added. The median duration of combined treatment in 11 evaluable patients was 26 days. Total doses of both drugs varied widely. Most patients received amphotericin B intravenously. Four patients had adverse side effects necessitating withdrawal of treatment. The overall rate of improvement or cure was 88%. Eighty-two percent of patients were clinically and mycologically cured. Two premature neonates died of infection. One patient who relapsed received ketoconazole; another was cured by a longer course of combined treatment. One surviving infant exhibited developmental retardation. Three infants developed hydrocephalus. One patient later developed learning difficulty and a seizure disorder.

Combined treatment with amphotericin B and 5-fluorocytosine appears to benefit patients with *Candida* meningitis. Synergism can be demonstrated both in vitro and in experimental infections due to *Candida*. A lower dose of amphotericin B may be necessary with the combined approach, reducing the risk of toxicity. Psychomotor retardation and hydrocephalus may occur less often in infants given combined drug treatment.

▶ The authors address the important therapeutic issue of whether combination chemotherapy is advantageous in severe fungal infections, in this case *Candida* meningitis. Only 5 of the 17 patients discussed were adults. While the high recovery rate is similar to the few previous reports using amphotericin B alone in both children and adults, there may be situations in which this combination will prove superior to amphotericin monotherapy for *Candida* meningitis.—M.K.

High-Dose Ketoconazole Therapy and Adrenal and Testicular Function in Humans

Allan Pont, John R. Graybill, Philip C. Craven, John N. Galgiani, William E. Dismukes, Richard E. Reitz, and David A. Stevens
Arch. Intern. Med. 144:2150–2153, November 1984

3–5

Ketoconazole has produced gynecomastia in some patients, and has been shown to transiently block testosterone synthesis and blunt the cortisol response to corticotropin. Testicular and adrenal function was examined in adult patients receiving ketoconazole, often in doses of 800 mg daily or above. Twenty-four patients were examined for gynecomastia. Five of them had readily detectable gynecomastia that had not been noted before treatment. Five of the 24 patients reported impotence, and 3 others described a decrease in libido starting after the initiation of ketoconazole therapy.

Six of the 9 patients studied had low sperm counts, and 2 were azoospermic. Counts rose when ketoconazole was discontinued in 1 case, and again declined when treatment was reinstituted. All patients with decreased sperm counts had received at least 800 mg of ketoconazole daily for more than 4 months. Some men had consistently low bound and free testosterone levels, but little relation with ketoconazole dose was apparent. Urinary cortisol excretion was depressed, and responses to corticotropin were impaired. The blockade appeared related to the serum ketoconazole level. Monitoring of 111 patients showed no clinical or laboratory features of hypoadrenalism

Ketoconazole in high dosage can reduce testosterone and cortisol secretion. Some patients exhibit functional hypogonadism which seems to be reversible. The efficacy of ketoconazole in the treatment of serious fungal disease must be balanced against its side effects. Hormone-related side effects are rare with doses of 200 to 400 mg daily. There is preliminary evidence that ketoconazole is effective in the treatment of advanced prostatic carcinoma.

▶ To the astute eye, unwanted side effects can, on occasion, be turned to advantage. While this paper appropriately emphasizes the need to remember that patients receiving ketoconazole have lowered testosterone synthesis and have blunted cortisol responses to ACTH, the authors have applied these effects of ketoconazole on hormones to the treatment of advanced, hormone-sensitive prostate cancer (Ponts A., Trachtenberg, J.: *Clin. Res.* 32:421A, 1984). If only we could think of something good to say about aminoglycoside nephrotoxicity!—M.K.

Estrogens Inhibit Mycelium-To-Yeast Transformation in the Fungus *Paracoccidioides brasiliensis:* Implications for Resistance of Females to Paracoccidioidomycosis

Angela Restrepo, Maria E. Salazar, Luz E. Cano, E. Price Stover, David Feldman, and David A. Stevens
Infect. Immunity 46:346–353, November 1984

3–6

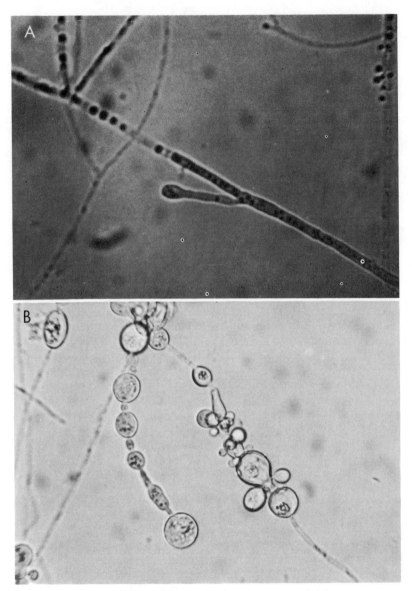

Fig 3–2.—Mycelium-to-yeast transformation of *P. brasiliensis*. **A,** mycelial fragments, none transformed. Appearance of microcultures before incubation and when transformation is blocked by hormone. **B,** transformation of mycelial fragments to yeast form after incubation at 36 C for 5 days in agar microcultures. Initial step is formation of rounded structures that then develop into individual yeast cells, as can be seen in figure. Yeast cells then reproduce by multiple budding, and some mother cells with several attached daughter cells can also be seen. For reference to all structures seen, diameter of individual yeast cells is 5 to 15 μ. (Courtesy of Restrepo, A., et al.: Infect. Immunity 46:346–353, November 1984.)

Paracoccidioidomycosis is an endemic disorder caused by the dimorphic fungus *Paracoccidioides brasiliensis* which is seen much more frequently in males in Latin America, although skin test studies indicate that infection is equally common in females. Fungi pathogenic for humans may be influenced by mammalian steroid hormones, and an estrogen-binding protein has been found in cytosol from the yeast form of *P. brasiliensis*. Estrogens now have been found to suppress the transition between the mycelial and yeast forms of the fungus in vitro, which must occur in the initial establishment of infection. The effects of various hormones on mycelium-to-yeast transformation were examined using patient isolates of *P. brasiliensis*.

Mycelium-to-yeast conversion occurred in 35% to 80% of cells in the absence of added hormones (Fig 3–2). Transformation was consistently inhibited by 17 β-estradiol in all 3 isolates studied extensively, and a clear dose-response relationship was evident. Similar findings were obtained with diethylstilbestrol, but not with testosterone, 17β-estradiol, tamoxifen, or corticosterone. Yeast-to-mycelium transformation and yeast growth and reproduction by budding were unaffected by 17β-estradiol. The cytosol binder was found to be protein in nature. Binding of ^{3}H-estradiol was reversible.

A binding protein is present in cytosol from the yeast form of *P. brasiliensis* which can recognize mammalian estrogens. The ability of estrogen to delay or reduce mycelium-to-yeast transformation at the initial site of infection may explain the marked resistance of females to paracoccidioidomycosis. The presence of this binding protein suggests conservation through evolution of eukaryotes, almost certainly unrelated to the property of binding vertebrate hormone. The ligand-receptor system may be related to mating processes in the dimorphic fungi.

▶ This study suggests a novel mechanism of accounting for male predominance in the clinical expression of paracoccidioidomycosis following infection; namely, sex hormone inhibition of the transformation of the organism from mycelial to yeast phase growth. The interesting aspect in this case is that host factors are acting directly on the organism rather than on the host.—G.K.

Immunologic Responsiveness and Safety Associated With the *Coccidioides immitis* Spherule Vaccine in Volunteers of White, Black, and Filipino Ancestry
Paul L. Williams, David L. Sable, Steven P. Sorgen, Demosthenes Pappagianis, H. B. Levine, Stephanie K. Brodine, Byron W. Brown, F. Carl Grumet, and David A. Stevens
Am. J. Epidemiol. 119:591–602, April 1984   3–7

Previous studies in animals have shown the efficacy of the spherule phase of the organism as an immunogen. Studies in humans suggested safe and tolerable vaccine doses. A trial of killed *Coccidioides immitis* spherule vaccine was undertaken with 151 healthy adult volunteers with negative skin tests and controls. The authors sought to evaluate the safety of selected regimens and the induction of humoral and cell-mediated immune responses, and to determine if there was immunogenetic differences in these responses. Large subgroups of volunteers of white, black, and Filipino ancestry were included in order to study correlations with ancestry.

The doses used were calculated from a determination of the dry weight of the material utilizing a 7 mg/ml suspension. A second dose was given one week later and a third booster dose 6 to 7 weeks thereafter. Three 3.5 mg doses of vaccine was given in the first group and three 1.75 mg doses were given in the second group. No severe systemic symptoms were noted, although 3% of 3.5 mg doses were associated with severe local reactions. Nearly 50% of subjects in both groups had skin test conversions with 15% persisting for more than 6 months. There was an increased conversion rate associated with more severe vaccine reaction. Persons of black or Filipino ancestry were more likely to convert their skin test reactivity. There was a trend to immune response in persons of O blood type (6 patients) and with some HLA phenotypes. Two-thirds of patients showed increased lymphocyte blastogenesis in vitro and 16% of patients given three 3.5 mg doses developed antibody. There was no evidence of deficient response to vaccination in subpopulations known to respond to coccidioidal infection poorly.

Three 1.75 mg doses and three 3.5 mg doses were equally capable of stimulating cell-mediated immunity as shown be delayed-type hypersensitivity and lymphocyte blastogenesis. However, the authors suggest a series of three 1.75 mg doses as a satisfactory regimen to avoid unacceptable severe local reactions seen in three 3.5 mg doses. This regimen would be suitable for all subpopulations to be studied, including those at greater risk for coccidioidal infection.

▶ The clustering of cases of coccidioidomycosis in defined racial groups (e.g., those of Filipino ancestry) and geographic areas (e.g., Arizona, California, New Mexico) as well as the lack of an effective treatment for disseminated coccidioidomycosis make the development of a safe, effective vaccine for targeted prevention programs an activity of high interest. This report suggests that three intradeltoid doses over 8 weeks of a vaccine against the spherule phase of the organism is both safe and immunogenic. While the safety and immunogenicity of this vaccine may predict efficacy, we should recall the optimistic early studies on a safe, immunogenic, but not terribly efficacious cholera vaccine. Nevertheless, we eagerly await the vaccine efficacy study which will certainly follow from these carefully done studies.—M.K.

Successful Treatment of Chromoblastomycosis With Topical Heat Therapy

Hachiro Tagami, Masumi Ginoza, Shunsuke Imaizumi, and Shoko Urano-Seuhisa (Hamamatsu Univ., Japan)

J. Am. Acad. Dermatol. 10:615–619, April 1984   3–8

The above researchers report 4 female patients with chromoblastomycosis who were completely cured by prolonged topical applications of tolerable heat from pocket warmers. Two types of pocket warmers were used that could emit constant heat to keep the skin surface temperature about 43 C.

CASE 1.—Woman, 42 years old, had a painful pruritic eruption on the left buttock for 6 years. After constant application of a pocket warmer at home for 2 months, the lesion disappeared, leaving an atrophic scar.

CASE 2.—Woman, 58 years old, had an asymptomatic skin eruption on the back for 2 years. Topical heat therapy with a pocket warmer was applied on an outpatient basis and complete cure was confirmed 3 months later. No recurrence was noted after 2 years, 6 months.

CASE 3.—Woman, 78 years old, had a painful, erythematous plaque on the right forearm for 6 years. After persistent application of heat with a pocket warmer for 5 months, the skin lesion gradually improved. No recurrence occurred after 1 year.

CASE 4.—Woman, 59 years old, had a painful pruritic, lesion on the right elbow for 3 years. Application of heat therapy resulted in a complete cure of the lesion after 2 months.

Results of in vitro studies showed the thermosusceptibility of the *Fonsecaea pedrosoi* isolated from Patients 1, 3, and 4, withstood persistent heating at 42.5 C for more than 1 month. This suggested that heat killing of the causative organisms is unlikely to have been the sole reason for the effectiveness of this simple therapeutic modality.

The authors suggest that it may be worthwhile to try heat therapy in combination with other therapeutic agents such as amphotericin B, thiabendazole, 5-fluorocytocine, or ketoconazole, in order to increase the efficacy of these drugs by improving local circulation as well as preventing undesirable side effects.

▶ Tropism of skin infections may, in some instances, reflect a preference of the organism for the cooler temperature of this tissue. In addition to leprosy and cutaneous leishmaniasis, chromoblastomycosis appears to be another such infection. In this report, 4 patients showed marked improvement with local heat treatment.—G.K.

4 Parasitic Infections

Helminths

Biliary Ascariasis: A Common Cause of Biliary and Pancreatic Disease in an Endemic Area
Mohammad Sultan Khuroo and Showkat Ali Zargar (Soura, Srinagar, Kashmir, India)
Gastroenterology 88:418–423, February 1985   4–1

Ascaris invasion of the biliary tree can produce recurrent pyogenic cholangitis, cholecystitis, and pancreatitis. The role of ascariasis in biliary and pancreatic disease in an endemic area was examined in 134 patients seen in a 6-month period in Srinagar, India, among a total of 2,836 patients evaluated for gastrointestinal symptoms. Biliary or pancreatic disease was proved in 109 patients, and 40 cases (37%) were found to be related to ascariasis. Studies included both endoscopic retrograde cholangiopancreatography and scintiscanning with ^{99m}Tc-sulfur colloid.

Biliary ascariasis occurred predominantly in adult women. The mean duration of symptoms was about 5 years. Nearly all patients had biliary colic associated with recurrent pyogenic cholangitis. Patients frequently vomited roundworms during attacks of biliary colic. Sixteen patients had had biliary operation and often were found to have acalculus cholecystitis. Stool studies were positive for *Ascaris* ova in 38 patients. All 21 patients with proved biliary ascariasis had radiographic evidence of roundworms in the biliary tree (Figs 4–1 and 4–2). Five of 29 patients had abnormal pancreatograms. All patients received anthelmintic treatment with Mebendazole. Thirty-eight patients were free of symptoms after a mean follow-up of 7½ months. Worms had left the biliary tree in all 11 patients who were restudied. Six of the 40 study patients (15%) had pancreatitis, presumably due to blockage of the sphincter of Oddi by worms entering the bile duct.

Biliary ascariasis is treated conservatively with fluids, antibiotics, and antispasmodics. Worms migrating into the duodenum are amenable to anihelmintic therapy. Surgical procedure is planned if repeat cholangiopancreatography after 2 weeks shows that worms still are present in the biliary tree and symptoms are present. Anthelmintic treatment for 2 months is necessary to prevent recurrences in an endemic area.

► Ascariasis is highly prevalent (at least one quarter of the world's population is infected) but generally considered to cause little morbidity. However, even if a very small percentage of patients develop complications, such as biliary duct obstruction, the number affected would be rather large. This study demonstrates that biliary ascariasis is a common cause of biliary disease in an area highly endemic for *Ascaris,* and also shows that conservative management

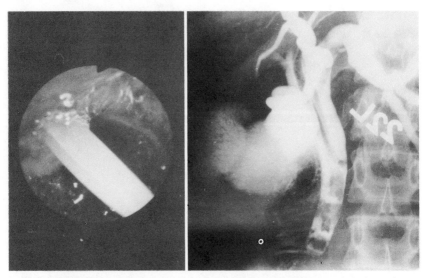

Fig 4–1 (left).—Photograph taken during duodenoscopy that shows biliary ascariasis. A roundworm is visualized in the duodenum and has entered the ampulla of Vater. Endoscopic retrograde cholangiopancreatography revealed the remaining portion of roundworm in the common bile duct.

Fig 4–2 (right).—Endoscopic retrograde cholangiopancreatography. Biliary ascariasis. Two smooth, long, linear filling defects are seen in the upper half of the common bile duct and extend up into the hepatic ducts. The lower half of the common bile duct reveals three defects of varying shapes (stones). Gallbladder is dilated but free of worms or stones.

(Courtesy of Khuroo, M.S., and Zargar, S.A.: Gastroenterology 88:418–423, February 1985. Reprinted by permission of Elsevier Science Publishing Co., Inc. Copyright 1985 by the American Gastroenterology Association.)

without surgery may result in clinical improvement. It is a reminder to physicians in the United States to search for *Ascaris* in patients originating from endemic regions of the world within the previous 3–5 years (the usual life span of adult worms) presenting with unexplained biliary colic or acalculous cholecystitis.—G.K.

Acute Gastric Anisakiasis: Analysis of 178 Cases

Keizo Sugimachi, Kiyoshi Inokuchi, Toshio Ooiwa, Takahiro Fujino, and Yoichi Ishii
JAMA 253:1012–1013, Feb. 15, 1985   4–2

Acute gastric anisakiasis caused by gastric mucosal penetration by *Anisakis* larvae is relatively frequent in Japan where raw fish is commonly eaten. A total of 178 cases were seen since 1969. All patients presented with acute, severe abdominal pain after eating raw fish. The 107 male and 71 female patients were aged 15–75 years. Some patients became symptomatic within an hour of ingesting raw fish. Nausea was the rule, and more than one third of the patients vomited. Raw mackerel had most often been eaten. More than two thirds of the cases occurred during the spring months.

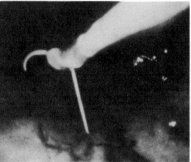

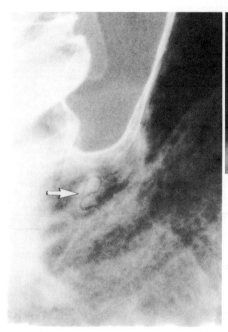

Fig 4–3 (left).—Roentgenographic findings. Typical threadlike filling defect caused by *Anisakis* larva is shown at gastric angle in double-contrast study *(arrow)*.
Fig 4–4 (above).—Endoscopic findings. *Anisakis* larva being removed with biopsy forceps.
(Courtesy of Sugimachi, K., et al.: JAMA 253:1012–1013, Feb. 15, 1985; copyright 1985, American Medical Association.)

Upper gastrointestinal (GI) radiography was done in 130 cases, and showed threadlike gastric filling defects about 30 mm long in nearly half of them (Fig 4–3). The shapes occasionally changed. Small, round collections of barium were seen where the larvae became fixed and penetrated the mucosa. Mucosal edema was usually present, and compression films helped identify the worms. A broad edematous gastric fold itself was highly suggestive of anisakiasis. The worms were removed with biopsy forceps (Fig 4–4) in all patients. Worms were found in all areas of the gastric mucosa, and local and generalized mucosal edema was present in most cases. Tumor formation was evident in 43% of the cases.

Recognition of acute gastric anisakiasis as a cause of sudden severe gastric symptoms can avoid laparotomy for acute abdomen. Symptoms resolve rapidly after endoscopic removal of the larvae. Anisakiasis can be avoided by eating only well-cooked fish. The upper gastrointestinal findings on radiography may simulate gastric cancer which makes endoscopy an effective diagnostic procedure.

▶ *Anisakis* worms are ascarid roundworm parasites of marine mammals. Their complex life cycle involves two intermediate hosts, and infectious larvae are present in viscera and muscle of fish or squid. Big fish eat little fish, and as a result, the larvae grow bigger and move up the food chain. Humans are attacked when we eat infected raw fish or squid, and as sushi eating is becoming more popular in the United States, more cases are being seen. Two types are involved: *Phocanema,* which infects many species of fish and causes a self limited mild gastritis, and *Anisakis,* which infects only Pacific salmon and true herrings (*Culpea* sp.) in United States waters but causes more severe and persistent symptoms until the larvae are mechanically removed.—G.K.

Meandering Ocular Toxocariasis
Edward M. Sorr (St. Francis General Hosp., Pittsburgh)
Retina 4:90–96, Spring 1984   4–3

The report details the first photographically documented and serologically substantiated occurrence of a migrating subretinal *Toxocara canis* larva.

Boy, 16, presented in 1978 with painless blurred vision of 3 weeks duration in the left eye. He worked on occasion in his father's slaughterhouse. Visual acuity was 20/50 in the left eye. There was a subretinal pigmented tract that led to a white subretinal equatorial nodule or capsule. From this capsule a second pigmented tract led toward the disc subretinally and entered the substance of the retina, coursing along the inferonasal branch vein to the optic nerve head where the tract ended. The nerve head was edematous with subretinal fluid evident, and a prominent macular star of hard exudates was present. An enzyme-linked immunosorbent assay titer was positive for *T. canis* in July 1978. Medrol given at an initial dose of 16 mg twice daily, improved vision to 20/25 in the left eye with improvement in the fundus picture.

After a 2-year symptom-free absence, the patient returned in 1980 with painless

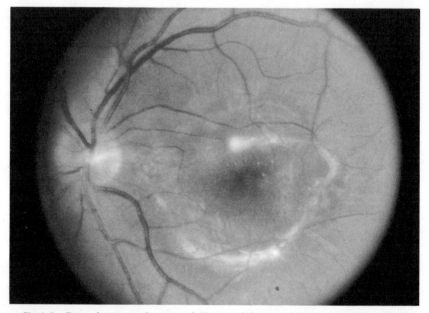

Fig 4–5.—Forward migration has stopped. Tenting of the internal limiting membrane appears to indicate possible entrance into the vitreous. The retinal vessels over the old, empty, and collapsed cyst are now flat. Pigment has appeared at the site of the empty capsule as had occurred at previous resting sites deep in the retina. (Courtesy of Sorr, E.M.: Retina 4:90–96, Spring 1984.)

loss of vision in the left eye and visual acuity of 20/300. A new tract had appeared; it began in the nerve head and continued deep into the retina beneath the maculopapillary bundle. A smooth, dome-shaped, yellow-orange capsule was present deep in the retina. Despite thiabendazole treatment, the larva left the capsule and traveled within the nerve fiber layer of the retina. A yellow-white retinal opacification prevented visualization of the 400-μm organism. Two months later, visual acuity had improved to 20/25 + 2 on no medication. Focal tense elevation of the internal limiting membrane at the leading edge of the tract suggested that the larva might burrow into the vitreous (Fig 4–5). The larva continued to move, variously affecting visual acuity until it was possible to destroy it 18 months later with Xenon photocoagulation.

During the 4-year observation there were several periods of migration of the larva. At no time was the organism or its movement visible; whenever it burrowed, it was enveloped in a cloak of opacified pigment epithelium or retina. Despite intense and prolonged treatment, thiabendazole was ineffective in destroying the organism and argon blue-green laser was also ineffective. Xenon photocoagulation ultimately killed the larva.

▶ It must be frustrating to directly observe ocular larva migrans with fluctuating visual acuity loss for so long a period, and have no effective treatment. In this case, the larva was finally killed when "zapped" by xenon photocoagulation. The value of ELISA for diagnosis is also of note. The reason why *Toxocara* affects the eye without visceral involvement in older subjects, and results in visceral larva migrans in young children, remains an intriguing mystery.—G.K.

Diagnostic Features of Zoonotic Filariae in Tissue Sections
Y. Gutierrez (Case Western Reserve Univ.)
Hum. Pathol. 15:514–525, June 1984   4–4

Several species of filarial parasites from wild and domestic animals can accidentally infect human beings. Zoonotic infections are being seen with increasing frequency, especially in areas free of human filariasis. Filariae capable of reaching adulthood and producing microfilariae cause infection in endemic regions. Other infections are caused by filariae that do not mature under normal conditions. They are found in human beings in larval or young adult stages and are usually unfertilized.

Dirofilariae are distributed worldwide in primates, carnivores, and rodents. Most human infections by *Dirofilaria immitis* have involved the lungs in asymptomatic patients. Symptoms such as cough and chest pain may accompany embolization of dying young filariae into pulmonary artery branches. *D. repens* can cause subcutaneous or conjunctival swelling with pain and inflammation. Similar features are associated with *D. tenuis* infection. *Dirofilaria ursi* infection follows the distribution of bears in North America (Fig 4–6) and Asia.

Many species of *Onchocerca* inhabit the connective tissues of wild and domestic animals throughout the world. *Onchocerca volvulus* naturally affects human beings in endemic tropical areas. *Brugia* species are parasites

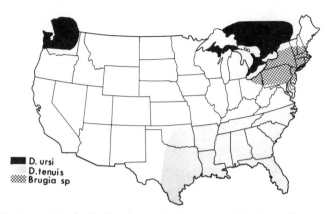

Fig 4–6.—Approximate distribution of zoonotic subcutaneous and lymphatic filariasis in the United States. (Courtesy of Gutierrez, Y.: Hum. Pathol. 15:514–525, June 1984.)

of the lymphatic system of primates, carnivores, and insectivores. A few cases of zoonotic *Brugia* infection are recorded in the American literature, involving healthy patients who have enlarged lymph nodes.

▶ Most clinicians are unaware that invasive systemic roundworm infections of humans occur in the United States, including not only visceral and cutaneous larva migrans (caused by animal *Ascarid* worms or hookworms, respectively) but also filarial worms for which the human is not a definitive host. *Dirofilaria immitis,* for example, can result in single or multiple coin lesions in the lung and should be included in the differential diagnosis.—G.K.

American Paragonimiasis Treated With Praziquantel

Constance T. Pachucki, Roland A. Levandowski, Valerie A. Brown, Brigitta H. Sonnenkalb, and Michael J. Vruno
N. Engl. J. Med. 311:582–583, Aug. 30, 1984 .   4–5

Infection from American *Paragonimus* has rarely been documented. However, the authors report data on a patient infected with a *Paragonimus* species.

Man, 19, ate the raw flesh of a crayfish during a canoe trip in Missouri. Fever, fatigue, and malaise appeared within 2 weeks. Infectious mononucleosis was suspected because Epstein-Barr-virus (EBV) capsid IgG in serum was 1:256. Erythromycin and prednisone were administered with minimal symptomatic improvement. Dyspnea, left pleuritic chest pain, and a left pneumothorax developed within 2 weeks. The EBV-IgG titer rose to 1:1,024, peripheral white blood cell count was 6,900, with 59% band forms, 13% neutrophils, 19% lymphocytes, and 6% eosinophils. The spleen was enlarged on radionuclide scan. Subsequently, the pneumothorax and fever resolved spontaneously, but the pleuritic pain, dyspnea, and malaise persisted. Prednisone (60 mg/day) brought about gradual symptomatic relief.

Six months after the initial presentation, development of hemoptysis led to cytologic examination of the patient's sputum. Numerous operculated ova of a *Paragonimus* species, most probably *Paragonimus kellicotti,* were identified in the sample. Complement fixation titers for *Paragonimus* were positive at a dilution of 1:64. The stool examination yielded no ova.

The patient received praziquantel orally, 75 mg/kg of body weight per day, in 3 divided doses on 2 consecutive days. No adverse reaction occurred. Dyspnea, pleuritic chest pain, cough, sputum production, and hemoptysis resolved within 4 weeks. Three months after therapy, the infiltrates and adenopathy had resolved and minimal residual left pleural thickening persisted. Complement-fixation titers for *Paragonimus* remained at a dilution of 1:64.

Paragonimus species are the cause of infection in wild and domestic animals in North and South America; distribution parallels that of the two intermediate hosts, the operculate snail and crayfish. Identification is most reliably based on the pattern of branching of the ovaries and testes of the mature flukes. Presentation and course of the infection in this patient were very similar to those in the illnesses described for *Paragonimus westermani* which is associated with consumption of encysted Asian freshwater crabs.

American paragonimiasis should be part of the differential diagnosis of any patient with eosinophilia, eosinophilic pneumonia, hemoptysis, or fever of unknown origin after travel to or residence in an endemic area, particularly when the patient has eaten raw or undercooked crayfish. Praziquantel appears to be safe and effective for this debilitating disease.

▶ Paragonimiasis conjurs up images of lung fluke infection in faraway exotic regions of the world. This patient developed a severe illness due to a species of the worm native to North America. After 6 months, parasite eggs were finally identified in sputum, and drug therapy produced a rapid clinical response.—G.K.

Acute Cholangitis Caused by Ruptured Hydatid Cyst
Amnon Ovnat, Jochanan Peiser, Eliezer Avinoah, Yechiel Barki, and Ilan Charuzi (Beer-Sheva)
Surgery 95:497–500, April 1984   4–6

Acute cholangitis caused by ruptured hydatid cyst is a rare event. The authors present their experience in the management of 4 patients with acute cholangitis caused by ruptured echinococcal cyst.

The patients presented with fever, jaundice, and pronounced rigidity over the right upper abdominal quadrant. Treatment was begun with fluid resuscitation, nasogastric tube insertion and antibiotics before diagnostic procedures were done. Ultrasonography showed a hydatid cyst and an enlarged common bile duct filled with scolecesin in 3 patients (Fig 4–7). Surgical intervention was done in all patients within 8 hours after admission. The operative procedures adopted were cholecystectomy, choledochotomy, choledochoduodenostomy, and cystectomy in 3 patients and removal of the hydatid cyst in 1 patient. Follow-up ranged from 18 months to 5 years and revealed no mortality or recurrence of cholangitis. Only 1

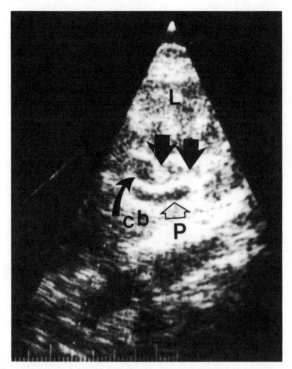

Fig 4–7.—Ultrasonic view in left lateral decubitus position at the level of the common bile duct shows daughter cysts within the dilated common duct *(large arrows)*. L, liver; cb, common bile duct; P, portal vein. (Courtesy of Ovnat, A., et al.: Surgery 95:497–500, April 1984.)

patient needed reoperation in the case in which the cyst was left untouched originally followed by removal of the cyst.

Diagnosis is established best by ultrasonography. Surgical intervention should not be delayed unnecessarily and choledochoduodenostomy with cholecystectomy constitutes an appropriate surgical intervention.

▶ Hydatid cyst disease affects a sizable number of people in the highly endemic regions of Europe (including Greece, Spain, Italy, and Turkey), the middle east, South America, and elsewhere where sheep husbandry is prevalent. Because of migration, more cases are being imported into the United States. This paper presents 4 patients with acute cholangitis due to hydatid cysts in which the diagnosis was made by ultrasonography. This information was important to the surgeon in advance of surgical intervention.—G.K.

Protozoa

Rigid Membranes of Malayan Ovalocytes: A Likely Genetic Barrier Against Malaria
N. Mohandas, L. E. Lie-Injo, M. Friedman, and J. W. Mak
Blood 63:1385–1392, June 1984   4–7

Nonhemolytic hereditary ovalocytosis is prevalent in Malayan aborigines and may reflect reduced susceptibility of affected persons to malaria. Kidson et al. found that ovalocytes from Melanesians in Papua New Guinea are resistant to infection in culture by *Plasmodium falciparum*. An attempt was made to define the mechanism of this protection by examining the membrane and cellular deformability characteristics of the cells with an ektacytometer. Blood samples were obtained from 7 Malayan aborigines known to have hereditary ovalocytosis and 4 normal Malayans.

The ovalocytic red blood cells exhibited markedly reduced deformability at all levels of applied shear stress. The ovalocytes had a more favorable surface area-to-volume ratio and, therefore, increased osmotic resistance. Accelerated loss of deformability in the hypertonic region suggested that increased internal viscosity may contribute to the reduced whole cell deformability of ovalocytes, but this could not be confirmed. Direct evidence for increased ovalocyte membrane rigidity was obtained by measuring the deformability characteristics of membranes rather than whole cells. An in vitro invasion assay using *P. falciparum* merozoites showed that the extent of inhibition was closely related to the reduction in membrane deformability. Normal red blood cells treated with glutaraldehyde became less deformable, and their susceptibility to infection decreased at the same time.

The resistance of Malayan ovalocytes to parasitic invasion appears to result from a genetic mutation causing increased membrane rigidity. The molecular and biochemical basis of the increased membrane rigidity remains to be determined, but further studies may elucidate the role of skeletal proteins and their interactions in the regulation of red blood cell membrane properties.

▶ A number of genetic red blood cell defects appear to provide some protection against malaria. In this paper, the basis for inate resistance of hereditary ovalocytosis erythrocytes to invasion by falciparum malaria was investigated. Invasion was inhibited in proportion to the intrinsic resistance of the cells to membrane deformability, and is probably related to the dramatic deformations of the erythrocyte which occur during the invasion process.—G.K.

Structure of the Gene Encoding the Immunodominant Surface Antigen on the Sporozoite of the Human Malaria Parasite *Plasmodium falciparum*
John B. Dame, Jackie L. Williams, Thomas F. McCutchan, James L. Weber, Robert A. Wirtz, Wayne T. Hockmeyer, W. Lee Maloy, J. David Haynes, Imogene Schneider, Donald Roberts, Greg S. Sanders, E. Premkumar Reddy, Carter L. Diggs, and Louis H. Miller
Science 225:593–599, Aug. 10, 1984   4–8

Monoclonal antibody to the circumsporozoite (CS) protein of *Plasmodium berghei* has protected mice from challenge by infected mosquitoes. The gene for the CS protein of *Plasmodium falciparum* now has been cloned, and the amino acid sequence of the protein has been deduced from the nucleotide sequence of the gene. The gene encodes a protein of 412 amino acids. The protein contains 41 tandem repeats of a tetrapeptides; 37 are Asn-Ala-Asn-Pro, and 4 are Asn-Val-Asp-Pro. Monoclonal antibodies against the protein were inhibited from binding to the protein by synthetic peptides of the repeat sequence. The CS protein of *P. falciparum* and that of a simian malaria parasite, *Plasmodium knowlesi*, were found to have 2 regions of homology, 1 on either side of the repeat. One region contains 12 of 13 identical amino acids, and 25 of 27 nucleotides are conserved within the sequence of this region.

The conservation of regions in parasites widely separated in evolution suggests that they may have a function, such as binding to liver cells, and may therefore represent an invariant target for immunity. The conserved regions, as well as the repeating epitope, may be targets for sporozoite vaccines. If the region in question is conserved in other human malarias and is exposed to the immune system, immunization with the region from *P. falciparum* may protect against other species of human malaria. If the homologous region is involved in reception for liver invasion, the malarial parasite may not be able to vary the sequence in this region.

▶ This paper is one of several of this past year that report startling progress towards the goal of malaria vaccine development. In this study, the gene for the dominant sporozoite antigen, CS, has been cloned, and from this the amino acid sequence determined. Structurally, the antigen is very interesting, containing multiple tandem repeats of a tetrapeptide, which may serve as the basis for a peptide vaccine to prevent sporozoite invasion of liver cells, as the first stage in malaria infection.—G.K.

Identification and Expression in *Escherichia coli* of Merozoite Stage-Specific Genes of the Human Malarial Parasite *Plasmodium falciparum*
Michael J. McGarvey, Esmail Sheybani, Michel P. Loche, Luc Perrin, and Bernard Mach (Univ. of Geneva)
Proc. Natl. Acad. Sci. USA 81:3690–3694, June 1984   4–9

Attempts are underway to clone genes for parasite antigens and express them in bacteria in order to prepare *Plasmodium falciparum* proteins for use in vaccination. A major problem is identifying recombinant DNA clones corresponding to the schizont merozoite specific polypeptides involved in immunity against malaria. Studies in a cDNA library now have led to the identification of recombinant clones corresponding to genes expressed specifically at the late schizont merozoite stage of *P. falciparum* development.

A total of 132 cDNA clones were identified from among 10,000 in the library that correspond to 12 different genes which probably represent most of the major schizont merozoite specific genes. The stage-specific cDNAs are efficiently expressed in *Escherichia coli* cells. The protein products of some of these clones are recognized by monoclonal antibodies specific for late schizont merozoite proteins. Hybridization studies suggested that activation of new genes at the transcriptional level takes place during parasite development. Both the enzyme-linked immunosorbent assay and electrophoretic transfer blot assay showed that the protein product of some stage-specific cDNA clones reacts with monoclonal antibodies specific for schizont merozoite polypeptides.

The maturation of *P. falciparum* appears to be associated with the selective activation of a relatively small set of genes. The protein product of some stage-specific cDNA clones is recognized by monoclonal antibodies specific for some of the relevant merozoite proteins. Preparation in bacteria of the protein products corresponding to the merozoite specific genes will permit evaluation of their capacity to protect against malaria in vivo.

▶ Theoretically, the problem with a sporozoite malaria vaccine is that if one sporozoite escapes the immune response and reaches the liver, it could multiply and initiate the erythrocytic cycle of the infection, which would result in clinical disease. Hence, there is continuing interest in a merozoite vaccine. This paper reports an essential step in this process, the identification and cloning of genes for merozoite specific antigens.—G.K.

Immune Sera Recognize on Erythrocytes A *Plasmodium falciparum* Antigen Composed of Repeated Amino Acid Sequences

Ross L. Coppel, Alan F. Cowman, Robin F. Anders, Albert E. Bianco, Robert B. Saint, Klaus R. Lingelbach, David J. Kemp, and Graham V. Brown (Melbourne)
Nature 310:789–792, Aug. 30, 1984   4–10

Protective immune responses against the asexual stages of *Plasmodium falciparum* presumably are directed against exposed antigenic determinants on the surface of the free merozoite or the infected red blood cell, making antigens at these sites candidates for components of a molecular vaccine. A method has been developed of expressing *P. falciparum* proteins in *Escherichia coli* as fused polypeptides. Antigen-producing clones are detected by screening with immune human sera. Antibody against the fused polypeptide expressed by one clone has been found to react with a *P. falciparum* protein synthesized late in schizogony, which later is present on the surface of the ring-infected erythrocyte.

The clone in question produced a large fused polypeptide with a molecular weight of 156 K, presumably composed of 116K of β-galactosidase sequence and 40K of *P. falciparum* sequence. The *P. falciparum* antigen corresponding to this fragment was identified as an acidic protein of 155K MW. Reactive erythrocytes were infected with ring forms; all cells so infected appeared to have the antigen. Fully mature schizonts were reactive, but fluorescence was localized to the parasite. Mature trophozoites showed minimal reactivity. The protein was present in all isolates of *P. falciparum* examined. It was composed of repeating subunits of 8, 4, and 3 amino acids.

The exposed location of ring-infected erythrocyte surface antigen (RESA) on the surface of infected red blood cells presumably makes it vulnerable to immune attack. Anti-RESA antibodies are found in some sera from immune persons. An immune response to the RESA could interfere with merozoite invasion or prematurely lyse recently infected cells. The antigen could have a role in protective vaccination, although not all parts of the molecule may be equally immunogenic.

▶ This paper reports another essential step in the road to a malaria merozoite vaccine by the use of convalescent patient sera to identify important parasite antigens as potential protective antigens. By this means, the authors have identified an erythrocyte surface parasite antigen present on infected red blood cells that may serve as a target to attack these cells and preclude the maturation of the parasite to a form in which it can infect new cells, and thus interrupt the clinical phase of the disease.—G.K.

Antidepressants Cause Lethal Disruption of Membrane Function in the Human Protozoan Parasite *Leishmania*

Dan Zilberstein and Dennis M. Dwyer (Bethesda)
Science 226:977–979, Nov. 23, 1984   4–11

The tricyclic antidepressant drugs imipramine and 3-chlorimipramine efficiently inhibit serotonin uptake in mammalian cells and also uncouple oxidative phosphorylation. In high concentration they inhibit H^+ adenosinetriphosphatases in mammalian mitochondria, and this activity is present in the surface membrane of the trypanosomatid protozoan *Leishmania donovani*, the cause of human visceral leishmaniasis. The effects of clomipramine and nitroimipramine on extracellular promastigotes of both *L. donovani* and *Leishmania major* were examined. The growth of amastigotes of both parasites, within peritoneal macrophages was assessed.

Clomipramine and nitroimipramine killed extracellular promastigotes of both *L. donovani* and *L. major*. Clomipramine also killed amastigotes of both species within murine macrophages with no apparent toxic effect on the host cells. The amastigotes were more sensitive than the promastigotes to clomipramine. A concentration of 100 μ/L inhibited L-proline transport in promastigotes. Synergistic inhibition of L-proline transport was observed with clomipramine and either valinomycin or nigericin.

The cytotoxic effects of clomipramine on *Leishmania* appear to result from disruption of the proton electrochemical gradient in the surface membrane of the parasite. Similar energy transduction processes may occur in other parasitic protozoa that suggests clomipramine and compounds with a similar mode of action may prove to be useful antiparasitic agents.

▶ Although leishmaniasis does not exist in the United States we see cases imported both by American travelers to endemic areas and natives from such regions. Current therapy for the disease depends heavily on pentavalent antimonials, available from the Centers for Disease Control, and is less than satisfactory. There is no vaccine. This study opens up new possibilities for treatment with available drugs used for other purposes, and is a direct result of understanding metabolism in the parasite and selection of potential inhibitors. The clinical value of the tricyclic antidepressants as anti-protozoal agents remains to be determined.—G.K.

Cryptosporidiosis in an Urban Community
D. A. Hunt, R. Shannon, S. R. Palmer, and A. E. Jephcott
Br. Med. J. 289:814–816, Sept. 29, 1984   4–12

Cryptosporidium is an important pathogen in immunocompromised patients and those individuals with acquired immune deficiency syndrome. It is now being reported more often as a cause of self-limited gastroenteritis in immunologically normal persons. Stool specimens collected from 867 patients who presented in a 3-month period with gastrointestinal symptoms were examined for *Cryptosporidium oocysts*. Fecal smears were fixed with alcohol and stained by a modified Ziehl-Neelsen method. Oocysts were found in 5% of the samples (table). *Cryptosporidium* was second only to *Campylobacter* as an enteric pathogen. Seven percent of children, younger than age 5 years, in the series excreted *Cryptosporidium oocysts*. Positive samples were associated with mild gastroenteritis and 4–6 watery, mucoid, foul-smelling stools daily that lasted 1 to 2 weeks. Some patients had abdominal pain. Only 1 patient had blood in the stool. The median duration of diarrhea was 2 weeks.

Cryptosporidium apparently can cause a self-limited gastroenteritis in immunocompetent persons. The source of the present infections was not identified, but direct contact with farm animals was not observed. No association with a common water supply was apparent. Two small clusters of cases were identified in day nurseries. Stool specimens were obtained from 24 household contact of 10 index cases. Four of the contacts from 3 households excreted *Cryptosporidium oocysts* in their stools. Only symptomatic treatment and rehydration are necessary. *Cryptosporidium* should be included with the enteric pathogens routinely sought in patients with

FECAL PATHOGENS IDENTIFIED IN PEOPLE WITH
GASTROINTESTINAL SYMPTOMS*

Age of patients (years)	No (%) with *Cryptosporidium*	No (%) with *Salmonella*	No (%) with *Shigella*	No (%) with *Campylobacter*	No (%) with *Giardia*
<1 (n=78)	6 (7·7)	3 (3·8)		3 (3·8)	
1-4 (n=251)	18 (7·2)	4 (1·6)	1 (0·4)	8 (3·2)	5 (2·0)
5-9 (n=49)	2 (4·1)	3 (6·1)			1 (2·0)
10-14 (n=16)	1 (6·3)	2 (12·5)		2 (12·5)	
15-24 (n=128)	8 (6·3)	6 (4·7)		11 (8·6)	2 (1·6)
25+ (n=278)	8 (2·9)	16 (5·8)	5 (1·8)	17 (6·1)	8 (2·9)
Unknown (n=67)		3 (4·5)	1 (1·5)	8 (11·9)	1 (1·5)
Total (n=867)	43 (5·0)	37 (4·3)	7 (0·8)	49 (5·7)	17 (2·0)

*From October 24, 1983, to January 31, 1984.
(Courtesy of Hunt, D.A., et al.: Br. Med. J. 289:814–816, Sept. 29, 1984.)

diarrhea because of the simple diagnostic procedures and the possible importance of *Cryptosporidium* as a pathogen in human beings.

▶ In a few years, *Cryptosporidium* has gone from an unknown parasite to a readily diagnosed cause of 5% of acute diarrheal disease throughout the world. While the parasite is currently not specifically treatable, it causes a self-limited illness in the immunocompetent host. The problem is in the immunocompromised patient. The establishment of the life cycle in cell culture a year ago (see Current, W. L., and Haynes, T. B.,: *Science* 224:603–605, 1984) offers the hope of developing and testing drugs for this parasite.—G.K.

Issues in Clinical Parasitology: The Treatment of Giardiasis
Richard A. Davidson (Univ. of North Carolina)
Am. J. Gastroenterol. 79:256–261, April 1984   4–13

Symptomatic infection with *Giardia lamblia* is now the most common parasitic infection in the United States that causes an acute diarrheal illness with malabsorption and marked dehydration. As many as 86% of infected patients may spontaneously clear the infection through circulating antibodies or mononuclear leukocytes, but many patients require chemotherapy with antiprotozoal agents. The author examines the efficacy of these drugs, their side effects, and risk of long-term carcinogenesis.

Quinacrine, an antimalarial, was the first clearly effective drug. It may cause side effects, especially nausea and vomiting, and may also cause hemolysis in glucose-6-phosphate dehydrogenase-deficient individuals. Standard dosage for adults is 100 mg 3 times daily for 5 days. For children it is 6 mg/kg/per day in 3 divided doses for 5 days. Metronidazole is presently not approved for treatment of giardiasis in the United States. Its side effects include a metallic taste, nausea, lassitude, and drowsiness. The recommended dosage for adults is 250 mg three times daily for 5 days. For children it is 15 mg/kg per day in 3 divided doses for 5 days. Furazolidone, a minimally absorbed nitrofuran derivative, is the only effective drug available in a liquid suspension. It has some of the same side effects as quinacrine and metronidazole. Adult dosage is 100 mg 4 times daily for 7 days and the recommended pediatric dosage is 5 mg/kg per day in 4 divided doses for 10 days.

The trials available for review suffered from unclear methods, variability in study populations and total dosage of medication used, inaccuracy in determining outcomes, and inadequate sample sizes.

Of 139 patients treated with quinacrine in 4 studies, 129 were cured (92.8%). Long courses of metronidazole were given to 238 patients in 7 studies; 219 (92%) were cured. In 6 studies, 177 patients were given furazolidone and 150 (84%) were cured. With regard to side effects, approximately 7.1% of metronidazole-treated patients, 9.6% of furazolidone-treated patients, and 23% of quinacrine-treated patients had side effects that were reported.

To date, no adequate, well-controlled study has been done regarding the carcinogenicity of metronidazole. It has been suggested that in children who have an expected long latency period, possible carcinogens should be avoided. Thus, quinacrine would be the drug of choice; however, its toxicity may cause a lack of compliance. The slight long-term risk of metronidazole may be preferable under these circumstances.

▶ In spite of the cure rates of 85%–92% suggested by the studies reviewed, treatment of giardiasis is not wholly satisfactory. Many of us have seen patients who fail on repeated courses of metronidazole and cannot tolerate quinacrine. There is a need for new drug development for this common protozoan infection in the United States.—G.K.

5 Mycobacterial Infections

Possible Role of Mycobacteria in Inflammatory Bowel Disease
Rodrick J. Chiodini, Herbert J. Van Kruiningen, Walter R. Thayer, Richard B.
Merkal, and Jessica A. Coutu
Dig. Dis. Sci. 29:1073–1085, December 1984   5–1

I. An unclassified Mycobacterium *species isolated from patients with Crohn's disease.*—Crohn's disease is a granulomatous enteritis resembling tuberculosis. Its response to sulfasalazine also prompts consideration of a possible causative role of mycobacteria. An unclassified *Mycobacterium* species was isolated from a girl, aged 15 years, with Crohn's disease in 1982, and chronic ileitis was produced by oral inoculation of the organism in a goat. A similar *Mycobacterium* species subsequently was isolated from a boy, aged 12 years, with a diagnosis of Crohn's disease.

The organism is an acid-fast, mycobactin-dependent *Mycobacterium* that belongs to Runyon group III. It is most closely related to *Mycobacterium paratuberculosis*. The organism is pathogenic for mice when injected intravenously or intraperitoneally, producing hepatic and splenic granulomas that contain numerous acid-fast mycobacteria. The goat inoculated orally developed humoral and cell-mediated immunologic responses as well as granulomatous disease of the distal small bowel. A single organism was found in each of two microgranulomas in a mesenteric lymph node, and the organism was reisolated from the node but not from the bowel. Findings from inoculation studies of rats, guinea pigs, rabbits, and chickens were negative.

Similar mycobacteria have not been isolated from 11 patients with Crohn's disease or 3 with ulcerative colitis. The organism is an exceptionally fastidious one that requires long incubation on complex media. The organism appears to be sparse in tissues. The use of mycobactin specifically prepared from the organism may enhance its isolation. The organism can produce granulomatous disease of the intestine in the goat, and it may be related to the intestinal disease of the patients examined.

II. Mycobacterial antibodies in Crohn's disease.—Thayer, Coutu, Chiodini, Van Kruiningem, and Merkal recently isolated a *Mycobacterium* species from the diseased bowels of 2 patients with Crohn's disease. The organism, which may be related to *Mycobacterium paratuberculosis*, produced granulomatous ileitis when given orally to a newborn goat. The animal developed an immunologic response to the organism with considerable cross-reactivity to *M. paratuberculosis*. Antibodies now have been sought to the organism and to *M. paratuberculosis* using serums from patients with Crohn's disease and ulcerative colitis, and serums from control subjects. An enzyme-linked immunosorbent assay was used.

Serums were obtained from 56 patients with Crohn's disease, 34 patients with ulcerative colitis, 67 healthy purified protein derivative (PPD)-negative subjects, and 41 PPD-positive subjects. Eighteen resected patients with Crohn's disease also were evaluated. Titers against *M. paratuberculosis* more than 2 SD above the control mean were found in 23% of patients with Crohn's disease and in none of those with ulcerative colitis. Comparable results were obtained in PPD-positive and negative patients. Positive-PPD controls also had elevated levels of antibody to *M. paratuberculosis*. Positive responses in Crohn's disease patients were not related to the area of gut involvement or to the activity of Crohn's disease. Forty-three percent of patients positive for antibody to *M. paratuberculosis* also were positive to *Mycobacterium kansasii*, but none were positive with *M. tuberculosis*.

These findings lend preliminary support to a role for the unclassified *Mycobacterium* species in the pathogenesis of Crohn's disease. Serums from patients with Crohn's disease appear to recognize an antigen present in *M. paratuberculosis* and *M. kansasii*, and probably also present in the unclassified *Mycobacterium* species. The response of Crohn's disease patients cannot be explained by reactivity to PPD.

▶ We would love to believe that the etiologic agent of Crohn's disease has at last been discovered! Certainly, it is tempting to believe the *Mycobacterium* connection. The pathology, with its granuloma formation and altered cell-mediated immunity, resembles that caused by this group of organisms. In addition, there is a remarkable counterpart in ruminants known as Johne's disease, which is caused by a *Mycobacterium*.

The problems with the first report, however, are legion: the organism has been isolated in fact from only 2 of 11 patients with Crohn's disease. There is no discussion of isolation attempts in tissues from normal controls. The inoculation study in animals, while intriguing, is not entirely convincing, since it is known that such granulomatous reactions can be induced by inoculation of a variety of foreign antigens, both living and dead, into experimental animals. Again, there were no controls of other forms of protein inoculations. Also, several other animal species tested failed to demonstrate pathogenicity with this *Mycobacterium*.

The antibody studies, recounted in the second paper failed to convince this reader. Only 23% of Crohn's patients had measurable antibody to this organism. Similar results, however, were observed in PPD-positive controls. These findings suggest that contact with *Mycobacterium* is found in at least some Crohn's patients. The question is whether this organism is the true pathogen or whether it is an idle bystander in the intestinal microflora. The intestinal mucosa of Crohn's patients is abnormal, and there seems to be increased sampling of antigen within the intestinal lumen. Thus, such patients have higher antibody levels to a variety of intestinal bacteria and viruses, some of which are pathogens, and others merely eating at the same table. Despite its obvious flaws, these papers represent an intriguing line of investigation, one which should be pursued with vigor. We are closing in on the pathogen of Crohn's disease, but the enigma still remains.—S.G.

Pulmonary Infection With *Mycobacterium xenopi:* Review of Treatment and Response
J. Banks, A. M. Hunter, I. A. Campbell, P. A. Jenkins, and A. P. Smith
Thorax 39:376–382, May 1984   5–3

There has been no report that accurately assesses the effect of chemotherapy or surgical procedure on the long-term prognosis of patients with pulmonary infection with *Mycobacterium xenopi.* The authors studied 47 patients, 82% were men with a mean age of 61.5 years (range 36–84 years) with *M. xenopi* infection presenting over a 10-year period to assess their response to treatment and prognosis for cure as well as to identify a form of successful therapy.

Preexisting lung disease was present in 35 cases (75%) of which healed *Mycobacterium tuberculosis* infection, chronic bronchitis, and emphysema were most common. In 21 of 43 patients who presented with respiratory symptoms, the disease was characterized by a subacute illness developing during 2 to 4 months with increasing cough and sputum, loss of weight, and malaise. Another 20 patients gave longer history of chronic respiratory symptoms sometimes associated with slowly progressive changes on chest x-ray films. Eleven patients (23%) were cured with chemotherapy; 6 patients were cured while receiving a combination of rifampicin, isoniazid, and ethambutol despite relatively poor in vitro sensitivity results. Another 12 patients (26%) showed satisfactory responses initially to at least 9 months of drug therapy, but eventually relapsed. Eleven patients who received less than 9 months of chemotherapy eventually had unfavorable results. Retreatment in 4 patients resulted in curing 3 patients and a relapse in the fourth patient. Four patients had progressive diseases while receiving prolonged courses of chemotherapy. Resection was performed in 5 cases with resultant cure in 4.

Overall, the response to treatment was poor and unpredictable, and was not related to the results on in vitro sensitivity tests, preexisting lung disease, or mode of onset of symptoms. In 23% of patients cured, the best drug regimen appeared to be rifampicin and isoniazid combined with either streptomycin or ethambutol. An adequate period of therapy was not determined, but a course of less than 9 months was not favorable. Since the prognosis with chemotherapy alone is so unpredictable in pulmonary infection with *M. xenopi,* it is suggested that resection may be a part of first-line therapy in some patients who fail to respond to initial chemotherapy or patients who relapse.

▶ The large number of patients with *Mycobacterium xenopi* pulmonary infections and the substantial follow-up period (up to 13 years) makes this a valuable paper to refer to in this clinical situation. The relatively poor cure rate (26%) contrasts with many published reports and textbook descriptions of the good prognosis for this pathogen. The close antigenic relationship it has with *M. avium-intracellulare* makes me think that this paper more accurately reflects the problematic natural history of *M. xenopi* infections.—M.K.

Disseminated Infection With *Mycobacterium avium-intracellulare:* A Report of 13 Cases and a Review of the Literature
Charles R. Horsburgh, Jr., Ulysses G. Mason III, Diane C. Farhi, and Michael D. Iseman (Denver)
Medicine 64:36–48, January 1985   5–4

Thirteen cases of disseminated *Mycobacterium avium-intracellulare* (MAI) infection seen in 1940–1984 were reviewed, along with 24 cases reported in the literature since 1940. The incidence of disseminated MAI was 5% of the incidence of pulmonary MAI disease. All age groups were affected, but 7 patients were younger than age 3 years. Common physical findings included fever, enlarged reticuloendothelial organs, and skin lesions. Generalized symptoms were present in 26 patients, pulmonary symptoms in 10 patients, and gastrointestinal symptoms in 5 patients. Most patients were anemic, but only 4 were thrombocytopenic. The mean duration of symptoms before MAI infection was diagnosed was about 5 months.

No single serotype predominated. The bone marrow, sputum or lung, and lymph nodes were the most frequent culture-positive sites. Acid-fast bacilli were found on histologic study of biopsy or autopsy material in 30 of 37 cases. Twenty-four of 33 evaluable patients responded to antimycobacterial chemotherapy, but 4 later relapsed and died despite additional therapy. All 3 untreated patients died. Patients who responded received a mean of about 5 drugs. Therapy with cycloserine as part of the regimen was more frequent in patients who responded than in those who did not. Normal and immunocompromised patients responded equally well to treatment. Children and patients who had large numbers of acid-fast bacilli in their tissues were less likely to respond to treatment. Four patients who responded to treatment later died of another infection.

The portal of entry of MAI into the human host is not certain. Disseminated MAI infection usually results in diffuse involvement of the reticuloendothelial system. Optimal treatment of disseminated MAI infection remains to be established, but multidrug therapy seems indicated. Favorable results have been obtained in patients who were simultaneously given 2 or more drugs to which their organisms were sensitive in vitro.

▶ *Mycobacterium avium-intracellulare* is receiving considerable attention now because it is one of the frequent opportunistic infections in acquired immunodeficiency syndrome (AIDS) patients (see Fauci, A. S., et al.: *Ann. Intern. Med.* 102:800–813, 1985). In this paper, a review of 13 patients seen at one center from 1940–1984 and of 24 patients reported in the literature since 1940 spans the pre-AIDS era to the present time. It is of interest because 10 patients were less than 10 years of age (most less than 3 years) and 17 of the 37 patients were not known to be immunosuppressed. The problems of drug therapy of this infection are well illustrated and appear to be characteristic of the organism and independent of host immune status except for the AIDs patients who are unresponsive regardless of drug regimen.—D.S.

Tuberculosis Mimicking Cancer: A Reminder
Silvio D. Pitlik, Victor Fainstein, and Gerald P. Bodey (M. D. Anderson Hosp. and Tumor Inst.)
Am. J. Med. 76:822–824, May 1984   5–5

Tuberculosis is a protean disease that can mimic other disease entities, especially cancer. The authors reviewed the cases of 26 patients who were referred with a presumptive diagnosis of neoplasm and who were ultimately found to have only tuberculosis. Twenty-six patients, 14 males and 12 females, mean age 54 years (range 15 to 85 years) were studied. Twenty-one patients were born in the United States, and only 3 patients had a history of exposure to tuberculosis. Twenty-two patients presented with few symptoms, i.e., cough, anorexia, cervical mass, and weight loss. Average duration of symptoms was approximately 3 months. Underlying conditions were found in 8 patients and alcoholism was the most common. The most frequent diagnosis on admission was lung cancer (42%), lymphoma (23%), nasopharyngeal carcinoma (12%), and breast cancer (8%). Chest x-ray abnormalities were present in 16 patients and showed multilobar infiltrations, right upper lobe infiltrations, and pleural effusions. Cavitation was seen in only 1 patient and a "coin" lesion was found in another. Although some of the patients had undergone nondiagnostic biopsy procedures before referral, none had skin tests for tuberculosis. Laboratory abnormalities were found in only 9 patients with 8 patients showing increased platelet counts. *Mycobacterium tuberculosis* was cultured from only one site in 24 patients, with the sputum as the most common site of isolation. The most common form of tuberculosis diagnosed was pulmonary (14 patients) followed by lymphadenitis (9 patients).

Tuberculosis continues to be an elusive disease even in countries with advanced medical technology. Despite the protean manifestations of tuberculosis in this study, the diagnosis of tuberculosis was established in most of the patients with relatively simple procedures. Physicians must be aware that this disease may mimic other disease entities, especially cancer.

▶ Prior to the development of antituberculous therapy, tuberculosis was considered to be the cause of illness in many patients with a wide variety of clinical presentations. This report reminds us that patients with tuberculosis need not have many of the typical signs of inflammation usually associated with an infectious disease. Thus, in patients thought to have a malignant disease, who have an atypical presentation, tuberculosis must be considered in the differential diagnosis.—S.M.W.

Extrapulmonary Tuberculosis Revisited: Review of Experience at Boston City and Other Hospitals

Salvador Alvarez and William R. McCabe
Medicine 63:25–55, January 1984   5–6

Extrapulmonary tuberculosis has a very broad clinical spectrum, which may be referable to almost any organ system. The proportion of extrapulmonary cases has increased significantly in recent years. Specific forms of extrapulmonary involvement, apart from disseminated miliary disease, include tuberculous meningitis, tuberculous peritonitis, and genitourinary tuberculosis. Tuberculous lymphadenitis and osseous and articular tuberculosis also are encountered. A few cases of pericardial tuberculosis and adrenal disease have been encountered. Miscellaneous sites of disease have included the ear, dental tissues, larynx, and anus. Tuberculin skin testing has been positive in about three fourths of the cases. About 60% of patients have had abnormal chest roentgenographic findings of active or inactive tuberculosis. Biopsy specimens have yielded a positive diagnosis in half of all patients studied.

Fourteen of 103 patients with extrapulmonary tuberculosis who were followed up died, 7 resulted from causes other than tuberculosis. Four deaths, 2 with miliary tuberculosis and 2 with meningeal disease, occurred before the initiation of antituberculosis chemotherapy. Nineteen percent of 27 patients with miliary tuberculosis and 2 of 10 patients with tuberculous meningitis died. The overall mortality attributable directly to tuberculosis was 7%. Current ATS guidelines are cautious in using short-term treatment for extrapulmonary disease. The value of steroids in the treatment of meningeal and other extrapulmonary forms of tuberculosis remains to be established and, at present, they are recommended only for cerebral edema in the most seriously ill patients with impending spinal or ventricular obstruction.

▶ Extrapulmonary tuberculosis can be a diagnostic dilemma and a therapeutic emergency. Although most institutions will see no more than a case or two a year, the prevalence of these infections has not decreased even though pulmonary tuberculosis is less frequent now. In this review of 136 patients with extrapulmonary tuberculosis from several Boston hospitals seen over the period 1968–1977, the pitfalls and problems likely to be encountered are described and the diagnostic yield of various procedures is detailed. The relative proportion of extrapulmonary to pulmonary tuberculosis, which is about 1 in 10 in the general population, is markedly increased in AIDs patients (70%–80%) and includes both *M. tuberculosis* and atypical strains such *M. avium-intracellulare* (see Pitchenik, A. E., et al.: *Ann. Intern. Med.* 101:641–645, 1985).—D.S.

Rapid Diagnosis of Tuberculous Meningitis by Latex Particle Agglutination

Elias Krambovitis, Michael B. McIllmurray, Paul E. Lock, William Hendrickse, and Helen Holzel
Lancet 2:1229–1231, Dec. 1, 1984
5–7

Tuberculous meningitis remains an important cause of morbidity and mortality in children. Early treatment is essential. Latex particle agglutination (LPA) is a simple, rapid, and sensitive means of detecting bacterial antigens associated with acute pyogenic meningitis. The test was evaluated in 18 pediatric cases of tuberculous meningitis in which cerebrospinal fluid (CSF) samples were available. Control samples were obtained from 38 children who had acute pyogenic meningitis due to other organisms and 96 who had various infective and noninfective disorders.

Six of the 18 study patients died. Widely varying laboratory findings were present at admission (Table 1), but a mononuclear reaction generally was associated with normal or low glucose levels. *Mycobacterium tuberculosis* was cultured from 13 CSF samples. *Mycobacterium tuberculosis* plasma membrane antigen was detected in initial samples from all patients but one who later had positive findings. Only 1 of 134 control samples was positive (Table 2). The positive control subject had *Hemophilus influenzae* type b meningitis and a subdural abscess.

The LPA test holds much potential for diagnosing tuberculous meningitis. It could be especially useful in developing countries since it is inexpensive and requires no special equipment. The LPA test might be helpful

TABLE 1.—CSF Findings on Admission

	Protein (g/l)	Glucose (mmol/l)	White cells (× 10^6/l)	% mono- nuclear	FM	TB culture	TB antigen	Duration of therapy*
1	0·98	4·2	189	99	+	+	+	None
2	0·62	3·1	36	100	–	–	+	6 wk (R, I, E)
3	1·0	1·4	365	86	+	+	+	8 wk (I, S, P)
4	1·6	1·5	314	100	+	–	+	None
5	1·25	2·9	370	48	+	+	+	None
6	0·61	1·2	446	95	–	–	+	3 d (R, I, S)
7	0·15	0·38	250	50	+	+	+	1 wk (R, I, S)
8	1·1	1·1	710	100	+	+	+	2 wk (R, I, S)
9	6·0	0·94	290	99	+	–	+	None
10	1·47	1·1	223	98	+	+	+	None
11	0·82	3·0	52	100	+	+	+	None
12	0·64	3·5	47	98	–	–	–	1 d (R, I, S)
13	1·0	0·8	99	94	+	+	+	1 d (R, I, S)
14	2·2	0·7	163	52	+	+	+	2 d (R, I, S)
15	3·0	1·1	173	48	+	+	+	4 d (R, I, S)
16	1·1	2·7	196	36	+	+	+	1 wk (R, I, S)
17	0·1	3·4	154	60	+	+	+	10 d (R, I, S)
18	1·6	2·1	35	98	+	+	+	8 wk (R, I)

*Duration of antituberculous therapy on admission. E = ethambutol, I = isoniazid, P = para-aminosalicylic acid, R = rifampin, S = streptomycin.
†FM = fluorescence microscopy.
(Courtesy of Krambovitis, E., et al.: Lancet 2:1229–1231, Dec. 1, 1984.)

TABLE 2.—Control Patients Tested for
Mycobacterium tuberculosis Antigen in CSF

n

Bacterial meningitis*	38†
Acute leukaemia	28
Febrile illness	19
Neurodegenerative disease	14
Hydrocephalus	11
Encephalitis	8
Myelographic investigation	5
Febrile convulsion	5
Glioma	3
Head injury	2
Near-miss cot death	1

Hemophilus influenzae b = 18, *Streptococcus pneumoniae*
= 12, *Neisseria meningitidis* = 6, streptococcus group B = 2.
†1 positive sample from a child with *H. Influenzae* b meningitis.
(Courtesy of Krambovitis, E., et al.: Lancet 2:1229–1231,
Dec. 1, 1984.)

in monitoring patient responses to chemotherapy and in detecting mycobacterial antigens in other body fluids.

▶ There is a clear need for a rapid test for tuberculous meningitis. The diagnosis is generally made on the basis of the clinical picture and the evolving CSF
findings. Once diagnosis is made, treatment is intensive, expensive, and prolonged. This simple procedure shows promise as a cost-effective aid to early
detection and therapy of this otherwise lethal infection, and would be of great
use in developing countries with a high incidence of the disease.—G.K.

Rifampicin in Tuberculous Meningitis: A Retrospective Assessment
P. Latorre, M. Gallofré, J.-R. Laporte, and J. Massons
Eur. J. Clin. Pharmacol. 26:583–586, July 1984   5–8

Rifampicin is actively bactericidal against *Mycobacterium tuberculosis*
at relatively low concentrations, and standard doses produce therapeutic
levels in the cerebrospinal fluid (CSF). A review was made of data on
treatment of tuberculous meningitis (TBM) with a rifampicin-isoniazid
combination and with other regimens. Data on 143 cases seen at 4 hospitals
in 1967–1980 were reviewed. Children younger than age 10 years were
excluded from the study. In 37 cases tubercle bacilli were demonstrated
in the CSF. Sixty-four patients received treatment including rifampicin,
and 79 received treatment with other antituberculosis drugs, most frequently isoniazid. Rifampicin was given in a daily dose of 600 mg. Twelve
rifampicin-treated patients and 20 others received isoniazid in a daily dose
of at least 15 mg/kg. The two treatment groups had comparable prognostic
characteristics.

Overall mortality was 15%. It was 3% in rifampicin-treated patients and 24% in the other patients, a significant difference. The difference in mortality remained significant when patients dying during the first 48 hours after the start of treatment were excluded. Mortality was similar in the patients given rifampicin plus isoniazid and those given isoniazid without rifampicin. Neurologic sequelae at 6 months were more severe in patients not given rifampicin. Four of the 5 patients with clinical evidence of hepatitis were taking rifampicin plus isoniazid, and 1 was taking isoniazid without rifampicin.

These results suggest the value of adding rifampicin to isoniazid in the treatment of TBM. Isoniazid should be used in a dose no lower than 8 mg/kg in patients with TBM. Whether there is an unacceptable risk of hepatotoxicity when rifampicin is used with higher doses of isoniazid remains to be determined. Neurologic sequelae were less marked in rifampicin-treated patients in the present study.

6 Infections in the Compromised Host

Trimethoprim-Sulfamethoxazole in the Prevention of Infection in Neutropenic Patients
EORTC International Antimicrobial Therapy Project Group
J. Infect. Dis. 150:372–379, September 1984   6–1

Neutropenic patients are at an increased risk of serious infection. The European Organization for Research on Treatment of Cancer undertook a multicenter, prospective, randomized, double-blind, placebo-controlled trial of trimethoprim-sulfamethoxazole (TMP-SMX) as a means of preventing such infection in patients with fewer than 1,000 circulating granulocytes/µL, or expected to become neutropenic within a few days. Patients were assigned randomly to receive 2 tablets of 160 mg of TMP and 800 mg of SMX twice daily or placebo tablets. Children received 150 mg of TMP and 750 mg of SMX/sq m. Treatment was continued as long as granulocytopenia persisted. Febrile patients received nystatin, amphotericin B, ketoconazole, or miconazole. Those patients who were febrile at the outset received β-lactam and aminoglycoside antibiotics as well as the trial drug.

The occurrence of infection in patients given prophylaxis and placebo patients among the 342 evaluable patients at 12 centers is shown in Table 1. Infection was significantly less frequent in patients given prophylaxis. The distribution of organisms causing bacteremia in the 2 groups was fairly similar. Infection was not less frequent in patients with acute nonlymphocytic leukemia who received prophylaxis (Table 2). Overall infection was comparably frequent in other patients, but bacteremia was more frequent in placebo patients (Table 3). Prophylaxis was well tolerated; no serious side effects were observed.

TABLE 1.—Occurrence of Infections Among Placebo- and TMP-SMZ-Treated Patients

Treatment group	Total no. of patients	No. (%) of patients with	
		Any infection	Bacteremia
Placebo	165	64 (39)*	32 (19)[†]
TMP-SMZ	177	46 (26)*	22 (12)[†]

*$P = .016$.
[†]$P = .106$.
(Courtesy of EORTC International Antimicrobial Therapy Project Group: J. Infect. Dis. 150:372–379, September 1984.)

TABLE 2.—Occurrence of Infection in Patients With Acute Nonlymphocytic Leukemia Treated With or Without Orally Administered Nonabsorbable Antibiotics. Where Indicated, Data Are Number of Patients (%)

Treatment group	Oral nonabsorbable antibiotics			No oral nonabsorbable antibiotics		
	Patients	Infection	Bacteremia	Patients	Infection	Bacteremia
Placebo	32	14 (49)	3 (9)*[†]	32	21 (66)	12 (39)*[‡]
TMP-SMZ	37	13 (35)	8 (22)[†]	38	18 (47)	10 (26)[‡]
Total	69	27 (39)	11 (16)[§]	70	39 (56)	22 (32)[§]

*P = .016.
†P = .29 (difference NS).
‡P = .94 (difference NS).
§P = .05.
(Courtesy of EORTC International Antimicrobial Therapy Project Group: J. Infect. Dis. 150:372–379, September 1984.)

TABLE 3.—Occurrence of Infection in All Patients Excluding Those With Acute Nonlymphocytic Leukemia

Treatment group	No. of patients	No. (%) of patients with	
		Infection	Bacteremia
Placebo	101	29 (29)*	17 (17)[†]
TMP-SMZ	102	15 (15)*	4 (4)[†]

*P = .038.
†P = .005
(Courtesy of EORTC International Antimicrobial Therapy Project Group: J. Infect. Dis. 150:372–379, September 1984.)

A modest reduction in the occurrence of infection and bacteremia is observed in patients with malignancies other than acute nonlymphocytic leukemia who are neutropenic and are given TMP-SMX prophylaxis. Bacteremia in this setting is likely to be due to organisms resistant to these drugs, and routine prophylaxis is not warranted in patients with acute nonlymphocytic leukemia.

Infection Prophylaxis in Acute Leukemia: Comparative Effectiveness of Sulfamethoxazole and Trimethoprim, Ketoconazole, and a Combination of the Two
Elihu Estey, Andrew Maksymiuk, Terry Smith, Victor Fainstein, Michael Keating, Kenneth B. McCredie, Emil J. Freireich, and Gerald P. Bodey (Houston)
Arch. Intern. Med. 144:1562–1568, August 1984   6–2

Both fungal and bacterial infections have been the principal cause of death in patients with acute leukemia during the last 20 years. The authors determined if either sulfamethoxazole (SFX) and trimethoprim (TMP), ketoconazole alone, or SFX and TMP plus ketoconazole would reduce morbidity and mortality from infection during induction therapy of acute leukemia.

One hundred forty-seven patients were randomized to receive either of the following: (1) 38 patients were given no prophylaxis; (2) 35 patients were given SFX and TMP, one double-strength tablet twice daily; a total of 320 mg of TMP and 1,600 mg of SFX 5 times daily; (3) 32 patients were given ketoconazole, 200 mg twice daily; or (4) 45 patients were given a combination of SFX, TMP, and ketoconazole in doses noted previously. All patients received therapy as outpatients or inpatients in a hospital. Infection was considered present if fever and either a clinical site of infection, i.e., cellulitis, pharyngitis, or a positive finding in blood or urine culture was present.

Both SFX and TMP and the combination of SFX, TMP, and ketoconazole substantially reduced the overall incidence of infection consequent to a marked decrease in bacterial infection. However, major fungal infections occurred more in patients receiving SMX and TMP, whereas ketoconazole decreased this complication. Because of the shorter period of time on study, the number of episodes of infection per 100 days on study was calculated. These calculations showed that patients receiving SMX and TMP with or without ketoconazole had a significantly lower number of episodes of infection. Considering fungal infections alone, the highest number of episodes of infection per 100 study days was observed in patients using SMX and TMP alone and was lowest in patients receiving ketoconazole alone. The addition of ketoconazole to SMX and TMP eliminated the increased risk of fungal infections. There were no significant differences in the infectious mortality rate or complete remission rates between groups. Also, there were no significant differences in the percent of patients who failed to obtain complete remission because of infection, as opposed to hemorrhage or resistant leukemia.

This study shows that infection prophylaxis reduces the risk of infection but fails to affect the complete remission or fatality rates in patients with acute leukemia receiving remission induction therapy. The authors suggest that the combination of SMX, TMP, and ketoconazole offers substantial advantages in reducing morbidity in patients with acute leukemia undergoing remission induction therapy.

▶ There have now been several trials of prophylactic antibiotics during leukemia remission induction chemotherapy. Trimethoprim-sulfamethoxazole has been particularly scrutinized as a combination to prevent bacterial infections and, with the increasing awareness of how frequently fungal infections occur in the granulocytopenic, leukemic patient, attention has broadened to also include antifungal prophylaxis. While the concept of antimicrobial prophylaxis is appealing, it clearly does not hold the entire answer. The overall complete remission rate as well as the rate of failure to achieve complete remission because of infection have not been substantially altered in most studies of prophylactic antibiotics. In abstract 6–2, there was also no reduction in mortality from infection comparing any of the treatment groups to nonprophylaxed patients. In the large, multicentered EORTC study, a significant benefit from TMP-SMX prophylaxis was only seen in patients with diagnoses other than acute nonlymphocytic leukemia. Even in this group the major benefit was to reduce the occurrence of bacteremia with only a modest reduction in the overall occurrence of infection. The deaths attributable to infection and the complete remission rates were not reported in this study. Despite some pessimism, we need to continue the search for measures to prevent infections in such patients, especially as our oncology colleagues improve regimens to achieve complete remission and improve survival.—M.K.

Treatment of *Pneumocystis Carinii* Pneumonitis: A Comparative Trial of Sulfamethoxazole-Trimethoprim Versus Pentamidine in Pediatric Patients With Cancer—Report From the Children's Cancer Study Group
Stuart E. Siegel, Lawrence J. Wolff, Robert L. Baehner, and Denman Hammond (Los Angeles)
Am. J. Dis. Child. 138:1051–1054, November 1984   6–3

Pentamidine has been preferred for the treatment of *Pneumocystis carinii* pneumonia, but it has a number of significant adverse effects. Treatment with sulfamethoxazole-trimethoprim (SMX-TMP) would have the advantages of ready availability, greater safety, and oral administration. A randomized trial comparing SMX-TMP with pentamidine was undertaken in 25 pediatric cancer patients with biopsy-proved *P. carinii* pneumonia. The organism was demonstrated in all cases by staining of lung biopsy tissue or aspirated material. Fifteen patients were assigned to receive TMP and SMX in respective daily doses of 20 and 100 mg/kg for 2 weeks, whereas 10 were assigned to 4 mg/kg of pentamidine daily by intramuscular injection. Most patients in both groups had acute lymphocytic leukemia. The median age of both groups was 3–4 years. Clinical features were similar except for more frequent cyanosis in the SMX-TMP group.

There were no differences in clinical or roentgenographic responses or in the final outcome in the two treatment groups. All patients but 1 recovered from pneumonia, and none had a recurrence. Most patients received long-term prophylaxis with SMX-TMP. Two patients in the pentamidine group were changed to treatment with SMX-TMP because of a deteriorating clinical status. One of them died after 2 weeks of treatment with progressive pulmonary involvement. Toxicity was similarly frequent in the two groups. Two patients in the SMX-TMP group had mild liver enzyme level elevations. Three patients in the pentamidine group had a rise in serum creatinine or serum urea nitrogen levels.

The SMX-TMP is effective in the treatment of *P. carinii* pneumonia. Its ready availability and relative ease of administration support the use of SMX-TMP as the agent of first choice for *P. carinii* infection in immunocompromised children and adults. Pentamidine will remain useful as a secondary agent for the few patients who fail to respond to SMX-TMP.

▶ In children with *Pneumocystis* infection, a high cure rate (96%) was observed with either regimen, and both drugs seem to be equally effective. This story is considerably different from that seen in AIDS patients since these patients suffer a high failure rate and a high incidence of drug-related side effects.—S.G.

Single Drug Versus Combination Empirical Therapy for Gram-Negative Bacillary Infections in Febrile Cancer Patients With and Without Granulocytopenia
M. Piccart, J. Klastersky, F. Meunier, H. Lagast, Y. Van Laethem, and D. Weerts (Univ. of Brussels)
Antimicrob. Agents Chemother. 26:870–875, December 1984   6–4

Safer single drug therapy is preferable to multidrug empirical treatment in infected cancer patients if a sufficiently broad antimicrobial spectrum and adequate bactericidal activity can be realized. A prospective study was done comparing the third-generation cefoperazone alone with a combination of cefoperazone and amikacin in both neutropenic and nongranulocytopenic cancer patients with a temperature above 38.5 C. Patients received either 6 gm of cefoperazone twice daily, intravenously, or 2 gm of cefoperazone plus 500 mg of amikacin twice daily. These regimens have exhibited identical bactericidal activities against common gram-negative bacilli in volunteer subjects. Twenty-nine infectious episodes were microbiologically documented in neutropenic patients, including 23 gram-negative bacteremias. Twenty-seven of 61 documented episodes in nonneutropenic patients were gram-negative bacteremias.

The two regimens were comparably effective in neutropenic patients, whether response or overall cure was considered. Cefoperazone alone was effective in 78% of the episodes of gram-negative bacteremia, and combined treatment was effective in 81% of the episodes. Only 3 treatment failures occurred in nonneutropenic patients with gram-negative bacteremia. Superinfection was more frequent in the patients given combined treatment. Both regimens were well tolerated. No diarrhea was observed.

Cefoperazone alone is an effective and safe empiric treatment for cancer patients suspected of having gram-negative bacillary sepsis, whether or not they are neutropenic. The findings lend support to the concept of single drug empirical therapy with new cephalosporins in cancer patients with suspected gram-negative bacillary sepsis. This approach might, however, have to be revised if resistance of gram-negative bacilli to these agents becomes more prevalent.

▶ This small scale study will need to be confirmed before single drug therapy for suspected gram-negative bacillary infections in cancer patients can be recommended.—D.S.

Bronchoalveolar Lavage in the Diagnosis of Diffuse Pulmonary Infiltrates in the Immunosuppressed Host

Diane E. Stover, Muhammad B. Zaman, Steven I. Hajdu, Michael Lange, Jonathan Gold, and Donald Armstrong (New York City, N.Y.)
Ann. Intern. Med. 101:1–7, July 1984   6–5

Pulmonary complications of many types cause morbidity and mortality in immunosuppressed patients. Accurate diagnosis and prompt treatment can be effective in many instances. The clinical features are usually non-specific. Cutting-needle biopsy has a high complication rate, and needle aspiration is inadequate in diffuse disorders. Bronchoalveolar lavage was evaluated in 97 immunosuppressed patients seen in a 2-year period who underwent fiberoptic bronchoscopy. The patients had a diagnosis of cancer, had received a bone marrow transplant, or were receiving chemotherapy or other immunosuppressive agents. A volume of 210 ml of normal saline was lavaged in 30-ml aliquots, and at least 3 transbronchial and brush biopsy specimens were taken from at least 2 different lobes of the same lung, including the segment in which the lavage was done. In 74 cases the diagnosis was confirmed by tissue examination.

Two patients had the bronchoscopic procedure twice. Hematologic malignancy was the most common underlying disorder. A total of 92 specific diagnoses were made in 83 patients, the most common being malignancy, *Pneumocystis carinii* pneumonia, drug toxicity, and viral pneumonia. The diagnostic yield of bronchoalveolar lavage is shown in the table. All but 4 of 22 cases of *P. carinii* pneumonia were correctly diagnosed by bronchoalveolar lavage. Cytomegalovirus pneumonia was diagnosed in 10 of 12 cases, and fungal pneumonia was seen in 5 of 6 cases. There were no major complications, although 18 patients with respiratory failure were on ventilatory assistance at the time of bronchoscopy and lavage, and 35 patients had severe thrombocytopenia. One patient having transbronchial biopsy had a pneumothorax and another had major pulmonary hemorrhage, but there were no deaths.

Bronchoalveolar lavage is a safe and useful diagnostic procedure in

DIAGNOSTIC YIELD OF BRONCHOALVEOLAR
LAVAGE IN 83 IMMUNOSUPPRESSED
PATIENTS

Disease	Yield* n/n (%)
Infection	38/46 (83)
Hemorrhage	7/9 (78)
Malignancy	10/22 (46)
Drug toxicity	6/15 (40)

*In the value given, the numerator represents the number of patients whose diagnosis was made by bronchoalveolar lavage. The denominator represents the total number of patients with a diagnosis determined by bronchoscopic, open lung biopsy, or postmortem findings.

(Courtesy of Stover, D.E., et al.: Ann. Intern. Med. 101:1–7, July 1984.)

immunosuppressed patients with diffuse pulmonary infiltrates. It should be strongly considered as the initial procedure when opportunistic infection or pulmonary hemorrhage is likely. The additional use of bronchial washings, brushings, and transbronchial biopsy is recommended when the clinical circumstances permit.

▶ We continue to strive for better prevention, diagnosis, and treatment of infections in abnormal hosts. In this paper, the use of bronchoalveolar lavage for identifying the cause of diffuse pneumonias in these patients is discussed. Several points deserve emphasis. The advantages, disadvantages, and utility of this procedure may be highly dependent on the patient population. For example, patients in this series had a 1% incidence of bacterial pneumonia and a 24% incidence of *P. carinii* to account for their diffuse pneumonias. This is distinct from the acutely febrile, granulocytopuric patient receiving trimethoprim-sulfamethoxazole prophylaxis during induction chemotherapy for acute nonlymphocytic leukemia. Here the incidence of bacterial pneumonia is higher and, in many institutions, the incidence of *P. carinii* may be much lower. Nevertheless, under the right circumstances bronchoalveolar lavage should be considered in the diagnostic armamentarium. We need all the help we can get.—M.K.

Invasive *Fusarium* Infections in Bone Marrow Transplant Recipients
Bruce R. Blazar, David D. Hurd, Dale C. Snover, Jack W. Alexander, and Philip B. McGlave (Univ. of Minnesota)
Am. J. Med. 77:645–651, October 1984   6–6

The fungus *Fusarium* was first implicated in human disease in 1913 when contamination of food caused a plague-like illness in Russia. Subsequent reports of disease in human beings have described mainly local infections of the cornea, skin, and nails. Only rarely has *Fusarium* been implicated as a cause of invasive disease. Three patients were found to have culture-proved invasive *Fusarium* infections after allogeneic bone marrow transplantation. *Fusarium* was cultured from discrete skin nodules in one patient, the maxillary sinus in a second patient, and the blood and excised nasal septum in a third patient. All 3 isolates were resistant to 5-fluorocytosine, but 2 were susceptible to amphotericin B. All the patients died, 2 after clearance of the *Fusarium* infection. Two of the patients had *Aspergillus* infection as well.

Burn-injured patients are at an increased risk of *Fusarium* infection. Diabetics also may be at risk. Invasive disease has been limited to immunocompromised hosts such as bone marrow transplant recipients. *Fusarium* infection in an immunocompromised host does not, however, necessarily imply that the disease will become disseminated. The present patients had recently received chemotherapy and also received polymicrobial antibiotics for bacterial septicemia. Successful treatment of *Fusarium* infection depends on the site and extent of infection and on the antifungal sensitivity of the species present. Immunocompromised patients appear to have a poor prognosis. Amphotericin B presently is the preferred treatment for invasive *Fusarium* infection. Virtually all isolates have been resistant to 5-fluorocytosine. It may be useful to add rifampin to amphotericin B in some cases. Leukocyte transfusions may be indicated for granulocytopenic hosts. Localized *Fusarium* infection is managed by surgical removal.

▶ Tissue sections alone are inadequate to make a diagnosis of *Fusarium* since the acute angle branched, septate hyphae are indistinguishable from *Aspergillus*. In all 3 patients described in this report, multiple other pathogens were also present. The prognosis in patients with this unusual fungal infection is poor.—D.S.

Complement Deficiency States and Infection: Epidemiology, Pathogenesis, and Consequences of Neisserial and Other Infections in an Immune Deficiency
Stephen C. Ross (Univ. of Michigan) and Peter Densen (Univ. of Iowa)
Medicine (Baltimore) 63:243–273, September 1984   6–7

Serum proteins in the complement sequence have an important role in generation of the normal inflammatory response and in host defense against a wide variety of microorganisms. Deficiency states have been described for most of the 19 known complement components and regulator proteins. A review was made of data on 242 homozygotes or hemizygotes with an inherited absence of a complement protein, excluding cases of C1 esterase deficiency and hereditary angioneurotic edema. Most homozygotes have deficiencies of classic pathway components. Virtually all the collagen-vascular and autoimmune diseases are represented among patients with complement deficiencies. Four percent of the patients had had active infection by an intracellular pathogen such as *Mycoplasma tuberculosis*. Several syndromes have been described in which individual parts of the complement sequence are markedly depressed.

Neisserial infections are prominent in patients with complement deficiencies, especially those with a late component deficiency. One fourth of the present patients had systemic infection with either *Neisseria meningitidis* or *Neisseria gonorrhoeae*. The 61 patients had a total of 90 distinct episodes of meningococcal meningitis or meningococcemia and 23 episodes of disseminated gonococcal infection. Complications of meningococcal disease included arthritis in 12% of the patients and disseminated intravascular coagulopathy in 6%. The case-fatality rate was 6.9%.

The optimal management of complement-deficient patients is uncertain. Fresh frozen plasma has a short period of effectiveness in most patients, and antibody production may limit the value of subsequent treatment. It would seem reasonable to vaccinate patients with meningococcal and pneumococcal vaccines. Long-term antibiotic prophylaxis would likely be ineffective in complement-deficient patients. Protection is especially important for properdin-deficient patients who develop fulminant meningococcal infections with high mortality.

Infections in Burn Patients: A Paradigm for Cutaneous Infection in the Patient at Risk

Jeffrey A. Gelfand (Tufts-New England Med. Center, Boston)
Am. J. Med. 76:158–165, May 15, 1984   6–8

Infection is a major complication of thermal injury and the burned patient is, in many respects, the typical immunosuppressed host. The evolution of infection parallels the changes in infections seen in other immunocompromised hosts. Antimicrobials have shifted infections from primarily gram-positive cocci to gram-negative bacilli, especially *Pseudomonas aeruginosa*. Both local burn wound infections and burn wound sepsis develop in patients. Burn patients, especially those with tracheobronchitis or shock lung, are particularly vulnerable to pneumonia from the airborne or hematogenous route. In destroying the skin, burn injury removes a major host defense. The depth and extent of injury are important determinants of the degree of total disruption produced.

Serum immunoglobulin levels are depressed early after burn injury, but reduced serum antibody titers generally correlated poorly with the incidence of infection. Fibronectin levels also are lowered often before sepsis develops, and infusion of fibronectin-rich cryoprecipitate may improve the clinical outcome. Burn injury results in massive complement activation, primarily by the alternate complement pathway. This may contribute to impaired host defense against gram-negative pathogens for which the patient has no preformed antibody. Complement activation floods the immune system with anaphylatoxins which may have multiple effects on other immune functions.

Neutrophils from burn patients are partially deactivated. Abnormal cell-mediated immunity and lymphocyte function have been described. In addition to Enterobacteriaceae with high antimicrobial resistance, methicillin-resistant *Staphylococcus aureus* infections have become a problem in some burn units. Opportunistic pathogens such as fungi and herpesviruses are causing more infections in burn-injured patients.

▶ Infections continue to be a major cause of morbidity and mortality in burned patients. Recent studies from the author's laboratory and those of others have clearly shown that thermal injury results in a profound acquired immunodeficiency state. Understanding of these defects and the development of immunotherapeutic approaches should lead to immunologic reconstitution of the patient at risk as well as prevention of infection.—S.M.W.

Inadequate Interleukin 2 Production: A Fundamental Immunologic Deficiency in Patients with Major Burns

J. Jeremy Wood, Mary L. Rodrick, John B. O'Mahony, Steven B. Palder, Inna Saporoschetz, Philip D'Eon, and John A. Mannick (Brigham and Women's Hosp., Boston)
Ann. Surg. 200:311–320, September 1984   6–9

Interleukin 1 (IL-1) is produced by most cells of the monocyte-macrophage series, whether fixed or circulating; it is released in response to foreign antigens, including bacteria and their products, particularly endotoxin. Many immunologic reactions require the rapid proliferation of a small number of cells into several million, which is largely initiated and controlled by Interleukin 2 (IL-2). Because Interleukin 2 appears also to be involved in the development of T cells and the promotion of specific T cell cytotoxicity and nonspecific natural killer cytotoxicity, it follows that IL-1 and IL-2 are crucial in the immune response to foreign antigens and the defense against microbial invasion.

Seven female and 16 male patients (mean age 48.9 years) with a mean burn area of 33.1% in the Burn Unit at Longwood Area Trauma Center and 23 matched controls were studied. Serial measurements of IL-1 production were made by adherent mononuclear cells after stimulation with lipopolysaccharide and of IL-2 production by lymphocytes after stimulation with phytohemagglutinin (PHA).

Interleukin 2 production was clearly reduced in the burn patients. Eighty determinations in 13 patients with burns exceeding 30% of total body surface area (TBSA) revealed a mean IL-2 production of 0.71 μ as compared with 1.24 μ for the 10 patients with less than 30% burns. At each time interval, patients with larger burns had lower IL-2 values than did those with smaller burns; this difference was significant only 40–49 days postinjury. Compared to the controls, the larger burns had significantly less IL-2 production from immediately after injury until 60 days postburn. Those with smaller burns had a significant reductions in IL-2 only 20–29 and 30–39 days postburn.

Lymphocyte responses of burn patients to the mitogens PHA and ConA were suppressed. Burn patients with greater than 50% impairment of lymphocyte responsiveness to PHA as compared to normal controls produced less IL-2 (median 0.2 μ) than burn patients with less than 50% suppression of the PHA response (median 0.7 μ). A highly significant correlation was found between ConA suppression and IL-2 production (r = 0.371, P < 0.01, 80 df).

Examination of circulating T cell subsets in patients after thermal injury revealed a persistent reduction in the relative concentration of OKT4 positive helper cells. Interleukin 2 is a T cell product, principally produced by T_4-cells. Compared to controls, burn patients showed a significant reduction in number of circulating OKT3 cells up to 49 days postburn; OKT4 positive cells were also significantly reduced for most of the first 49 days postburn. No significant reduction in OKT3 and OKT4 cells was found 50–59 days postburn. As compared with controls IL-1 production was significantly elevated early after injury but was subsequently within normal range regardless of burn size. The Il-2 values in septic patients were lower than in nonseptic patients after 5 days postburn; the differences were significant only for the period 10–29 days. The IL-2 production during periods of sepsis was significantly lower than Il-2 production after recovery (mean 0.4 μ versus mean 1.78).

The study demonstrates a profound and persistent reduction in the ability of peripheral blood mononuclear cells of burn patients to produce IL-2. This is probably caused by the reduction in lymphocyte blasto-genesis in response to mitogens and specific antigens. The data provide theoretical support for a trial of IL-2 therapy in patients with major burns.

▶ With the use of modern technology we will soon have a variety of purified and well-characterized products, such as IL-1 (Auron, P. E., et al.: *Proc. Natl. Acad. Sci. USA* 81:7907–7911, 1984). Such materials will allow for better detection systems and new information regarding such important clinical matters as deficiency states. Furthermore, such materials will be in adequate supply for reconstitution of a deficient host. Thermal injury obviously disturbs many aspects of the immune response (see abstract 6–8). Better understanding of these changes should lead to real improvement in our treatment of burned patients.—S.M.W.

Proteins of the Cystic Fibrosis Respiratory Tract: Fragmented Immunoglobulin G Opsonic Antibody Causing Defective Opsonophagocytosis
Robert B. Fick, Jr., Gary P. Haegel, Susan U. Squier, Robert E. Wood, J. Bernard L. Gee, and Herbert Y. Reynolds
J. Clin. Invest. 74:236–248, July 1984   6–10

In the disease cystic fibrosis (CF), pulmonary infection with *Pseudomonas aeruginosa* is a common clinical complication that determines most morbidity and almost all excess mortality. The authors postulated that a defect in *Pseudomonas*-reactive IgG antibodies may contribute to chronic *Pseudomonas* infections. Bronchoalveolar lavages were performed on 13 patients (9 men and 4 women; aged 9–27 years; mean age, 17 years) with CF, 7 patients (3 men and 4 women; aged 59 ± 5.4 years) with chronic bronchitis characterized by recurrent *Pseudomonas* infections, and 4 normal volunteers (3 men and 1 woman; aged 29 ± 3.5 years). The levels of various proteins important to host defenses and proteases were determined; enzyme inhibition studies were performed. The CF respiratory immunoglobulin levels were significantly elevated when compared with chronic bronchitis. Albumin and transferrin levels were decreased in the CF lung fluids. The CF elastolytic activity was strikingly elevated (mean, 6.02 µg/mg total protein) and the inhibitory profile suggested such activity resembled a serine-proteinase. Alpha-1-antitrypsin antigenic levels were not altered in CF respiratory fluids. There was a tendency for the lagate IgG to fall as elastase levels rose.

The IgG opsonins for 2 *Pseudomonas* immunotypes were isolated with affinity chromatography for functional and immunochemical studies. Bacterial phagocytic rates in the presence of these *Pseudomonas*-reactive IgG opsonins derived from CF lavage fluid were depressed (0.3% uptake per unit time) when compared with similarly titered positive controls (uptake = 1.3% per unit time). Additionally, normal pulmonary macrophage intracellular killing of *Pseudomonas* was severely altered in the presence of opsonins derived from CF respiratory fluids. At some time points, less than

30% of the bacteria were killed. The CF IgG opsonins contain a cleavage fragment with antigenic determinants similar to the Fab portion of IgG. The presence of such a fragment was inversely correlated with phagocytic functional activity. Intact IgG comparised as little as 18% of the CF lavage fluid specimens. Aliquots of intact human IgG, when mixed with the CF opsonins, augmented *Pseudomonas* uptake and improved intracellular killing. Conversely, peptide fragments derived in vitro, duplicated in the study system the defect observed with opsonins derived from CF lung fluids; bacterial uptake was inversely related to the concentration of F (ab') 2 and to a greater degree, to Fc present in the opsonic mixture.

Commercially prepared enzyme-digested IgG preparations are suitable only for intramuscular administration and the dose that can be given is limited. As is the case with CF respiratory IgG opsonins, those commercial preparations lack the Fc region of IgG and thus have suboptimal opsonizing activity. In contrast, use of the cold ethanol extraction method results in IgG antibodies of which 94% are monomeric and all of the opsonizing and antigen-binding properties are intact. With such preparations, intravenous administration is possible and larger amounts may be given more frequently. If defects in CF opsonins are confirmed by others, replacement therapy might be cautiously undertaken in the proper clinical setting.

▶ This is a very well done study that sheds some light on a serious problem. The opsonic defect in CF patients probably plays a role in the major host defense abnormalities present in the lungs of these patients. Although the concept of giving intravenous immunoglobulin to such patients will be worth a try (if this work is confirmed), one wonders whether the active material will get to where it is needed (i.e., the lung).—S.M.W.

Association of Respiratory Viral Infections With Pulmonary Deterioration in Patients With Cystic Fibrosis
Elaine E. L. Wang, Charles G. Prober, Barbara Manson, Mary Corey, and Henry Levison (Univ. of Toronto)
N. Engl. J. Med. 311:1653–1658, Dec. 27, 1984   6–11

The role of bacterial agents in pulmonary deterioration of patients with cystic fibrosis remains uncertain, but viruses are the most common cause of respiratory infections and have been linked with pulmonary exacerbations in other chronic respiratory disorders. They also may predispose to bacterial infections. The role of viral infection was assessed in a 2-year prospective study of 49 patients with cystic fibrosis and 19 normal siblings. Both groups had a mean age of 14 years. Quarterly assessments were performed that included nasal washes for viral isolation and blood sampling for respiratory viral serologic studies. Lung function was evaluated at least twice a year.

Mean lung function and clinical scores were moderately below normal in the cystic fibrosis patients. More illnesses were reported for the patients, but the incidence of viral seroconversions each year was almost the same in the 2 groups. Forty percent of infections in the patient group were asymptomatic. Parainfluenza viruses accounted for most infections. The incidence of viral infection did not correlate closely with bacterial colonization. The annual incidence of viral infections in patients correlated significantly with all measures of disease progression, including decline in the Shwachman score, forced vital capacity and FEV_1, and hospitalization for respiratory exacerbations. Nearly 40% of all hospitalizations were temporally associated with viral seroconversions.

The frequency of viral respiratory infection is closely associated with pulmonary deterioration in patients with cystic fibrosis. A strong correlation was found in this 2-year study between declining clinical status and pulmonary function, and the frequency of viral infection. Better viral diagnostic methods could improve the hospital and outpatient care of patients with cystic fibrosis, and place antibiotic use on a more rational basis. The causes of respiratory illnesses that are not attributable to viral infection remain to be determined.

Immunoglobulins in the Hyperimmunoglobulin E and Recurrent Infection (Job's) Syndrome: Deficiency of Anti-*Staphylococcus aureus* Immunoglobulin A

Stephen C. Dreskin, Paul K. Goldsmith, and John I. Gallin (Bethesda)
J. Clin. Invest. 75:26–34, January 1985   6–12

Patients with Job's syndrome of hyperimmunoglobulin E and recurrent infections (HIE) typically have frequent cutaneous and respiratory infections caused by *Staphylococcus aureus*. The ear, mastoid, and bronchi also are frequent sites of bacterial infection in this disorder. The finding of anti-*S. aureus* IgE suggests that other humoral immune abnormalities may contribute to the marked predisposition to *S. aureus* infection in this syndrome. A set of enzyme-linked immunosorbent assays, that use whole *S. aureus* and highly specific, affinity-purified enzyme conjugates of immunoglobulin antibodies, was used to determine *S. aureus*-specific immunoglobulin levels in 11 patients with "classic" HIE and 39 healthy subjects. Five patients were evaluated 1–3 weeks after onset of an *S. aureus* infection. Fifteen patients with chronic granulomatous disease (CGD), 3 with Chediak-Higashi syndrome, and 5 with eczema and recurrent superficial *S. aureus* infections also were evaluated.

Increased serum levels of both IgE and IgD were found in the HIE patients, and the patients with eczema and recurrent *S. aureus* infections also had elevated IgE levels. Anti-*S. aureus* IgE level was elevated in 9 of 10 patients with HIE. Levels of anti-*S. aureus* IgG were elevated in patients with CGD and those with eczema and recurrent superficial *S. aureus* infections. Anti-*S. aureus* IgA levels are compared in Figure 6–1. Levels of anti-*S. aureus* IgM were increased in the HIE group. Levels of naturally occurring IgA antibody against *Escherichia coli* lipopolysaccharide and the antigens of pneumococcal vaccine were normal. The rate of mucosal and model infections correlated inversely with the serum anti-

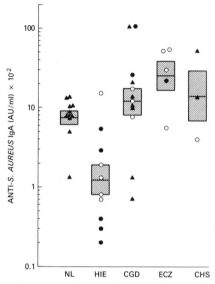

Fig 6–1.—Anti-*S. aureus* IgA. Serums were assayed at dilutions ranging from 1:60 to 1:32,000. Solid circles denote patients with acute *S. aureus* infections; open circles, other patients with history of recent (within 2 years) infections; and solid triangles, normal controls *(NL)* and patients with no history of recent *S. aureus* infections. Geometric mean and relative SE are shown for each group. To simplify figure, only one SE is shown for CGD patients. However, for statistical comparison, these patients can be considered as whole (CGD) or as two groups, those with recent *S. aureus* infections (CGD)* and those without recently documented *S. aureus* infections (CGD)‡. HIE vs. NL (*P* < .001), CGD (*P* < .01), CGD‡ (*P* < .05), CGD* (*P* < .01), ECZ (*P* < .001), and CHS (*P* < .02) patients. CGD* vs NL (*P* < .02) patients. ECZ vs. NL (*P* < .01) patients. Other statistical comparisons were not significant. (Courtesy of Dreskin, S.C., et al.: J. Clin. Invest. 75:26–34, January 1985; copyright of the American Society for Clinical Investigation.)

S. aureus IgA and IgE levels and with the total serum IgE and IgD levels.

An immunoregulatory defect in patients with HIE may contribute to the increased susceptibility to infection characterizing these patients. Serum total and anti-*S. aureus* IgE and total IgD may be protective. The deficit of anti-*S. aureus* IgA is not explained solely by lower total serum IgA levels.

▶ Perhaps because of the colorful early designation of Job's syndrome patients with recurrent, usually staphylococcal, skin and respiratory tract infections associated with extremely high serum IgE levels have become widely recognized by specialists in infectious diseases and dermatology. This paper, which describes a deficiency of serum and salivary IgA (as well as anti-*Staphylococcus aureus* IgA), adds to the growing list of "host defense" abnormalities that have been reported in these patients. While the precise mechanism of mechanisms that result in this syndrome remain unknown, the search for a unifying theory continues to be fueled by the hope that a fundamental understanding of these relatively uncommon patients will offer clues linking antigen specific IgE and IgA biosynthesis, T cell function, neutrophil chemotaxis, and monokine production. Certainly much rarer diseases of the normal host response to microorganisms have opened whole new vistas for biomedical research (e.g., chronic granulomatous disease).—M.K.

Immunoglobulin A From Bronchopulmonary Secretions Blocks Bactericidal and Opsonizing Effects of Antibody to Nontypable *Hemophilus influenzae*

Daniel M. Musher, Allen Goree, Robert E. Baughn, and Holly H. Birdsall (Houston)

Infect. Immun. 45:36–40, July 1984   6–13

Patients with chronic bronchitis are colonized by and may develop acute bronchopulmonary infection due to nontypable *hemophilus influenzae* (NTHI) despite the presence of bactericidal and opsonizing antibody to the infecting organism. To test the hypothesis that secretory immunoglobulin A (IgA) contributes to colonization or infection, secretory IgA was extracted from bronchopulmonary secretions of 5 patients with NTHI pneumonia and also from 4 patients not infected with NTHI to serve as control. The NTHI was incubated with IgA before or during incubation with each patient's own serum or normal human serum (NHS).

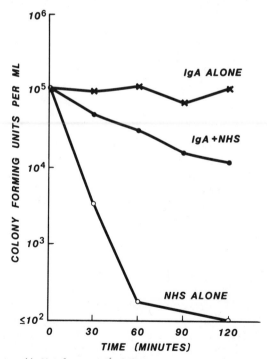

Fig 6–2.—Nontypeable *H. influenzae* (10^5/ml) from a patient with NTHI pneumonia was incubated with 0.4 mg of IgA per ml extracted from the patient's own sputum after which 10% NHS was added. Bacteria was also incubated with IgA alone and with 10% NHS alone. (Courtesy of Musher, D.M., et al.: Infect. Immun. 45:36–40, July 1984.)

Preincubation with IgA extracted from bronchopulmonary secretions of 4 patients with NTHI pneumonia blocked the bactericidal activity of pooled NHS or the patient's own serum against his own or another patient's NTHI. Prior incubation with IgA caused a 2.1 $\log_{10}$ (99.2%) decrease in bacterial killing at 1 hour (Fig 6–2). The IgA isolated from bronchopulmonary secretions of 3 patients blocked opsonization of their own NTHI by NHS and their own serum. Studies with fluorescein-labeled goat antiserum to IgA or ^{125}I-labeled rabbit antihuman IgA showed that incubation of NTHI with secretory IgA led to deposition of IgA on the bacterial surface. The blocking effect was still present despite repeated washings of NTHI incubated with IgA before the addition of NHS. The IgA from bronchopulmonary secretions of uninfected patients showed no blocking effect.

The results suggest that blocking of the interaction between bactericidal or opsonizing antibody and NTHI by secretory IgA may contribute to the occurrence of NTHI colonization and pneumonia in individuals despite adequate antibody against the infecting organism. Binding of IgA to the surface of NTHI is thought to be responsible for the blocking effect. However, it is still not known whether this occurs at antigenic sites responsible for bactericidal or opsonizing activity, or whether interaction with adjacent antigenic sites and subsequent steric interference is responsible.

▶ The immune response may be a double-edged sword at times. In this instance, secretory IgA blocking antibodies are functioning to inhibit the effect of bactericidal and opsonizing antibodies and permit infection to occur in an otherwise protected host. The implications of this for mucosal immunization and the role of microbial IgA proteases in the complex interaction of host and pathogen remain to be clarified.—G.K.

Correlation Between Opsonic Activity for Various Microorganisms and Composition of Gammaglobulin Preparations for Intravenous Use

R. van Furth, P. C. J. Leijh, and F. Klein
J. Infect. Dis. 149:511–517, April 1, 1984   6–14

Modifications of gammaglobulin preparations to prevent vasoactive reactions and anaphylaxis might alter the structure of the gammaglobulin molecule and change its opsonic effect. A comparative study of the opsonic activity of a large number of gammaglobulin preparations currently used intravenously was undertaken. Twelve commercial immunoglobulin preparations designed for intravenous use were examined with regard to opsonic activity for various strains of *Staphylococcus aureus*, *Escherichia coli*, *Streptococcus pyogenes*, and group B streptococci. Both microbiologic and morphological assays for opsonic activity were used. In addition, concentrations of unsplit IgG molecules, IgG fragments, and IgG aggregates (dimers) were determined.

Four preparations treated with enzyme or by reduction and alkylation had almost no opsonic activity. The others were as effective as inactivated serum. Opsonic activity of the various organisms correlated well with the concentration of intact IgG molecules in a given preparation. The concentration of IgG fragments correlated negatively with opsonic activity. Most of the preparations did not have strong bactericidal activity in the phagocytosis assay used, indicating that the reduction in viable extracellular organisms was due mainly to ingestion of organisms by granulocytes.

Preparations of IgG should be tested for functional activity before being accepted for clinical use. Preparations that exhibited good functional activity in vitro can be expected to also have good functional activity in vivo. Good opsonic activity does not reflect the presence or absence of potentially harmful aggregates. A high proportion of the 7S fraction does not necessarily indicate good functional activity.

Decline of Serum Antibody in Splenectomized Children After Vaccination With Pneumococcal Capsular Polysaccharides

G. Scott Giebink, Chap T. Le, and Gerald Schiffman
J. Pediatr. 105:576–582, October 1984   6–15

Overwhelming pneumococcal sepsis is a risk in children and adults with anatomical or functional asplenia. Serious pneumococcal disease from vaccine types has occurred in a number of asplenic children given pneumo-

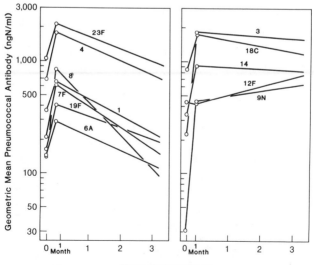

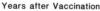

Years after Vaccination

Fig 6–3.—Increase and decline in geometric mean pneumococcal antibody values after pneumococcal vaccination in 23 children who underwent splenectomy because of trauma. Slope of antibody decline after 1 month was calculated by type-specific analysis in each patient; slopes were averaged to obtain mean percentage antibody decline per year. Last serum specimen from these patients was obtained 2.5 to 4.1 years (mean, 3.3) after vaccination; hence, declines are projected to 3.5 years. (Courtesy of Giebink, G.S., et al.: J. Pediatr. 105:576–582, October 1984.)

coccal vaccine. The duration of protective antibody levels after vaccination is largely unknown. This was investigated in a series of 33 children, aged 5–15 years, who were selected to receive either a 12-valent vaccine or a 14-valent preparation with types 2 and 25 added. Twenty-three children had had splenectomy after traumatic splenic laceration, and 10 had the procedure for the treatment of hereditary spherocytosis (HS). The respective mean ages were 12 and 10½ years. Type-specific pneumococcal antibody was measured by serum radioimmunoassay.

Mean increases in antibody levels were comparable in the trauma and HS groups. Vaccination appeared to be more efficient in the HS group. The decline in geometric mean antibody after vaccination was significant only in the trauma group, but type-specific analysis indicated highly significant differences in rates of antibody decline among the various antibody types in both patient groups. Most antibody types in both groups declined, and most were independent of baseline antibody levels as shown in Figure 6–3. The antibody types that declined significantly would be expected to reach baseline values 1½ to 5½ years after vaccination.

One means of preventing pneumococcal disease in asplenic persons might be to modify the pneumococcal polysaccharides, possibly by conjugation with proteins, to elicit a greater IgG response. Revaccination of asplenic children with types 7F, 8, and 19F polysaccharides about 1–2 years after initial vaccination might increase antibody levels to within the protective range, but monovalent pneumococcal polysaccharide vaccines are not presently available.

▶ It has been known for many years that splenectomized animals do not achieve normal serum antibody levels after immunization with polysaccharide antigens. These studies done in children are noteworthy since there were differences in responses between two different groups of splenectomized patients (posttrauma and hereditary spherocytosis) and marked differences between antigenic types of pneumococcal polysaccharides. Although these observations should be extended to larger groups of subjects, this paper nonetheless demonstrates the need for follow-up evaluation in splenectomized patients for possible booster injections.—S.M.W.

Prevention of Pneumococcal Infection in Children With Homozygous Sickle Cell Disease
A. B. John, A. Ramlal, H. Jackson, G. H. Maude, A. Waight Sharma, and G. R. Serjeant (Univ. of the West Indies)
Br. Med. J. 288:1567–1570, May 26, 1984   6–16

Prophylaxis against pneumococcal infection in children with homozygous sickle cell (SS) disease depends on penicillin or pneumococcal vaccines. The authors present an interim report including the first 5 years of a randomized, controlled trial comparing the efficacy of pneumococcal vaccine and prophylactic penicillin in young children with SS disease.

Two hundred and forty-two children with SS disease, aged 6 months to

3 years, were randomized into four treatment groups: (1) pneumococcal vaccine and penicillin; (2) pneumococcal vaccine alone; (3) *hemophilus influenzae* B vaccine and penicillin; and (4) *H. influenzae* B vaccine alone. The 14 valent pneumococcal vaccine and *H. influenzae* vaccine were each given as a single intramuscular dose of 0.5 ml on admission. Benzathine penicillin was given in a dose of 600,000 units by monthly intramuscular injections at home. Blood cultures were performed during feverish illness and at necropsy.

During the first 5 years, pneumococcus from blood or cerebrospinal fluid was isolated in 13 children. Eleven isolations occurred in children given the pneumococcal vaccine, and 10 were by serotypes present in the vaccine. Type 23 accounted for 5 of these 10 vaccine failures. Among 62 children given the pneumococcal vaccine in their first, second, and third years, the incidence rate of infections was 3.4, 1.5, and 2.0, respectively. No pneumococcal infections occurred in children receiving penicillin prophylaxis, although 4 isolations occurred within a year after stopping penicillin administration when the patient was aged 36 months. Adverse reactions to pneumococcal vaccine were minimal. Penicillin was well tolerated and no allergic reaction occurred.

Penicillin offers the most effective prophylaxis against pneumococcal infection. However, it must be continued after age 3 years because this age group remains hypersusceptible to subsequent infections due to lack of acquired immunity. The data also suggest that pneumococcal vaccine does not protect against pneumococcal infection. The age at which it should be given must await further data on antibody response and clinical efficacy in these patients.

Impaired Antipneumococcal Antibody Production in Patients Without Spleens

Franco Di Padova, Michael Durig, Felix Harder, Carlo Di Padova, and Carlo Zanussi
Br. Med. J. 296:14–16, Jan. 5, 1985   6–17

Pneumococcal infection remains an important cause of morbidity and mortality in asplenic children and patients whose spleens have been removed for therapeutic reasons or after trauma. Many immune defects have been described in this setting. Previous studies with pneumococcal vaccine suggested that the spleen has a central role in controlling circulating lymphocyte subsets that can synthesize antipneumococcal capsular polysaccharide antibodies. Fifteen splenectomized and 15 normal subjects were studied, in the absence of intentional immunization, for pokeweed mitogen-induced synthesis of these antibodies in vitro by peripheral blood mononuclear cells. The subjects were males aged 22–65 years. Splenectomies had been done for trauma 2 months to 23 years previously. No subject had evidence of immunologic or hematologic disorders, and all were healthy at the time of study.

The blood mononuclear cells from splenectomized subjects were relatively incapable of secreting antipneumococcal capsular polysaccharide antibody of the IgM class. Antibody of the IgG class was found only occasionally in samples from both splenectomized and normal subjects. The synthesis of polyclonal IgM and IgG was significantly reduced in the study group. Allogeneic coculture studies showed that the synthesis of both specific and polyclonal immunoglobulin by B cells clearly impaired in the splenectomized subjects, and was not enhanced by coculture with allogeneic helper T cells.

Absence of the spleen appears to produce a long-lasting B cell defect involving limitation of the ability of these cells to differentiate into antibody-secreting cells. The immune response to pneumococcal capsular polysaccharide is impaired at the cellular level in splenectomized subjects. The findings may help explain the reduced ability of such subjects to survive pneumococcal sepsis.

Anticore Endotoxin F(ab')$_2$ Equine Immunoglobulin Fragments Protect Against Lethal Effects of Gram-Negative Bacterial Sepsis
David L. Dunn, Patrick A. Mach, Richard M. Condie, and Frank B. Cerra (Univ. of Minnesota)
Surgery 96:440–446, August 1984   6–18

There is experimental evidence that antibody directed against a common component of the gram-negative bacterial cell wall can be effective in the treatment of gram-negative bacillary sepsis. Equine antibody directed against core endotoxin, a part of the bacterial outer membrane lipopolysaccharide (LPS) common to many gram-negative organisms, was evaluated in the present study. The IgG and IgG F(ab')$_2$ fragments were isolated from a horse immunized with *Escherichia coli* J5, which expresses core endotoxin on its cell surface. Mice received preimmune or immune IgG, F(ab')$_2$, or saline before intravenous challenge with viable organisms.

Immune IgG and F(ab')$_2$ possessed titers directed primarily against the immunizing organism. Only immune IgG enhanced the phagocytosis of gram-negative organisms in vitro. Both immune IgG and F(ab')$_2$ protected against lethal sepsis caused by *E. coli* J5, *E. coli* 0111:B4, *Klebsiella pneumoniae*, or *Pseudomonas aeruginosa*. Preimmune IgG and F(ab')$_2$ fragments provided minimal protection against intravenous septic challenge. The immune IgG and immune F(ab')$_2$ fragments provided comparable protection against lethal gram-negative sepsis.

These findings suggest that anticore lipopolysaccharide IgG and F(ab')$_2$ fragments protect against gram-negative sepsis in vivo through antitoxin activity rather than by opsonization and phagocytosis. Further experimental work is needed to determine the role of anticore LPS antibody in conjunction with antibiotics and perhaps steroids in the prophylaxis or treatment of gram-negative bacillary sepsis.

▶ Bacterial endotoxins are composed of a series of outer repeating polysaccharides attached to a core ("R core") which in turn is attached to a lipid moiety

("Lipid A"). The latter is thought to be responsible for many of the biologic effects of endotoxins. Certain rough mutants lack the polysaccharides, thus exposing the R core which is common to most endotoxins derived from gram-negative bacteria. Other authors have shown that sera from human volunteers immunized with a mutant of *E. coli* could decrease mortality rates in patients who received such sera and developed gram-negative infections (Ziegler et al.: *N. Engl. J. Med.* 307:1225–1230, 1982). This paper further strengthens the concept that the protection may be mediated by the antitoxin effects of the immunoglobulin rather than its classical antibody activity.—S.M.W.

Importance of Host Factors in Human Salmonellosis Caused by Multiresistant Strains of *Salmonella*
Lee W. Riley, Mitchell L. Cohen, Jerry E. Seals, Martin J. Blaser, Kristen A. Birkness, Nancy T. Hargrett, Stanley M. Martin, and Roger A. Feldman (Centers for Disease Control, Atlanta)
J. Infect. Dis. 149:878–883, June 1984   6–19

A review was made of antimicrobial resistance patterns of *Salmonella* isolates from subjects in randomly selected urban and rural counties in the United States in relation to clinical and epidemiologic host characteristics. The authors examined a total of 779 isolates from 58 counties in 20 states, representing 3.3% of the average number of human isolates reported annually to the Centers for Disease Control in 1969–1978. Sixteen percent of strains were resistant to antimicrobials, and 12% were multiply resistant. Eighteen percent of 317 strains of *Salmonella typhimurium* were resistant to 1 or more drugs. The rate was highest (60%) for *Salmonella heidelberg*.

The median age of the 542 evaluable patients was 6 years. Increased antimicrobial resistance could not be related to urban or rural residence, animal contacts, socioeconomic factors, or clinical factors, such as underlying illness. Significant factors associated with multiple resistance included infection by *S. heidelberg*, exposure to penicillins, and Hispanic origin. The ratio of the infection rate for multiresistant strains to that for sensitive strains was highest in subjects aged 55 years or older.

To cause disease, resistant organisms appear to be more dependent on host characteristics than sensitive organisms. There is no indication in the United States that hospitals, specific animal sources, or human beings are unique sources for resistant *Salmonella*.

▶ Multiresistant bacteria carrying R factors are therapeutic problems. In some instances, such isolates appear to be less intrinsically virulent than isolates lacking the R factor and therefore seem to selectively infect hosts with definable risk factors. This seems to be the case with *Salmonella*. What would be interesting, but not presented in this paper, is whether the clinical illness is similar or worse in patients with risk factors infected with a multiresistant strain compared to patients with or without risk factors who are infected with susceptible organisms. Do these characteristics of host and organism cancel or sum?—G.K.

Hypoprothrombinemia in Febrile, Neutropenic Patients With Cancer: Association With Antimicrobial Suppression of Intestinal Microflora

J. M. Conly, K. Ramotar, H. Chubb, E. J. Bow, and T. J. Louie (Manitoba, Canada)

J. Infect. Dis. 150:202–212, August 1984   6–20

Hypoprothrombinemia may occur in patients given antimicrobials, and it is suggested that the N-methyl-thiotetrazole-containing β-lactam antibiotics, such as moxalactam, may directly inhibit vitamin K production in liver microsomes. A prospective trial was performed to compare empirical treatment with moxalactam plus ticarcillin (M/T) and tobramycin plus ticarcillin (T/T) in 108 febrile, granulocytopenic patients with cancer. The dose of moxalactam was 2 gm given intravenously every 6 hours, tobramycin was 1.25 mg/kg every 6 hours, and ticarcillin was 3 gm given intravenously every 4 hours in both regimens. Treatment was given for at least 7 days, or 10 days when infection was documented. Parenteral cloxacillin, vancomycin, or erythromycin was added when clinically indicated.

Prothrombin times that were 2 seconds or more above control values developed in 30 of 54 patients given M/T therapy and 13 of 54 given T/T therapy. Serious bleeding was more frequent in the M/T group, occurring in 10 patients compared with 2 in the T/T group. The risk of bleeding is related to the degree of prothrombin prolongation in Figure 6–4. No deaths were directly attributable to bleeding, which was treated by red blood cell and platelet transfusions, fresh-frozen plasma, and parenteral vitamin K.

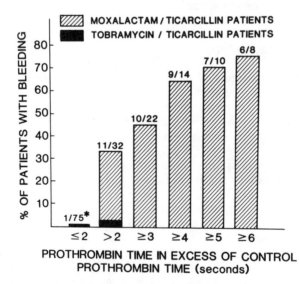

PROTHROMBIN TIME IN EXCESS OF CONTROL PROTHROMBIN TIME (seconds)

* No. PATIENTS BLEEDING / TOTAL

Fig 6–4.—Correlation of increase in prothrombin time over control prothrombin time and risk of clinical bleeding in 108 patients receiving M/T or T/T (54 patients per regimen). (Courtesy of Conly, J.M., et al.: J. Infect. Dis. 150:202–212, August 1984.)

Quantitative stool cultures showed that suppression of *Escherichia coli* and *Bacteroides* species was more frequent in the M/T group. Suppression of these organisms, which are major sources of synthesized menaquinones, was associated with a high rate of hypoprothrombinemia.

Menaquinones may have an important role in the maintenance of blood coagulation during dietary deficiency of phylloquinone. Inhibition of hepatic synthesis of vitamin K dependent procoagulants by antibiotics that have the N-methylthiotetrazole side chain may be a factor in some instances. Several other factors, including vitamin K turnover, hepatic and renal function, the state of the gastrointestinal tract, and genetic factors also may be important.

▶ The argument is whether moxalactam and related antibiotics cause prolongation of prothrombin time and encourage bleeding by depressing formation of the precursor (menaquinones) or by interfering with fibrin formation, either directly or indirectly. This paper clearly demonstrates that moxalactam has more inhibitory activity against the intestinal microflora than ticarcillin, presumably due to moxalactam's high biliary excretion and its resistance to β-lactamases in the gut. Thus, the intestinal microflora, particularly those organisms capable of synthesizing menaquinones, are reduced. Unfortunately, the authors could not show that menaquinone production in the intestinal flora was decreased, nor could they establish that reduction of menaquinones necessarily leads to hypoprothrombinemia, since dietary phylloquinones are still available as precursors. Despite these weaknesses, this paper represents an important advance in our knowledge, since it does establish the tremendous reduction in menaquinone-producing bacteria in the intestinal tract associated with moxalactam therapy.—S.G.

Infectious Peritonitis in Patients Receiving Intraperitoneal Chemotherapy
Robert A. Kaplan, Maurie Markman, William E. Lucas, Craig Pfeifle, and Stephen B. Howell (Univ. of California, San Diego)
Am. J. Med. 78:49–53, January 1985   6–21

Some chemotherapeutic agents are effectively administered intraperitoneally, but this approach carries a risk of infection during both initial catheter placement and subsequent catheter manipulations. Data on infectious complications were reviewed in 90 patients with histologically confirmed cancer who received intraperitoneal chemotherapy. Twelve patients with advanced cancer received cisplatin intraperitoneally with systemic thiosulfate protection of the kidneys. Ten patients with ovarian cancer received 20 dialysate exchanges. Sixty-eight patients with tumor chiefly confined to the peritoneal cavity received cisplatin and cytarabine, with or without doxorubicin, intraperitoneally at intervals of 3–4 weeks.

A total of 32 episodes of peritonitis were documented by positive findings in peritoneal fluid culture. Two episodes were due to perforation of the bowel during insertion of a dialysis catheter. *Staphylococcus epidermidis*

ORGANISMS CULTURED FROM
TWO CATHETER SYSTEMS

Catheter	Organism	Cases	
		Number	Percent
Tenckhoff	Staphylococcus epidermidis	14	56
	Staphylococcus aureus	5	20
	Streptococcus viridans	3	12
	Streptococcus sanguis	1	4
	Streptococcus bovis	1	4
	Clostridium perfringens	1	4
Total		25	
Subcutaneous	Staphylococcus epidermidis	8	89
port system	Staphylococcus aureus	1	11
Total		9	

(Courtesy of Kaplan, R.A., et al.: Am. J. Med. 78:49–53, January 1985.)

was the most frequent isolate. Standard Tenckhoff catheters were involved in two thirds of the episodes (table). Physical findings of infection were not always present in patients with peritonitis. Antibiotic therapy alone cured most episodes not related to bowel perforation, but catheter removal sometimes was necessary.

Bacterial peritonitis remains a problem with intracavitary chemotherapy, but the risk may be minimized by using subcutaneous ports and meticulous sterile technique during catheter manipulations. The usefulness of antibiotic prophylaxis in this setting remains to be confirmed. Cefazolin may be an effective first-line treatment in presumed cases of bacterial peritonitis not caused by bowel perforation. Intravenously administered antibiotic should be used for a week, and oral treatment should be given for another 3–7 days if the patient is afebrile and culture findings are negative.

7 Acquired Immunodeficiency Syndrome

Virology

Detection, Isolation, and Continuous Production of Cytopathic Retroviruses (HTLV-III) From Patients With AIDS and Pre-AIDS

Mikulas Popovic, M. G. Sarngadharan, Elizabeth Read, and Robert C. Gallo
Science 224:497–500, May 4, 1984   7–1

Epidemiologic data suggest that the acquired immunodeficiency syndrome (AIDS) is caused by an infectious agent that is horizontally transmitted by intimate contact or through blood products. Although the disease is manifested by opportunistic infections, predominantly *Pneumocystis carinii* pneumonia, and by Kaposi's sarcoma, the underlying disorder affects the patient's cell-mediated immunity, resulting in absolute lymphopenia and reduced subpopulations of helper T-lymphocytes (OKT4$^+$). Moreover, before a complete clinical manifestation of the disease occurs, its prodrome, pre-AIDS, is frequently characterized by unexplained chronic lymphadenopathy or leukopenia involving helper T-lymphocytes. This leads to the severe immune deficiency in the patient and suggests that a specific subset of T cells could be the primary target for an infectious agent. Although patients with AIDS or pre-AIDS are often chronically infected with cytomegalovirus or hepatitis B virus, for various reasons these appear to be opportunistic or coincidental infections. The authors have proposed that AIDS may be caused by a virus from the family of human T cell lymphotropic retroviruses (HTLV) that includes two major, well-characterized subgroups of human retroviruses, HTLV-I and HTLV-II. The most common isolate, HTLV-I, is obtained mainly from patients with mature T cell malignancies.

A cell system was developed by the authors for the reproducible detection of HTLV from patients with AIDS or pre-AIDS. The cells were specific clones from a permissive human neoplastic T cell line. Some of the clones grow permanently and continuously produce large amounts of virus after infection with cytopathic (HTLV-III) variants of these viruses. The HTLV-III was isolated from 4 patients by the cocultivation method and from 1 patient by cell-free infection of these T cell clones. The transmission was monitored by reverse transcriptase activity, electron microscopic examination, and expression of viral protein. When the H$_4$ cells thus infected were fixed with acetone and tested with rabbit antiserum samples to HTLV-III and with serum samples from patients, the percentage of positive

175

cells was 5% to 80%. The HTLV-III variant has also been isolated from a total of 48 patients by the more conventional methods for isolation of HTLV. Some of these isolates have now successfully been transmitted to the HT clones for production and detailed analyses. One cytopathic effect of HTLV-III in this system is the arrangement of multiple nuclei in a characteristic ring formation in giant cells of the infected T cell population.

The transient expression of cytopathic variants of HTLV in cells from AIDS patients and the previous lack of a cell system that could maintain growth and still be susceptible to and permissive for the virus represented a major obstacle in detection, isolation, and elucidation of the precise causative agent of AIDS. The establishment of T cell populations that continuously grow and produce virus after infection opens the way to the routine detection of cytopathic variants of HTLV in AIDS patients. It also provides the opportunity for detailed immunologic and molecular analyses of these viruses.

▶ This landmark paper presents the data that AIDS is caused by a human retrovirus, human T cell lymphotropic retrovirus, type III (HTLV-III). A wealth of other studies enumerated below have confirmed this virus to be the causative agent of AIDS. The HTLV-III has been shown to be the same agent as the lymphadenopathy-associated virus (LAV), which was first described by French investigators (Barre-Sinoussi, F., et al.: *Science* 220:868–871, 1983). Some investigators now call this virus HTLV-III/LAV.—D.S.

Frequent Detection and Isolation of Cytopathic Retroviruses (HTLV-III) From Patients With AIDS and at Risk for AIDS

Robert C. Gallo, Syed Z. Salahuddin, Mikulas Popovic, Gene M. Shearer, Mark Kaplan, Barton F. Haynes, Thomas J. Palker, Robert Redfield, James Oleske, Bijan Safai, Gilbert White, Paul Foster, and Phillip D. Markham

Science 224:500–503, May 4, 1984   7–2

The acquired immunodeficiency syndrome (AIDS) prodrome includes chronic lymphadenopathy or leukopenia with a reduction in helper T-lymphocytes. An association of members of the human T-lymphotropic retrovirus (HTLV) family with T-lymphocytes from some AIDS and pre-AIDS patients has been described. In this study, peripheral blood lymphocytes from patients with AIDS or pre-AIDS were grown in vitro with added T cell growth factor and tested for the presence of HTLV by viral reverse transcriptase activity; viral transmission on co-culture of T cells with irradiated donor cells; electron microscopic examination; and expression of viral antigen in direct immunofluorescence assays.

Retroviruses of the HTLV-III class were found in 18 of 21 samples from pre-AIDS patients, 3 of 4 from clinically normal mothers of juvenile AIDS patients, 3 of 8 from juvenile AIDS patients, 13 of 43 from adult AIDS

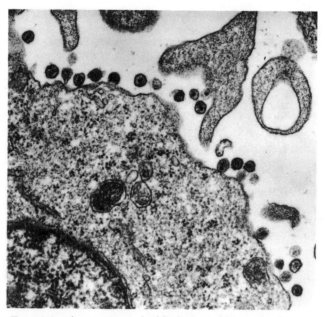

Fig 7–1.—Transmission electron micrograph of fixed, sectioned lymphocytes from patient with pre-AIDS; original magnification ×30,000. (Courtesy of Gallo, R.C., et al.: Science 224:500–503, May 4, 1984. Copyright 1984 by the American Association for the Advancement of Science.)

patients with Kaposi's sarcoma, and 10 of 21 from adult AIDS patients with opportunistic infections. Only 1 of 22 samples from homosexual male patients at presumably moderate risk of AIDS contained HTLV-III. This subject developed AIDS 6 months later. In none of 115 normal subjects was the virus isolated. Primary cells from patients usually produced virus (Fig 7–1) for 2 to 3 weeks. In some instances, viral release was reinitiated by adding antibody to α-interferon. The HTLV-III-producing cell cultures were mainly T-lymphocytes with a helper-inducer phenotype.

Highly infectious HTLV-III is produced by cultured T cells from patients with AIDS or pre-AIDS, as well as from some healthy subjects at risk of AIDS. The findings provide strong evidence for the causative involvement of HTLV-III in AIDS. There is evidence that serums from a high proportion of AIDS patients contain antibodies to HTLV-III.

▶ It is rare in the history of medicine that a clinical entity such as AIDS is recognized, and within a matter of a few years the causative agent is found. Using molecular biologic techniques, these authors and another group of authors in France (Barre-Sinoussi, F., et al.: *Science* 220:868–871, 1983) described a retrovirus (HTLV-III/LAV) that is the cause of AIDS and developed tests for antibody detection. The seroepidemiologic studies presented above as well as others show how common the exposure to these viruses has been in the groups at risk.—S.M.W.

Serologic Analysis of a Subgroup of Human T Lymphotropic Retroviruses (HTLV-III) Associated With AIDS

Jörg Schüpbach, Mikulas Popovic, Raymond V. Gilden, Matthew A. Gonda, M. G. Sarngadharan, and Robert C. Gallo

Science 224:503–505, May 4, 1984   7–3

The frequent finding of cell surface antigens encoded by human T lymphotropic retrovirus I (HTLV-I) in the serums of patients with acquired immunodeficiency syndrome (AIDS) or pre-AIDS suggests involvement of HTLV in these disorders. Another subgroup, HTLV-III, has now been isolated from many of these patients. Lysates of two immortalized and infected human T cell clones, H4/HTLV-III and H17/HTLV-III, were tested with serums from patients with AIDS or pre-AIDS, contacts of these patients, and homosexual and heterosexual male control subjects in a strip radioimmunoassay based on the Western blot technique.

Serums from patients with AIDS or pre-AIDS and from some homosexuals and heroin addicts recognized a number of specific antigens not detected in serums with heterosexuals. The antigens were similar in size to those found in other subgroups of HTLV. At least three serologically unrelated antigenic groups were represented. One was associated with the group-specific antigens p55 and p24 and another with envelope-related (p65) proteins. The antigens in the third group are of unknown affiliation. With a single exception, no antigen from uninfected clones reacted with patient serums. The reaction with p55 antigen occurred only in serums that also recognized p24, suggesting a relation between these antigens.

Viral or virus-induced antigens in cloned human T cells infected with HTLV-III are specifically recognized by antibodies in serums from patients with AIDS or pre-AIDS. Immunologic and nucleic acid data indicate that HTLV-III is a true member of the HTLV family and is more closely related to HTLV-II than to HTLV-I.

Antibodies Reactive With Human T Lymphotropic Retroviruses (HTLV-III) in the Serum of Patients With AIDS

M. G. Sarngadharan, Mikulas Popovic, Lilian Bruch, Jörg Schüpbach, and Robert C. Gallo

Science 224:506–508, May 4, 1984   7–4

Infections by T lymphotropic retroviruses can cause T cell proliferation and leukemia or T cell depletion and immunosuppression in cats. Both human T lymphotropic retrovirus I (HTLV-I) and HTLV-II can induce T cell proliferation in human beings, and a third subgroup of viruses, HTLV-III, has now been isolated from cultured cells of patients with acquired immunodeficiency syndrome (AIDS). Forty-three of 49 AIDS patients tested and 11 of 14 pre-AIDS patients had serum antibody to HTLV-III. Positive tests were also obtained in 3 of 5 intravenous drug users and 6 of 17 homosexual men. Only 1 of 164 normal subjects tested had antibody to HTLV-III. Immunologic analysis of the viral proteins indicated that the virus is a member of the HTLV family and is more closely related to HTLV-II than to HTLV-I. The major immune reactivity appeared to be directed against p41, the presumed envelope antigen of the virus. Titers to HTLV-III were widely variable in positive serum samples from AIDS patients. Serums from 2 young children reacted with HTLV-III, and the mother of 1 of them had reactive serum.

Infection by HTLV-III may cause an initial lymphoid proliferation and eventually kill the target lymphocytes, leading to an abnormal $T4^+$ to $T8^+$ ratio and loss of helper T cell functions, including antibody production by B cells. This could explain the low or absent serologic response in some cases of advanced AIDS. Positive serologic findings have been obtained in the mother of an infant with AIDS and in a long-term sex partner of a homosexual with AIDS. Recipients of blood products obtained from persons at risk of AIDS also have reacted to HTLV-III, and the virus has been isolated from several children with AIDS and from their mothers. Increasing evidence suggests that HTLV-III is the primary cause of AIDS.

Isolation of Human T Lymphotropic Retrovirus (LAV) From Zairian Married Couple, One With AIDS, One With Prodromes

A. Ellrodt, F. Barre-Sinoussi, P. Le Bras, M. T. Nugeyre, L. Palazzo, F. Rey, F. Brun-Vezinet, C. Rouzioux, P. Segond, R. Caquet, L. Montagnier, and J. C. Chermann (Paris)
Lancet 1:1383–1385, June 23, 1984   7–5

A new human T lymphotropic retrovirus, lymphadenopathy-associated virus (LAV), has been isolated from populations at high risk for acquired immune deficiency syndrome (AIDS) and from AIDS patients. Epidemiologic studies have suggested that LAV may have a role in the pathogenesis of AIDS. Isolation of the virus from African patients who lack the usual risk factors would support its role in the disease. A LAV-related virus now has been isolated from cultured lymphocytes of a Zairian couple living in France. The man had AIDS, and his wife had prodromal symptoms.

Infection with LAV was demonstrated in both subjects by isolation of the virus from cultured lymphocytes and by detection of specific antibodies in serum samples. The man had disseminated cryptococcosis; *Mycobacterium kansasii* tenosynovitis developed more recently. His wife lost weight, and oral thrush, chronic herpetic ulcers, and prurigo developed. Cervical lymphadenopathy subsequently developed. The man exhibited cutaneous anergy and had absolute lymphopenia with a marked reduction in OKT4-positive cells. The woman also had cutaneous anergy to multiple antigens and had an OKT4-OKT8 ratio of 0.02. Blastogenic responses to phytohemagglutinin and concanavalin A were very low.

There is strong evidence that AIDS is endemic in central and equatorial Africa. The finding of LAV in AIDS patients from Africa supports the hypothesis that this retrovirus is the etiologic agent of AIDS. A virus termed

HTLV-III, with characteristics similar to those of LAV, has been described as a possible etiologic agent. Whether HTLV-III and LAV are the same virus is under study.

► Lymphadenopathy-associated virus has been shown to be identical to HTLV-III. This study underscores the potential heterosexual transmission of AIDS.— D.S.

Lymphadenopathy-Associated Viral Antibody in AIDS: Immune Correlations and Definition of a Carrier State

Jeffrey Laurence, Françoise Brun-Vezinet, Steven E. Schutzer, Christine Rouzioux, David Klatzmann, Françoise Barré-Sinoussi, Jean-Claude Chermann, and Luc Montagnier
N. Engl. J. Med. 311:1269–1273, Nov. 15, 1984   7–6

Lymphadenopathy-associated virus (LAV) is a newly identified exogenous human T cell lymphotropic retrovirus recovered from the T cells of hemophiliacs and other patients with acquired immune deficiency syndrome (AIDS). Identification of IgG antibody to LAV core antigen was made in a large proportion of patients with unexplained generalized hyperplastic lymphadenopathy and risk factors for AIDS and in a smaller proportion of patients with opportunistic infections or malignant conditions characteristic of clinical AIDS. An attempt was made to determine whether serologic evidence of LAV correlates with the acquisition and transmission of AIDS. Serum samples were obtained from 25 patients with clinically documented AIDS, 17 adults and 8 children, aged 8–24 months. Five patients with an AIDS prodrome in whom AIDS developed within 2–11 months also were assessed, as were 8 homosexual men with generalized lymphadenopathy, 6 of whom met criteria for AIDS-related complex; 9 healthy subjects with risk factors for AIDS; and 23 patients with congenital immunodeficiencies.

Sixty-eight percent of the patients with AIDS were seropositive for anti-LAV antibody. All adults with cancer alone reacted positively, as did 6 of 12 adults and 6 of 8 children with opportunistic infections, with or without Kaposi's sarcoma. All 8 homosexual men with generalized adenopathy or AIDS-related complex and all subjects with AIDS prodromes also were seropositive. The patients with genetic immunodeficiency lacked anti-LAV antibody, as did 99 of 100 healthy blood donors. Studies of asymptomatic mothers with affected offspring suggested the probability of an AIDS carrier state through evidence of transfer of LAV to the offspring.

There is increasing evidence supporting an etiologic role for LAV in AIDS, and it appears to be at least a marker for AIDS. The virus may be carried and transmitted in the absence of clinical abnormalities or in vitro T cell abnormalities.

► Abstracts 7–6 and 7–7 are 2 important studies that confirm the presence of an asymptomatic carrier state in AIDS. Demonstrating the LAV antibody in mothers of infants with AIDS strengthens the hypothesis that there is a mother-to-infant transmission of LAV.

Abstract 7–7 below clearly demonstrates that HTLV-III may be carried in the peripheral blood lymphocytes or saliva of symptom-free, seronegative individuals. Almost 5% of high risk patients tested had HTLV-III infection without the presence of antibody, demonstrating the need for improved testing methods to detect the infected individual.—D.S.

HTLV-III in Symptom-Free Seronegative Persons
S. Zaki Salahuddin, Jerome E. Groopman, Phillip D. Markham, M. G. Sarngadharan, Robert R. Redfield, Mary F. McLane, M. Essex, Ann Sliski, and Robert C. Gallo
Lancet 2:1418–1420, Dec. 22/29, 1984   7–7

There is increasing evidence implicating human T cell leukemia virus type III (HTLV-III) or lymphadenopathy-associated virus in the development of acquired immunodeficiency syndrome (AIDS) and AIDS-related complex. The virus was isolated from peripheral blood cells in 96 patients with AIDS or AIDS-related complex, representing 50% and 85% of those tested, respectively, and from 20% of tested healthy donors at risk for AIDS. Four individuals had no detectable antibody to viral protein despite the isolation of HTLV-III from their lymphocytes. Three of these persons were symptom-free and 1 had lymphadenopathy. All 4 were sex partners of patients with AIDS or AIDS-related complex.

A minor population of seronegative persons apparently can harbor HTLV-III. Assays other than those detecting antibody to virus, perhaps based on the detection of viral antigens or immune complexes, may therefore be needed to identify all infected persons. It is possible that antibody may never develop in some infected persons, but none of the present individuals had evidence of impaired production of antibody to other viruses. A longitudinal study of such persons should help define the range of antibody responses to, and the clinical consequences of, HTLV-III infection in human beings. Screening methods based on determination of serum antibody HTLV-III levels should suffice to detect most potentially contagious persons.

HTLV-III in Saliva of People with Aids-Related Complex and Healthy Homosexual Men at Risk for AIDS
Jerome E. Groopman, S. Zaki Salahuddin, M. G. Sarngadharan, Phillip D. Markham, Matthew Gonda, Ann Sliski, and Robert C. Gallo
Science 226:447–449, Oct. 26, 1984   7–8

A primary pathogenic role for HTLV-III has been demonstrated in AIDS, a transmissible disorder, and in the AIDS-related complex (ARC). An attempt was made to identify the virus in peripheral blood mononuclear cells and saliva from 4 patients with AIDS. Ten patients with ARC and 6 healthy, asymptomatic homosexual men at risk of AIDS also were evaluated. Serum was tested for antibody to HTLV-III by the ELISA technique and a sensitive Western electroblot technique. All the patients with AIDS and ARC and 4 of the 6 healthy men had evidence of past exposure to HTLV-III indicated by antibody to HTLV-III. Infectious virus was isolated from the peripheral blood of 1 AIDS patient, 4 ARC patients, and 2 healthy men. It also was isolated from saliva in 4 ARC patients and 4 of the healthy men. Virus was identified ultrastructurally in material prepared from the saliva of one of the AIDS patients.

These findings suggest that, although AIDS does not seem to be transmitted by casual contact, the possibility of the transmission by saliva should be considered. The mechanism of viral survival in saliva has not been established, but cells producing virus as well as cell-free virus have been observed in patient saliva. Direct contact with saliva might best be avoided since saliva may form a protective matrix to support cell-free virus or virus-positive cells, and could facilitate horizontal transmission.

HTLV-III in the Semen and Blood of a Healthy Homosexual Man

David D. Ho, Robert T. Schooley, Teresa R. Rota, Joan C. Kaplan, Theresa Flynn, Syed Z. Salahuddin, Matthew A. Gonda, and Martin S. Hirsch
Science 26:451–453, Oct. 26, 1984.   7–9

The retrovirus human T-lymphotropic virus type III (HTLV-III) appears to be the etiologic agent of AIDS. Lymphadenopathy-associated virus appears to be identical with, or closely related to, HTLV-III. The virus was isolated from the semen of a healthy homosexual man who was seropositive for HTLV-III. The subject was a man aged 30 years, who participated in a prospective study of homosexual men with and without AIDS. He had a past history of gonorrhea, hepatitis, and sexual contact during the previous year with a man who later developed Kaposi's sarcoma. He had no localized or constitutional symptoms of AIDS. The T helper-suppressor ratio had ranged from 1.0 to 2.4. Serum was consistently positive for antibody to HTLV-III. The virus was isolated from both semen and blood. Isolation of HTLV-III was confirmed using murine monoclonal antibodies to HTLV-III core proteins in fixed-cell indirect immunofluorescence preparations. Ultrastructural confirmation also was obtained. The virus was recovered from the mononuclear-cell fraction of semen.

The isolation of HTLV-III in the semen of an asymptomatic subject at risk of AIDS supports the epidemiologic evidence that AIDS can be sexually transmitted. It is not clear why some HTLV-III carriers remain well while others develop AIDS, but asymptomatic carriers should be closely followed for the possible development of AIDS. Recent surveys suggest that HTLV-III/LAV seropositivity may occur in up to two thirds of urban male homosexuals, most of whom are healthy and without any obvious immune deficit. The frequency of HTLV-III carriers in this population is not known, but the carrier state may prove to be important in the dissemination of HTLV-III and, therefore, of AIDS.

Inactivation of Lymphadenopathy-Associated Virus by Chemical Disinfectants

B. Spire, F. Barré-Sinoussi, L. Montagnier, and J. C. Chermann (Paris)
Lancet 2:899–901, Oct. 20, 1984   7–10

There is epidemiologic evidence that an infectious agent, probably a virus, causes acquired immunodeficiency syndrome (AIDS). Lymphadenopathy-associated virus (LAV) has been isolated from patients with AIDS; it is a T lymphotropic retrovirus that exhibits selective tropism for T_4 lymphocytes. Reverse transcriptase (RT) activity of LAV was assayed after exposure of the virus to various standard chemical disinfectants in infected T lymphocyte cell cultures. The RT activity of the virus decreased in a dose-related manner on exposure to sodium hypochlorite. Inactivation was also produced by β-propionolactone, glutaraldehyde, and sodium hydroxide. Inactivation by different concentrations of ethanol was not linear or logarithmic. A 0.1% formalin preparation was ineffective.

Most of the disinfectants evaluated can inactivate LAV. Either 25% ethanol solution or 1% glutaraldehyde should be effective in disinfecting medical instruments. Benches and floors could be cleaned with 0.2% sodium hypochlorite solution. The effects of temperature, ultraviolet light, and gamma radiation are under study.

▶ This study of the inactivtion of the LAV, which is identical to HTLV-III, demonstrates that current recommendations for disinfecting instruments and laboratory areas are adequate to kill this virus. The preferred disinfectants are activated glutaraldehyde or sodium hypochlorite. The concentrations used to inactivate hepatitis B will also inactive LAV.—D.S.

Epidemiology

Longitudinal Study of Persistent Generalized Lymphadenopathy in Homosexual Men: Relation to Acquired Immunodeficiency Syndrome

Usha Mathur-Wagh, Roger W. Enlow, Ilya Spigland, Robert J. Winchester, Henry S. Sacks, Edwarda Rorat, Stanley R. Yancovitz, Michael J. Klein, Daniel C. William, and Donna Mildvan
Lancet 1:1033–1038, May 12, 1984   7–11

Apparently healthy homosexual men may have a syndrome of persistent generalized lymphadenopathy (PGL) of unknown cause. An attempt was made, in a group of 42 such subjects followed for up to 30 months, to determine whether the lymphadenopathy is an expression of a wider spectrum of acquired immunodeficiency syndrome (AIDS). The subjects were homosexual and bisexual men who had had unexplained lymphadenopathy for at least 3 months and involving at least two noncontiguous extrainguinal sites. Median age at presentation was 32 years. Most subjects had a history of multiple sexually transmitted diseases. Nonparenteral recreational drug use was frequent. The median duration of adenopathy at presentation was 18 months. About half the subjects had constitutional symptoms.

Splenomegaly was present in 12 subjects and hepatomegaly in 3. Seventeen were leukopenic and 6 had thrombocytopenia. Examination of enlarged nodes showed follicular hyperplasia in most cases, with capillary proliferation and prominent endothelial cells. Large numbers of interfollicular polymorphonuclear leukocytes were present in 5 instances. Hypergammaglobulinemia was present in three fourths of subjects. All but 5% of subjects had a decrease in helper T cells. Eight subjects developed AIDS during a median follow-up of 22 months. The median duration of lymphadenopathy before AIDS was diagnosed was 21 months. The development of AIDS was associated with heavy nitrate inhalant use, leukopenia, and a lower helper T cell count. Anergy and herpes virus isolation were also predictive factors.

The spectrum of diseases associated with AIDS appears to include PGL as well as such entities as symptomless immunodeficiency, autoimmune thrombocytopenia, and a syndrome of wasting, thrush, and diarrhea. The precise relation between AIDS and these entities will require ongoing longitudinal observations.

▶ Since AIDS is such a devastating illness, the full-blown syndrome has received most of the attention. Most research has been directed, and justifiably so, at the etiology and therapy of AIDS. However, patients with the AIDS-related complex surely must feel like they have the proverbial "sword of Damocles" hanging over their heads. Since a significant number of patients develops full-blown AIDS and others surely have the first symptoms of AIDS, this group of patients should prove to be a valuable resource in attempts to learn more about the pathogenesis and prevention of AIDS.—S.M.W.

Acquired Immunodeficiency Syndrome in Rwanda
Philippe Van de Perre, Dominique Rouvroy, Philippe Lepage, Jos Bogaerts, Philippe Kestelyn, Joseph Kayihigi, Anton C. Hekker, Jean-Paul Butzler, and Nathan Clumeck
Lancet 2:62–65, July 14, 1984   7–12

Most recently reported cases of acquired immune deficiency syndrome (AIDS) in Belgium have been in Zairian Africans, suggesting that AIDS may be endemic in central Africa. The occurrence of AIDS now has been examined prospectively in Rwanda, a central African country where Kaposi's sarcoma is endemic. Twenty-six patients seen in a 4-week period were assessed. The patients were obtained by asking clinicians at a central hospital for cases of either opportunistic infection or generalized or multifocal Kaposi's sarcoma or AIDS prodrome. Seventeen patients, 15 of them adults, had opportunistic infection or Kaposi's sarcoma associated with severe T cell defects, and 9 adults had severe T cell defects and nonspecific symptoms. All adult patients denied homosexuality and bisexuality, as well as intravenous drug use. Most men did acknowledge regular heterosexual contacts with different partners, often including prostitutes. No particular residential or socioeconomic features were noted.

The most frequent opportunistic infection was esophageal candidiasis. Frequent nonspecific symptoms included chronic fever, severe weight loss, generalized lymphadenopathy, and chronic diarrhea. The patients with lymphadenopathy had been symptomatic for an average of 11 months. The T cell ratio was inverted in all patients. An absolute increase in suppressor-cytotoxic T cells was present in 11 of the 17 patients with opportunistic infection or Kaposi's sarcoma and in 3 of the 9 with lymphadenopathy. Polyclonal hypergammaglobulinemia was a regular finding. Serologic evidence of *Treponema pallidum* and cytomegalovirus was frequently obtained, and several patients had antibodies to *Chlamydia trachomatis* and herpes simplex virus.

The existence of AIDS in Rwanda, a country east of Zaire, supports the endemic occurrence of the disease in central Africa. Possible risk factors for African AIDS include urban activity, a reasonable standard of living, heterosexual promiscuity, and contacts with prostitutes.

▶ This study confirms that AIDS can be transmitted through heterosexual contact and that the disease is endemic in Africa. The latter finding has prompted some investigators to suggest that the present epidemic in the United States was secondary to a virus originating in Africa.—D.S.

HTLV-I-Specific Antibody in AIDS Patients and Others at Risk
Marjorie Robert-Guroff, Douglas W. Blayney, Bijan Safai, Michael Lange, Edward P. Gelmann, Jordan W. Gutterman, Peter W. A. Mansell, James L. Goedert, Jerome E. Groopman, Neal H. Steigbigel, Gurdip S. Sidhu, Joyce M. Johnson, Alvin E. Friedman-Kien, Robert Downing, Anne C. Bayley, and Robert C. Gallo
Lancet 2:128–131, July 21, 1984   7–13

Several epidemiologic features of acquired immunodeficiency syndrome (AIDS) suggest that a transmissible agent is involved in its cause. One possible such agent has been the human T cell leukemia-lymphoma virus (HTLV) or a variant of it. Serum samples from a spectrum of risk groups for AIDS were obtained from collaborating institutions in areas where AIDS is epidemic. Serologic assays for HTLV-I-specific antibodies were performed by the enzyme-linked immunosorbent technique. Only serums the binding of which was significantly lessened by the HTLV-producer cell extract, but not by the extract of phytohemagglutinin (PHA)-stimulated lymphocytes or by fetal calf serum, were judged to contain HTLV-I-specific antibodies.

A total of 440 serum samples were assayed for specific antibodies to HTLV-I antigens. Specific antibodies were detected in 7% of AIDS patients, 7% of patients with lymphadenopathy, none of healthy homosexual men, and 12% of healthy Haitians. Prevalence among healthy American donors was less than 1%. When findings for homosexual men were analyzed separately, prevalence for those with lymphadenopathy was 7% and that for homosexuals with AIDS, 6%. Titers ranged from 77 to 74,000. There was no apparent difference in titers when lymphadenopathy or AIDS prodrome patients were compared with AIDS patients.

Data continue to implicate HTLV-I in AIDS as exemplified by the detection of HTLV-MA antibodies in Haitian mothers of children with AIDS. Also, HTLV-I has been isolated from T cells of AIDS patients. The isolations now point to opportunistic or coincidental infection with HTLV-I, whereas the antibody data may partly reflect, in serums with high titers, cross-reactivities with antigens of HTLV-III.

It appears that AIDS is also present in Africa as is Kaposi's sarcoma. Careful serologic studies may reveal not only HTLV-III-associated AIDS in Africa, but also the spectrum of HTLV family members, besides a broader spectrum of HTLV-associated disease.

▶ Although AIDS patients may be infected with HTLV-I as well as HTLV-III, these findings are more likely due to cross-reactivity between the two viruses.—S.M.W.

Clinical

Autopsy Findings in the Acquired Immune Deficiency Syndrome
Kevin Welch, Walter Finkbeiner, Charles E. Alpers, Walter Blumenfeld, Richard L. Davis, Edward A. Smuckler, and Jay H. Beckstead (Univ. of California, San Francisco)
JAMA 252:1152–1159, Sept. 7, 1984   7–14

Review was made of the medical and autopsy records of 36 patients with acquired immune deficiency syndrome (AIDS), most of them homosexual men. The series represents about 45% of all AIDS deaths occurring in the San Francisco Bay area up to mid-1983. All but 2 of the 34 adults were known to be homosexual men. One of the chilren was born to an intravenous drug abuser. The average age of the adults was 39 years. The most consistent premortem finding was lymphopenia. The mean ratio of T-helper to T-suppressor cells in 7 cases was 0.2.

Half the patients had a diagnosis of Kaposi's sarcoma, and 10 of the 18 had disseminated disease that contributed significantly to morbidity and mortality. Four patients (11%) had lymphoma. All patients but 1 had opportunistic infections, and the deaths of 33 of the 36 patients were related to infection by either an opportunistic agent or a bacterial pathogen. Oral candidiasis (81%) was the most common infection. Cytomegalovirus (69%) was the most common pathogen found at autopsy. Only 9 patients had an antemortem diagnosis of cytomegalovirus. *Pneumocystis carinii* was found in the lungs at autopsy in 13 cases, and was diagnosed by lung biopsy in 11 other patients. Acid-fast bacilli were identified in 8 cases. There were many unusual or opportunistic gastrointestinal tract infections. The most consistent and prominent autopsy finding was severe depletion of lymphoid tissues. Fatal infections most often involved the respiratory tract. Three patients died with widely metastatic Kaposi's sarcoma and secondary hemorrhage. The CNS was involved both clinically and pathologically in most cases. The adrenals, thyroid, and parathyroids were secondarily involved in some cases of systemic spread.

A wide spectrum of disease is found in patients dying of AIDS. The autopsy findings sometimes are even more protean than clinically suspected. *Pneumocystis carinii* and mycobacteria have persisted in some appropriately treated patients. The liver, endocrine organs, and CNS may be involved. Severe lymphoid depletion probably underlies the overwhelming infections that usually cause deaths in AIDS.

Opportunistic Infection Complicating Acquired Immune Deficiency Syndrome: Clinical Features of 25 Cases
Chester W. Lerner and Michael L. Tapper (Lenox Hill Hosp., New York)
Medicine (Baltimore) 63:155–164, May 1984   7–15

An increasing number of pathogens with a predilection for immunologically altered hosts have been recognized. Data on the opportunistic infections occurring in 25 patients with acquired immune deficiency syndrome (AIDS) seen in a 1½-year period in 1981–1982 were reviewed. Patients were followed up until death or for at least 1 year. There were 23 homosexual or bisexual men and 2 heterosexual intravenous drug users, including 1 woman, in the study. One homosexual man also was a drug user. The average age was 39.5 years. No patient had an underlying immunosuppressive disease.

Patients had been ill for an average of about 3 months before hospitalization. Eighteen patients had recurrent fevers. Thirteen of 14 patients with dyspnea had *Pneumocystis carinii* pneumonia. Five of 11 with diarrhea had cytomegalovirus colitis. All but 4% of patients were lymphopenic, and all 19 patients studied were anergic. Polyclonal hypergammaglobulinemia was a frequent finding; the IgA activity was most often elevated. In 22 cases, AIDS was initially diagnosed after opportunistic infection; in 4 of these patients, Kaposi's sarcoma later developed. Patients had an average of nearly three infections. Eighteen patients had *Pneumocystis carinii* pneumonia. Fourteen patients had cytomegalovirus infection, 19 had *Candida* infection, and 12 had mycobacterial infections, including 9 with atypical mycobacteriosis. There were 2 cases each of cryptococcosis and toxoplasmosis, and 1 each of cryptosporidiosis, herpes simplex infection, and progressive multifocal leukoencephalopathy. Twenty-two patients (88%) died an average of 7.4 months after presentation; another died more recently.

The most frequent causes of opportunistic infection in these patients with AIDS were *Candida albicans, P. carinii,* cytomegalovirus, and *Mycobacterium avium-intracellulare.* Disseminated atypical mycobacterial and cytomegalovirus infections were the leading causes of death. Pneumocystis pneumonia was more refractory to treatment than previously described.

▶ Anyone who cares for patients with AIDS is impressed with the array and severity of the opportunistic infections present in these patients. The infections are not only qualitatively different but, in quantitative terms, they are more impressive than any this observer has seen. To be able to see *P. carinii* on a throat swab or *M. avium-intracellulare* on a smear of a stool specimen is most impressive. However, we must remember when approaching patients with other immunodeficiency states that such techniques may not be rewarding, and we still must be aggressive in using our diagnostic procedures in such patients.—S.M.W.

Respiratory Cryptosporidiosis in the Acquired Immune Deficiency Syndrome: Use of Modified Cold Kinyoun and Hemacolor Stains for Rapid Diagnoses
Pearl Ma, Thelma G. Villanueva, David Kaufman, and John F. Gillooley
JAMA 252:1298–1301, Sept. 14, 1984   7–16

Cryptosporidium is a coccidial protozoan that recently has been recognized as a cause of disease in human beings. The organism is a frequent cause of diarrhea in mammals, birds, and reptiles. Intestinal disease is well documented in humans in both the uncompromised and immunocompromised states, but human respiratory cryptosporidiosis has not been described previously. Three respiratory cases are reported in patients with primary intestinal cryptosporidiosis and bilateral interstitial pneumonia. The diagnosis was made using two rapid-staining procedures, based on modified cold Kinyoun (MCK) solution and a Hemacolor set, and touch preparations of lung biopsy material, sputum, and stool. The finding of intracellular cryptosporidial oocysts in alveolar macrophages suggests possible hematogenous dissemination. Copious sputum production was a feature of the present cases. Two of the patients had concurrent cytomegalovirus infection, 1 with *Mycobacterium avium-intracellulare* infection as well; the third patient had concurrent pneumocystosis and Legionnaires' disease. One of the former patients died of respiratory failure.

Opportunistic cryptosporidiosis should be included in the differential diagnosis of pneumonia in patients with acquired immune deficiency syndrome (AIDS). A fourth case has been seen more recently in a patient with AIDS who had intestinal cryptosporidiosis. A case of disseminated cryptosporidiosis has been reported in an infant with combined immune deficiency. Acquisition of the infective agent by inhalation of oocysts is a possibility. The oocysts are very resistant to environmental changes and to a variety of commonly used disinfectants. *Cryptosporidium* may cause respiratory disease only in previously damaged lung tissue in immunodeficient patients. The MCK and Hemacolor methods can distinguish this pathogen from *Pneumocystis* and *Toxoplasma*. Current data suggest that cryptosporidiosis is an opportunistic infection by an organism of low virulence.

Toxoplasmic Encephalitis in Patients With Acquired Immune Deficiency Syndrome

Benjamin J. Luft, Robert G. Brooks, Frances K. Conley, Robert E. McCabe, and Jack S. Remington
JAMA 252:913–917, Aug. 17, 1984   7–17

An epidemic of toxoplasmic encephalitis is taking place in patients with acquired immune deficiency syndrome (AIDS). Review was made of 85 cases of cerebral toxoplasmosis encountered in the United States, Canada, and western Europe. All patients had clinical evidence of CNS involvement, and the organism was demonstrated histologically in brain tissue in all cases. Seventy patients were homosexuals, Haitians, or drug addicts with AIDS as defined by the Centers for Disease Control. The other 15 patients had immunosuppressive conditions such as Hodgkin's disease, lymphoma, or cardiac transplantation.

Conventional stains of brain tissue frequently were negative for *Toxoplasma* but all specimens were positive on peroxidase-antiperoxidase staining. Serologic titers did not indicate acute acquired infection except in 1 case. The ratio of agglutination titer to the Sabin-Feldman dye test titer appeared to be more predictive of active toxoplasmic encephalitis in the patients with AIDS than either test alone. Only 2 of 16 evaluable patients with AIDS had a significant rise in dye test titer on a repeat study at least 4 weeks after the first. The histologic picture was one of a profoundly destructive but fairly well-demarcated necrotizing process. Inflammatory infiltrates with arteritis and fibrinoid necrosis of vessel walls were present at the edges of necrotic foci. Neutrophils were more prominent in the cases of AIDS, whereas mononuclear cells predominated in the other cases.

Disorders of the CNS, including toxoplasmic encephalitis, cause substantial morbidity and mortality in patients with AIDS. Further knowledge of the pathogenesis of CNS toxoplasmosis in this setting may aid the development of new treatment modalities. More sensitive diagnostic methods are needed to detect the disease at an earlier stage.

▶ There are a number of neurologic problems associated with AIDS, including CNS toxoplasmosis, cryptococcal disease, CNS lymphoma, progressive multifocal leukoencephalopathy, atypical mycobacterial disease, *Candida,* cytomegalovirus, vascular complications, and other undiagnosed causes (see Snider, W. D., et al.: *Ann. Neurol.* 14:403–418, 1983).—D.S.

Enteropathy Associated With the Acquired Immunodeficiency Syndrome
Donald P. Kotler, Harold P. Gaetz, Michael Lange, Elena B. Klein, and Peter R. Holt
Ann. Intern. Med. 101:421–428, October 1984   7–18

Gastrointestinal symptoms are common in patients with AIDS, and some present with diarrhea and weight loss without evidence of a specific infectious agent. Gastrointestinal structure and absorption were evaluated in 12 homosexual men with AIDS and in 11 homosexual control subjects. Stool cultures for enteric pathogens were negative at the time of study by design. Seven of the AIDS patients had *Pneumocystis* pneumonia, and 3 had Kaposi's sarcoma. Two had progressive inanition associated with intestinal disease and viral infection. Five patients had evidence of other opportunistic infections. Ten of the control subjects presented with intestinal or hepatic symptoms. Three had unexplained diarrhea at the time of evaluation.

Significant diarrhea associated with weight loss occurred in 7 patients; it usually was intermittent, more severe at night, and made worse by food intake. Viruses, most often cytomegalovirus, were isolated from 9 of the immunodeficient patients. All study patients were malnourished and had lower body weights, serum albumin levels, and iron-binding capacities than the homosexual control subjects. Steatorrhea and xylose malabsorption were especially evident in patients with diarrhea. Jejunal biopsy specimens showed partial villous atrophy with crypt hyperplasia and an increase in intraepithelial lymphocytes. Rectal biopsy specimens showed intranuclear viral inclusions, mast-cell infiltration in the lamina propria, and focal cell degeneration near the crypt base. The crypt architecture was not abnormal.

Malnutrition and malabsorption appear to be common in patients with AIDS, and attention to the treatment of malnutrition seems necessary. Some patients may have severe intestinal damage not due to specific infection. Patients with severe intestinal involvement may require treatment in order to be rehabilitated. The potential role of malnutrition in the course of AIDS has not been sufficiently emphasized. Local immune responses in the gastrointestinal tract of patients with this syndrome could help clarify the relative roles of intestinal infection and immunologically mediated damage to the intestine.

Recurrent *Salmonella typhimurium* Bacteremia Associated With the Acquired Immunodeficiency Syndrome
Jordan B. Glaser, Linda Morton-Kute, Scott R. Berger, John Weber, Frederick P. Siegal, Carlos Lopez, William Robbins, and Sheldon H. Landesman
Ann. Intern. Med. 102:189–193, February 1985   7–19

Salmonella infection has been associated experimentally and clinically with deficient cell-mediated immunity. *Salmonella typhimurium* bacteremia was encountered in 8 patients with AIDS in a 28-month period. A total of 130 patients with proven AIDS was treated in this period; 40% were Haitians, 37% were intravenous drug abusers, and 19% were homosexual men. Seven Haitians and 1 patient with no identifiable risk factor for AIDS were infected with *Salmonella.*

All 8 study patients had, or eventually developed an opportunistic infection associated with AIDS. Three patients were bacteremic during or shortly after the diagnosis of other opportunistic infections, whereas 5 had their initial episode of *S. typhimurium* bacteremia 3–11 months before opportunistic infection. All 5 had evidence of abnormal immune function at the time of bacteremia. Seven patients had watery, nonbloody diarrhea.

Three patients had additional gastrointestinal pathogens. Stool culture was positive for *S. typhimurium* in only 1 case. Five patients had more than 1 episode of bacteremia. Studies for foci of infection were consistently negative. Recurrences were not prevented by treatment for 2–3 weeks with intravenously given ampicillin, chloramphenicol, or trimethoprim-sulfamethoxazole.

Salmonella typhimurium bacteremia, especially if recurrent, apparently can be added to the infections associated with AIDS. The bacteremia can present several months before AIDS is diagnosed, although other features of the syndrome usually are present at the time of infection. *Salmonella typhimurium* bacteremia still is most prevalent in patients without AIDS. The relative frequency of *S. typhimurium* bacteremia in Haitians compared with other risk groups may be related to increased exposure and subsequent asymptomatic carriage of the organism among immigrants.

▶ Several reports documenting *Salmonella* infections in AIDS patients have appeared (Jacobs, J. L. et al.: *Ann. Intern. Med.* 102:189–193, 1985; Smith, P. D., et al.: *Ann. Intern. Med.* 102:207–209, 1985). The organism has been very difficult to eradicate with antimicrobial therapy. Recurrent episodes of *Salmonella bacteremia* have been common and underscore the need for intact cell mediated immunity to cure salmonellosis.—D.S.

Pneumocystis carinii **Pneumonia: A Comparison Between Patients With the Acquired Immunodeficiency Syndrome and Patients With Other Immunodeficiencies**

Joseph A. Kovacs, John W. Hiemenz, Abe M. Macher, Diane Stover, Henry W. Murray, James Shelhamer, H. Clifford Lane, Carlos Urmacher, Christine Honig, Dan L. Longo, Margaret M. Parker, Charles Natanson, Joseph E. Parrillo, Anthony S. Fauci, Philip A. Pizzo, and Henry Masur
Ann. Intern. Med. 100:663–671, May 1984   7–20

Anecdotal reports have suggested that *Pneumocystis carinii* pneumonia in patients with acquired immunodeficiency syndrome (AIDS) has clinical features different from those in patients with previously known immunosuppressive illnesses. The authors compared the clinical features of 49 episodes of *P. carinii* pneumonia in patients with AIDS with those of 39 episodes in patients with other immunosuppressive diseases.

At presentation, patients with AIDS had a longer median duration of symptoms (28 days) than patients with other immunosuppressive diseases (5 days) ($P = .0001$). Patients with the syndrome were less likely to be febrile ($P = .08$), had a lower mean respiratory rate (23 vs. 30 breaths per minute) ($P = .005$), and were less hypoxemic on room air (69 vs. 52 mm Hg) ($P = .0002$), with a lower room air alveolar-arterial gradient (41 vs. 59 mm Hg) ($P = .0001$). There was no significant difference between the groups in leukocyte counts, chest x-ray findings, and histopathologic results. On the basis of histopathologic findings, other pathogens were not important contributors to pulmonary function. Overall survival rates from

1979 to 1983 were similar in the two groups, 57% and 50% respectively. In terms of response to treatment, there was no difference in median durations of fever and median number of days of treatment in the two groups. Trimethoprim-sulfamethoxazole (TMP-SMX) and pentamidine at conventional dosages were equally efficacious. Adverse effects of TMP-SMX, i.e., rash and leukopenia, were significantly more common in patients with AIDS. Patients with AIDS who initially had lower respiratory rates, higher room air arterial oxygen tensions, lower alveolar-arterial gradients, higher lymphocyte counts, and higher albumin concentrations were more likely to survive.

Pneumocystis carinii pneumonia in patients with AIDS is more insidious than in those with other immunosuppressive diseases, and therapy with TMP-SMX is complicated by frequent adverse reactions. The reasons for these differences are uncertain. Possibly some facet of the immunoregulatory defect in AIDS permits a different host-parasite relation from that usually seen in immunosuppressed patients undergoing treatment with corticosteroids or cytotoxic agents.

▶ *Pneumocystis carinii* pneumonitis in AIDS patients can be very insidious in onset and quite difficult to treat. Although this study suggests equal response rates to therapy of *P. carinii* comparing AIDS patients to other immunosuppressed patients, others show a lower response rate to treatment in AIDS patients. As the authors point out, therapy with TMP-SMX has frequently been associated with side effects (Gordin, F. M., et al.: *Ann. Intern. Med.* 100:495–499, 1984). In patients with reactions to TMP-SMX, pentamidine or an experimental agent, α-Difluoromethylornithine (DFMO) have been used (Golden, J. A., et al.: *West J. Med.* 141:613–623, 1984) with some success.—D.S.

Treatment of Intestinal Cryptosporidiosis With Spiramycin
David Portnoy, Mark E. Whiteside, Edward Buckley III, and Caroline L. MacLeod
Ann. Intern. Med. 101:202–204, August, 1984   7–21

In healthy persons, infection with *Cryptosporidium* usually results in acute self-limited episodes of diarrhea, whereas in immunosuppressed patients it can cause severe diarrhea and malabsorption, resulting in wasting and weight loss. Many drugs have been tried, but no effective treatment for cryptosporidiosis has been found. The authors report their experience in treating 10 immunosuppressed patients with enteric cryptosporidiosis and the favorable results achieved with spiramycin.

The 9 males in the study had either opportunistic infections or Kaposi's sarcoma, and results of immunologic studies were consistent with a diagnosis of acquired immunodeficiency syndrome. The 1 female developed cryptosporidiosis after allogeneic bone marrow transplantation for acute myeloblastic leukemia in relapse. All patients had severe, debilitating diarrhea. Stools were examined for *Cryptosporidium,* bacterial pathogen, ova, and parasites. Jejunal small bowel biopsy samples were obtained. All 10 patients were treated with spiramycin, 3 gm per day in divided doses, for 1 week or longer.

Diarrhea completely resolved in 6 patients. One patient required 16 weeks of treatment to eradicate the parasite from the stool. Another, who is asymptomatic, still has *Cryptosporidium* oocysts in the stool after 3.5 months of spiramycin therapy. In 2 patients the diarrhea persisted but was markedly decreased; stool specimens and small bowel biopsy samples showed no *Cryptosporidium*. In the other 2 patients, spiramycin treatment resulted in a decrease in the frequency of diarrhea, and *Cryptosporidium* oocysts remained on stool examination.

Jejunal biopsy samples may show villous atrophy besides organisms that appear as small (3 to 5 μ), round bodies adherent to the brush borders. These changes may be reversible, although prolonged or severe infection can produce mucosal damage that persists, resulting in continued diarrhea and malabsorption in the absence of *Cryptosporidium*.

Spiramycin is not approved for routine use by the FDA but can be obtained in Canada with special permission from the FDA.

▶ The grim course of opportunistic infection in AIDS is no less grim when *Cryptosporidium* is isolated. In contrast to self-limited infection in immunocompetent patients (see, for example, Wolfson, J. S., et al.: *N. Engl. J. Med.* 312:1278–1282, 1985), unrelenting, severe diarrhea has been the rule in AIDS, and no therapy has been useful. This paper suggests that spiramycin, a drug developed as an alternative to erythromycin, may be therapeutically effective in cryptosporidiosis. Given the present situation, it is certainly worth a try, but it seems unlikely that cryptosporidiosis will be controlled in this way.—G.K.

8 Sexually Transmitted Diseases

Nonsexual Transmission of Sexually Transmitted Diseases: An Infrequent Occurrence

Lawrence S. Neinstein, John Goldenring, and Sarah Carpenter (Los Angeles)
Pediatrics 74:67–76, July 1984   8–1

Results of several studies that evaluated the viability of *Neisseria gonorrhoeae* on commonly used fomites such as toilet seats and toilet paper indicated that transmission via washroom fomites seems to be rare. Reports indicated that nonsexual transmission of gonorrhea among adults or adolescents older than age 14 years occurred mostly as rare cases of conjunctivitis by accidental contamination in health professionals. In prepuberal children the disease is primarily sexually transmitted through sex play, sexual abuse, or intercourse, and all children with gonorrhea deserve a careful medical and social evaluation.

Among sexually active men, *Chlamydia* is a frequent cause of nongonococcal urethritis and epididymitis. Among women, it has been associated with purulent cervicitis, pelvic inflammatory disease, and a sterile dysuria-pyuria syndrome. Chlamydial neonatal conjunctivitis, pneumonia, or both, has its source in the birth canal of mothers with cervical chlamydial infections. When symptoms persist after penicillin treatment of prepuberal children with gonococcal infections, *Chlamydia trachomatis* should be suspected.

Primary genital herpes infections occur most frequently in adolescents and young adults; 85% of cases are due to herpes simplex virus type 2 (HSV2) and can be considered to be sexually transmitted. In evaluating a child, it is important to differentiate between HSV types 1 and 2; infections with the former are probably primarily transmitted nonsexually. Whenever possible, viral cultures from the vesicles should be obtained and acute and convalescent antibody titers determined.

Condyloma acuminata (veneral warts) appear singly or in clusters in the genital or anal region; they are caused by a DNA papilloma virus of which 11 subtypes may exist. A 62% infective rate has been documented in contacts of patients with venereal warts. In 21 cases reported in children since 1976, 11 were secondary to sexual abuse contact and 3 were due to contact during delivery.

Trichomonas vaginalis is a motile, single-celled flagellate protozoan. *Trichomonas vaginalis* vaginitis is a common sexually transmitted disease of high prevalence and infectivity. *Trichomonas* can survive on toilet seats for up to 1 hour and on wet clothes for at least 3 hours. In unhygienic circumstances *Trichomonas* can be transmitted by fomites such as a shared wet washcloth. Nonneonatal *T. vaginalis* infection is likely to result from sexual abuse or contact and is less likely to be transmitted via fomites.

More than 95% of cases of syphilis are sexually transmitted. Accidental transmission is possible (laboratory inoculation, operating room, blood transfusions). Prepuberal children with primary or secondary syphilis occurring beyond the neonatal period (transplacental transmission) should be presumed to be victims of sexual abuse.

Chancroid is caused by *Hemophilus ducreyi*. Once rarely seen, the incidence has increased with importation from Central America. There are no reports of chancroid in children.

Granuloma inguinale caused by *Calymmatobacterium granulomatis* is rare in the United States. It is manifest as granulomatous lesions of the perineum or perianal region.

In genital infections with the described organisms, the physician must establish that sexual abuse has not occurred. If one sexually transmitted disease is identified, tests for others must be performed.

Infection With *Chlamydia trachomatis* in Female College Students
William M. McCormack, Bernard Rosner, Dorothy E. McComb, John R. Evrard, and Stephen H. Zinner
Am. J. Epidemiol. 121:107–115, January 1985   8–2

Chlamydia trachomatis now is recognized as a major genital pathogen, but little is known of its prevalence and consequences in women. Between 1974 and 1975, a series of 500 college-aged women underwent examination, most of whom went to see a gynecologist for fertility control or routine physical examinations. *Chlamydia trachomatis* was isolated in 4.9% of genital specimens obtained from 431 evaluable participants whose mean age was 20.4 years. Most of the 21 women with chlamydial infection were asymptomatic, but 2 described dysuria, 3 reported abdominal pain, and 7 noted an abnormal vaginal discharge.

Chlamydial infection was more likely to occur in nonwhites and in women not using barrier contraceptive methods. Local chlamydial antibody was detected in secretions from 85% of 20 infected women and in 8% of women with negative culture results. Sexually inexperienced women were not infected and did not have local chlamydial antibody. Among women who had intercourse without using barrier contraception, infection or the local antibody concentration increased with the number of lifetime sexual partners. Other sexually transmitted organisms, e.g., *Mycoplasma hominis* and *Trichomonas vaginalis,* were more frequent in women with chlamydial infection.

About 5% of young women in this survey were infected by *C. trachomatis*. Both the presence of the organism and that of local chlamydial antibody increased in relation to the number of lifetime sexual partners in women using nonbarrier methods of contraception. Oral contraceptive users did not appear to be at a particular risk of chlamydial infection, but study of a larger sample would be definitive.

▶ In general, the frequency of asymptomatic carriers of *Chlamydia trachomatis* is similar to previous reports of carrier rates for gonococci. This study clearly establishes that *Chlamydia* infection is sexually transmitted in virtually all cases. How to identify such carriers, given the relative unavailability of such cultures, and whether to treat them once identified, remain unanswered questions.— S.G.

Lack of Association Between Genital Mycoplasmas and Infertility
Dieter W. Gump, Mark Gibson, and Taka Ashikaga (Univ. of Vermont)
N. Engl. J. Med. 310:937–941, April 12, 1984   8–3

The role of genital mycoplasma colonization was examined in 205 women from infertile couples who underwent extensive studies. All had involuntary infertility for at least 1 year. The mean age was 29 years. Nearly two thirds of the sample were nulliparous. All of the women were white, and most were of the upper and middle socioeconomic class. The minimum follow-up period was 18 months.

Women with a history of pelvic inflammatory disease had increased cervical carriage of *Mycoplasma hominis*, but not of *Ureaplasma urealyticum*. Cervical inflammation was not related to rates of colonization by either species of mycoplasma. Mycoplasmas were cultured from 5% of endometrial biopsy specimens, none of which showed signs of inflammation. Colonization with mycoplasmas did not influence either the number of sperm cells or the proportion of motile sperm present in cervical mucus on postcoital testing. Neither subsequent pregnancies nor pregnancy outcomes could be related to cervical carriage of mycoplasmas.

These findings fail to support a role for genital mycoplasmas in the pathogenesis of infertility caused by tubal abnormalities. They also indicate no adverse effect on other factors that might interfere with fertility.

Cytomegalovirus Infection in Sex Partners: Evidence for Sexual Transmission
H. Hunter Handsfield, Susan H. Chandler, Virginia A. Caine, Joel D. Meyers, Lawrence Corey, Edward Medeiros, and James K. McDougall (Seattle)
J. Infect. Dis. 151:344–348, February 1985   8–4

It has been proposed that sexual contact is an important mode of transmission of cytomegalovirus (CMV) in heterosexual adults, but the evidence has been largely circumstantial. A cultural and serologic survey was performed in 63 male sex partners of women seen at a sexually transmitted diseases clinic with or without CMV infection. Serologic evaluation utilized an enzyme-linked immunosorbent assay for antibody to CMV. Isolates from infected couples were compared by DNA restriction enzyme analysis.

Cytomegalovirus was isolated from a total of 46 women, including about one fifth of women in a total series of 327 who were seropositive and none who were seronegative. The cervix was culture positive in 35 women, and the urine in 18. Antibody to CMV was found in 74% of 42 partners of seropositive women and in 31% of 16 partners of seronegative women. Virus was isolated from urine or semen in 22% of partners of women shedding virus from the cervix or urine, and none of the partners of culture-negative women. Restriction enzyme typing of isolates from three pairs of sex partners showed that two couples were infected with common strains.

These findings support the hypothesis that CMV is sexually transmitted among heterosexual adults. The virus also appears to be sexually transmitted among homosexual men. Transmission of CMV probably requires overt exchange of secretions or excretions, which is common both in early childhood and during adult sexual activity. The risk in women in child-bearing age is significant since primary infection during pregnancy increases the risk of clinically significant congenital infection.

▶ This is a straightforward study of the sort we have come to expect from the group in Seattle who have contributed so much to our knowledge of sexually transmitted diseases. Since cytomegalovirus has been associated with congenital abnormalities in infants infected in utero, the observation that this agent is sexually transmitted is an important one.—S.M.W.

Epidemiology of Venereal Urethritis: Comparison of Gonorrhea and Nongonococcal Urethritis
J. Allen McCutchan (Univ. of California, San Diego)
Rev. Infect. Dis. 6:669–688, Sept.–Oct. 1984   8–5

Gonorrhea (GU) and nongonococcal urethritis (NGU) are by far the most common sexually transmitted diseases in men. Venereal urethritis has increased markedly in prevalence in most developed countries in the past 25 years. The clinical features of GU and NGU overlap enough to require laboratory differentiation. Once urethritis is diagnosed, differentiation of GU from NGU usually necessitates only a Gram stain. Simultaneous infection by *Neisseria gonorrhoeae* and *Chlamydia trachomatis* or other agents of NGU can give rise to postgonococcal urethritis after penicillin therapy for GU. *Chlamydia trachomatis* causes trachoma and lymphogranuloma venereum as well as NGU. Nongonococcal urethritis may also be caused by *Ureaplasma urealyticum*. No organism is isolated in about one fifth of cases of NGU.

Case ratios of NGU to gonococcal urethritis of about 2 have been reported. The findings shown in Figure 8–1 can be explained by the actual incidence of NGU roughly paralleling that of GU, with NGU being reported more often because of greater awareness of the disorder, changing diagnostic criteria, or changing patterns of seeking medical care. The reasons for the increased risk of gonococcal urethritis in blacks remain to be documented. The wide variations reported in secondary contacts might reflect variation in numbers of exposures.

Persons who are infectious but asymptomatic and those who remain

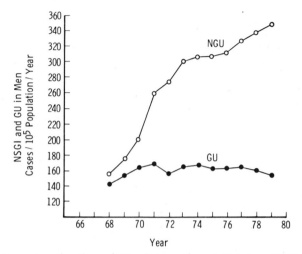

Fig 8–1.—Comparison of incidence of GU and nonspecific genital infections *(NSGI)* from 1968 to 1979. Before 1971, NSGI comprised NGU only, and thereafter, NGU predominantly. The doubling of the incidence of NGU during period of nearly constant incidence of GU is predominantly artifact of increased reporting and change in method of reporting in 1971. The roughly 2:1 ratio of NGU to GU between 1973 and 1979 has been found in individual clinics in Europe and North America throughout the decade. (Courtesy of McCutchan, J.A.: Rev. Infect. Dis. 6:669–688, Sept.–Oct. 1984.)

sexually active while symptomatic are the chief source of spread of both GU and NGU. The rapid spread of *N. gonorrhoeae* containing plasmids that code for penicillinases has reduced the likelihood that treatment will render patients noninfectious, and the posttreatment period may become an increasingly important public health factor. The recognition of prolonged asymptomatic carriage of *N. gonorrhoeae* by men may mandate reevaluation of strategies of contact tracing.

Hospitalizations for Pelvic Inflammatory Disease: Epidemiology and Trends in the United States, 1975 to 1981
A. Eugene Washington, Willard Cates, Jr., and Akbar A. Zaidi
JAMA 251:2529–2533, May 18, 1984   8–6

Several key factors influencing pelvic inflammatory disease (PID) rates (e.g., sexually transmitted organisms, sexual behavior, and contraceptive methods) have changed considerably since 1975. A review was made of data on estimated national trends in hospitalization for PID in the United States from 1975 to 1981 based on data derived from the Hospital Discharge Survey conducted by the National Center for Health Statistics.

An estimated 267,200 women, aged 15–44 years, were hospitalized annually for PID with the hospitalization rates averaging 5.3/1,000 women. Overall, both the estimated rate and number of hospitalizations for PID among women, aged 15–44 years, rose slightly. Women in their 20s had a twofold increased risk of being hospitalized for PID, with the age group 20–24 years having the highest average (7.0/1,000). Women younger than age 30 years accounted for 66% of the hospitalizations for PID among those of reproductive age. Nonwhite women had an average rate of hospitalization 2.5 times higher than that for white women. However, the trend of hospitalization remained stable among nonwhite women, whereas that in white women increased slightly. Regionally, average rates for PID hospitalizations were highest for women in the South and lowest in the Northeast, whereas rates were similiar between the North-Central and South regions and between the West and Northeast regions. Divorced and separated women were 70% more likely to be hospitalized for PID than were single or married women. The average duration of hospitalization for PID declined slightly from 7.2 days to 6.3 days since 1975.

Overall, more women experienced PID in the 1970s, leading to an increased rate of hospitalization for the disease. Recent changes in three key risk factors influencing PID rates accounted for this increased rate: the increase in nongonococcal agents (e.g., *Chlamydia trachomatis*) causing expansion of the sexually transmitted disease pool and leading to a larger percentage of nongonococcal PID; more liberal sexual behavior exposing young women to a greater risk of contracting PID; and shifting contraceptive measures by more young women away from methods that protect against sexually transmitted disease and PID. The increased rate of PID leads to increased rates of complications from PID, including ectopic pregnancies and infertility.

These data indicate that, rates for young white women have shown more pronounced increases although overall rates of hospitalization for PID have risen only slightly. Practitioners should be aware of the changes in risk factors influencing PID rates when counseling patients at high risk, or when examining and treating patients suspected of having PID.

▶ In recent years a more liberal policy of hospitalization for young women with PID has developed. One major reason is that teenagers with PID have a high rate of relapse, often due to noncompliance. Such relapses markedly diminish fertility, as well as increase the risk of ectopic pregnancies and even subsequent episodes of PID itself. This study reports data through 1981. It will be interesting to examine the more recent data when cost containment measures such as DRGs have taken effect in many states. An early casualty of a restricted hospital admission policy could be the vulnerable teenager, often without insurance and generally reluctant to come into the hospital at all. Therapy of PID will be forced into the outpatient area, and recidivism may become a major concern in this age group.—S.G.

Gonococcal Pili: Primary Structure and Receptor Binding Domain
Gary K. Schoolnik, Rosemary Fernandez, Joseph Y. Tai, Jonathan Rothbard, and E. C. Goschlich
J. Exp. Med. 159:1351–1370, May 1984   8–7

Gonococcal pili are surface appendages composed of identical polypeptide subunits termed pilin, which polymerize to form linear structures about 6 nm in diameter and 1,000–4,000 nm long. Pili bind epithelial cell receptor molecules and thereby promote mucosal colonization. They also interact with polymorphonuclear leukocytes and probably confer resistance to phagocytosis. Although pili from separate gonococcal strains and variants of the same strain exhibit similar functional and structural attributes, they may differ physically, chemically, and antigenically. To elucidate the molecular basis for epithelial adherence and antigenic diversity, Schoolnik et al. previously prepared cyanogen bromide (CNBr) fragments of pili from different gonococcal strains. The CNBr-2 fragment was found to be immunorecessive and to encompass a highly conserved region that mediates receptor binding function. The CNBr-3 fragment was found to be immunodominant and to comprise a variable region that confers type-specific antigenicity. The complete amino acid sequence of gonococcal pilin from the transparent opacity variant of strain MS11 is reported here.

The complete amino acid sequence of pilin from gonococcal strain MS11 and the sequence of constant and variable regions from strain R10 pilin were determined to elucidate the structural basis for adherence function, antigenic diversity, and polymeric structure. The MS11 pilin sequence consists of 159 amino acids in a single polypeptide chain with two cysteines in disulfide linkage and serine-bonded phosphate residues. The TC-2(31–111) sequence, a soluble monomeric pilus peptide prepared by arginine-specific digestion, binds human endocervical cells, but not buccal or HeLa cells, and therefore is postulated to encompass the receptor binding domain. Variable regions of CNBr-3 appear to confer antigenic diversity and comprise segments in which changes in the position of charged residues occur in hydrophilic, beta-turns. Residues 2–21 and 201–221 of gonococcal pilins and lower eukaryotic actins, respectively, exhibit 50% homology. When these residues are arranged at intervals of 100 degrees of arc on "helical wheels," the identical amino acids comprise a hydrophobic face on one side of the helix. This observation, the hydrophobic character of this region, and the tendency for TC-1 (residues 1–30) to aggregate in water suggest that this stretch interacts with other subunits to stabilize polymeric structure.

The differential binding of pili to endocervical and buccal epithelial cell surfaces indicates that the pilus receptor is likely tissue specific. It follows that receptor density and distribution may underlie the tissue tropism of gonococcal infections. These results are not consonant with Pearce and Buchanan's finding that whole, iodinated pili bind buccal and endocervical cells equally well. The discrepancy might be explained by the observations of Lambert et al. that some gonococcal pili appear to bind different receptor compounds. Alternatively, binding studies conducted with undenatured pili may lack specificity because the filaments readily associate with hydrophobic surfaces, including glass, plastic, latex beads, and synthetic lipid bilayers. Although these interactions are not chemically specific, they may be pertinent to the binding event. Hydrophobic binding may optimally position pilus filaments on cell surfaces, facilitating receptor-mediated binding.

Treatment of Penicillin-resistant *Neisseria gonorrhoeae* With Oral Norfloxacin

Steven R. Crider, Steven D. Colby, Larry K. Miller, William O. Harrison, Sharon B. J. Kerbs, and S. William Berg (Naval Hosp., San Diego)

N. Engl. J. Med. 311:137–140, July 19, 1984   8–8

Norfloxacin is an orally administered antibacterial organic acid that is structurally related to nalidixic acid. It has been shown to be highly active in vitro against penicillinase-producing *Neisseria gonorrhoeae,* with a mean minimal inhibitory concentration of 0.03 μg/ml or less. The authors compared the efficacy of norfloxacin with that of spectinomycin in men with uncomplicated gonococcal urethritis.

A total of 92 men with culture-proved gonococcal urethritis were included in the study. Norfloxacin was given orally in two 600-mg doses at 4-hour intervals to 28 subjects who had penicillinase-producing *N. gonorrhoeae* and 31 who had nonpenicillinase *N. gonorrhoeae.* Spectinomycin, 2 gm intramuscularly, was given to 14 patients who had penicillinase-producing *N. gonorrhoeae* and 19 who had nonpenicillinase-producing *N. gonorrhoeae.* All patients in both treatment groups had negative cultures for *N. gonorrhoeae* at follow-up. Complete resolution of symptoms occurred within 6 to 12 hours of initial dose of norfloxacin in 70% of patients, and complete resolution of symptoms occurred within 24 hours in all patients. The drug was well tolerated. No spherical or needle-shaped crystals were observed in posttreatment urine specimens. Minimal inhibitor concentration of norfloxacin, penicillin G, tetracycline, erythromycin, cefoxitin, and spectinomycin determined for 45 isolates of *N. gonorrhoeae* from this study and 65 additional isolates showed no differences between these groups. Ninety-eight percent of the isolates (108 of 110) were inhibited by 0.125 μg of norfloxacin per milliliter or less; there was no difference between producers and nonproducers of penicillinase.

This study shows that a two-dose, single day regimen of orally administered norfloxacin was markedly effective in the treatment of uncomplicated urethritis due to penicillin-resistant or penicillin-sensitive strains of *N. gonorrhoeae.* Compliance with the two-dose regimen is excellent, and the drug is well tolerated.

Mucopurulent Cervicitis: The Ignored Counterpart in Women of Urethritis in Men

Robert C. Brunham, Jorma Paavonen, Claire E. Stevens, Nancy Kiviat, Cho-Chou Kuo, Cathy W. Critchlow, and King K. Holmes

N. Engl. J. Med. 311:1–6, July 5, 1984   8–9

Criteria for diagnosing mucopurulent cervicitis was defined in a series of 100 randomly selected nonmenstruating women attending a clinic for sexually transmitted diseases. Twenty-five women attended because of relations with a man who had a sexually transmitted disease. The mean age was 22.5 years. The mean number of sexual partners was 13½. The most common symptom was vaginal discharge.

Chlamydia trachomatis alone was isolated from the cervix in 15 cases, and both *C. trachomatis* and *Neisseria gonorrhoeae* in 8 cases. *Chlamydia trachomatis* alone was isolated from the urethra in 4 women. Both visualization of yellow mucopurulent endocervical secretions on a white swab and the presence of 10 or more polymorphs per microscopic field at a magnification of 1,000 in a gram-stained endocervical smear correlated independently with cervical *C. trachomatis* infection, but not with gonorrhea or genital herpes. Mucopus was uncommon in women with *N. gonorrhoeae* infection alone. *Chlamydia trachomatis* was isolated from 20 of 40 women with either mucopus or 10 or more polymorphs per field, compared with 2 of 60 without these findings.

Mucopurulent cervicitis is a very common clinical disorder in women seen at a venereal disease clinic. Its prevalence approximates that of gonococcal and nongonococcal urethritis combined in heterosexual men. The present findings support the Centers for Disease Control recommendation that the syndrome be treated with a regimen used for chlamydial infection in adults, such as 500 mg of tetracycline given orally 4 times daily for at least a week.

Experimental Model for Activation of Genital Herpes Simplex Virus

Helena Wrzos and Fred Rapp (Pennsylvania State Univ.)
J. Infect. Dis. 151:349–354, February 1985   8–10

Recurrent herpesvirus infection is a major health problem, particularly in immunocompromised patients. The "skin-trigger" hypothesis of latent herpetic reactivation suggests that local scarring may facilitate the reactivation of latent virus. An attempt was made to reactivate latent herpes simplex virus-2 (HSV-2) infection in mice with visible signs of previous primary genital herpetic infection in the form of postinfection scarring. Latently infected C57Bl/6 mice were injected intraperitoneally with cyclophosphamide and antilymphocyte serum and were evaluated for reactivated virus or recurrent lesions. Primary infection was produced by inoculating mice with HSV-2 using cotton tampons soaked in an appropriate dilution of virus. The immunosuppressants are given twice weekly for as long as 2 months until external recurrent genital lesions appeared.

Latently infected mice subjected to immunosuppression exhibited neither recurrent lesions nor virus at the site of primary infection. Recurrent disease was, however, induced when mice were selected for immunosuppression on the basis of postinfection scarring. These mice presumably were latently infected by HSV-2. Recurrent lesions eventually developed in all mice with scars after immunosuppressive treatment. Spontaneous recurrent lesions were not seen in scarred mice not given immunosuppressive treatment, and virus was not isolated from the genital area in these animals.

Immunosuppression reactivates herpetic genital disease in this mouse model of persistent or latent HSV-2 infection. Recurrent disease is seen only in mice with postinfection scars that are subjected to immunosuppression. This model could be useful in testing antiherpetic agents in immunosuppressed animals. The present findings emphasize the importance of local factors in the reactivation of latent herpetic disease.

▶ Viral latency and reactivation, an important characteristic of the herpesvirus, is one of the most fundamental problems yet to be solved in the field of infectious diseases. The unusual tropism of herpesviruses for neural cells, the presence of HSV-2 DNA without other HSV-2 products within the neural cell, the unique resistance of neural cells to cytolysis by intact herpesviruses, and the propensity for reactivation to manifest near the site of primary infection and not uniformly in the area innervated by the latently infected cell all emphasize the complexities of this phenomenon. This paper calls attention to the interplay between local conditions, i.e., the presence or absence of scarring at the site of primary infection, as well as systemic immunosuppression. We certainly need to continue efforts that will provide newer and better models to study viral latency.—M.K.

9 Nosocomial Infections

Factors Causing Acute Shunt Infection: Computer Analysis of 1,174 Operations

Dominique Renier, Jacques Lacombe, Alain Pierre-Kahn, Christian Sainte-Rose, and Jean-François Hirsch (Paris)

J. Neurosurg. 61:1072–1078, December 1984   9–1

Infection continues to be the chief complication of shunt procedures for hydrocephalus; rates of 7%–10% generally are reported. Use of the surgical isolator has not eliminated the problem. Review was made of 1,174 operations for cerebrospinal fluid (CSF) shunt placement or revision, performed on 802 hydrocephalic children in 1975–1982. Cultures of CSF obtained during shunt operation were positive in 33 cases. The remaining operations included primary insertions and revisions. A ventriculoperitoneal shunt was placed primarily in nearly all cases, usually with a Hakin valve. Shunt infections were treated by removal of the shunt and antibiotic therapy for 3 weeks, with insertion of a new shunt when infection was eliminated.

The infection rate per surgical procedure was 7.9%. There were 56 cases of isolated meningitis, 17 of peritonitis, and 10 of wound infection. Only 2 cases of septicemia occurred. *Staphylococcus epidermidis* and *Staphylococcus aureus* accounted for more than two thirds of the infections. Gram-negative bacilli were relatively frequent in young infants. Infection in general was more frequent in patients, aged 1 year and younger, but the cause of hydrocephalus was not a significant factor. Patients with dermatitis or a scalp eschar were at an increased risk of infection, as were those with infection outside the CNS. Revisions had the lowest infection rate, and reinsertions after infection had the highest infection rate. Wound dehiscence or postoperative scalp necrosis increased the risk of shunt infection.

This uncontrolled trial showed that the occurrence of CSF shunt infections in children treated for hydrocephalus is related to intercurrent infections, infancy, poor preoperative skin condition, and the presence of wound dehiscence or scalp necrosis postoperatively. The number of shunt procedures was not a significant risk factor, but shunt reinsertions after previous infection carried a particular risk of infection.

Intravenous Therapy Team and Peripheral Venous Catheter-Associated Complications: A Prospective Controlled Study

J. Walton Tomford, Charles O. Hershey, Christine E. McLaren, Dan K. Porter, and David I. Cohen (Case Western Reserve Univ.)

Arch. Intern. Med. 144:1191–1194, June 1984   9–2

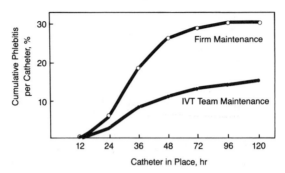

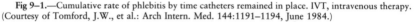

Fig 9–1.—Cumulative rate of phlebitis by time catheters remained in place. IVT, intravenous therapy. (Courtesy of Tomford, J.W., et al.: Arch Intern. Med. 144:1191–1194, June 1984.)

Most previous studies of an intravenous therapy (IVT) team have been retrospective or lacked proper controls. The present prospective controlled trial was conducted on four similar inpatient medical wards at a general teaching hospital. A total of 863 catheters were followed up in 445 patients seen in a 2½-month period. The IVT teams were organized by an experienced leader who was responsible for training and supervising the team members and for ensuring compliance with Centers for Disease Control guidelines. Catheters were to be withdrawn and reinserted after 48 to 72 hours if possible. All intravenous catheters were inspected daily by two investigators.

The occurrence of phlebitis was consistently reduced after participation by IVT teams; the overall effect was significant. Infiltrations were similar in the study and control groups. No catheter-related sepsis was observed. Both groups used plastic catheters in a majority of cases. The incidence of cellulitis and phlebitis was reduced from 2.1% to 0.2% in patients followed by the IVT. When all cases of infection were excluded, phlebitis occurred in 25% of control cases and 13% of IVT cases, still a significant difference. Lower rates of phlebitis were observed in the IVT group regardless of the duration of catheterization (Fig 9–1). Patients managed by the IVT team did not have more catheters than did control patients.

The rate of phlebitis related to peripheral IV catheters can be significantly reduced by institution of an IVT team. The team approach has improved house staff morale, and led to a more reliable and timely delivery of intravenously administered medications. That fewer complications occur seems to result from surveillance and maintenance of catheters by the IVT team rather than to insertional techniques. An IVT team can reduce morbidity and improve patient care. Financial costs may be reduced if hospital stays will be shortened. Experience in inpatient medical services should be applicable to other services.

Intravenous Tubing With Burettes Can Be Safely Changed at 48-Hour Intervals

Hector F. Gorbea, David R. Snydman, Annette Delaney, Jane Stockman, and
William J. Martin

JAMA 251:2112–2115, April 27, 1984   9–3

Recent studies showed low rates of fluid contamination in arterial and
peripheral intravenous (IV) infusion systems at 48 hours when used in
general medicine and operation settings. The safety of changing IV systems
containing inline burettes at 48 hours was investigated in an intensive care
unit. The study included 123 patients hospitalized in a surgical intensive
care unit at New England Medical Center Hospital in Boston. Patients
were assigned alternatively to have IV lines with an inline burette changed
at either 24-hour (64 patients), or 48-hour (59 patients) intervals. The IV
delivery system included a solution administration set, an extension tube,
an inline burette with a port, a three-way stopcock, and a cannula. A 2-
ml aliquot of burette fluid was obtained from each system for daily quantitative culture.

There were no differences between the two groups in mean age, sex
distribution, or length of stay in the intensive care unit. All patients had
multiple IV cannulae. The 24-hour-interval group had a greater number
of cannulae per patient and had more patients with infection as well as
more receiving antibiotics than was the case in the 48-hour group. Contaminated burette fluid was identified in 2% (95% confidence interval,
0.7% to 3.3%) of samples from 24-hour-interval burettes compared with
4% (95% confidence interval, 1.4% to 6.6%) of samples from 48-hour-
interval burettes (table). Bacterial contamination of fluid with at least 10
colonies per ml occurred in 1.1% (95% confidence interval, 0.14% to
2.1%) of the 24-hour-interval cultures and in 0.9% (95% confidence
interval, 0.3% to 1.5%) of the 48-hour-interval cultures. The type of
bacteria isolated *(Staphylococcus epidermidis* and *Staphylococcus aureus)*
and the distribution of colony counts were similar in the two groups. None
of the contaminated fluids was associated with primary bacteremia.

The overall burette fluid contamination rate did not differ significantly
between the 24-hour and 48-hour groups. Despite certain differences between the 2 groups (e.g., presence of infection on hospital admission and
use of antibiotics), the confidence intervals were narrow and reflected

CULTURE CHARACTERISTICS FROM THE 24-HOUR AND 48-HOUR
BURETTE CHANGE GROUPS

Characteristic	24-Hour Change No. (%)	48-Hour Change No. (%)
Total burettes	471 . . .	118 . . .
No. of burette cultures	452 . . .	224 . . .
Culture-positive burette fluid	9 (2.0)	9 (4.0)
Culture-positive burette fluid, colony counts ≥ 10	5 (1.1)	2 (0.9)

similar rates of contamination. Changing inline burettes in an intensive care setting at 48-hour intervals is safe and results in substantial cost savings.

Sepsis From Sinusitis in Nasotracheally Intubated Patients: Diagnostic Dilemma

Michael J. O'Reilly, Eddie J. Reddick, Waylon Black, Preston L. Carter, James Erhardt, William Fill, Delray Maughn, Anthony Sado, and Gordon R. Klatt (Tacoma, Wash.)
Am. J. Surg. 147:601–604, May 1984   9–4

Several patients with prolonged nasotracheal intubation and sepsis with no apparent origin recently were encountered. Study of the paranasal sinuses by computed tomography (CT) led to a diagnosis of sinusitis, and its aggressive treatment led to resolution of the sepsis. Eleven of 26 patients who had been intubated nasotracheally for longer than 5 days in a 6-month period in 1983 became septic. Seven of them had CT evidence of sinusitis. The 6 patients who survived had surgical sinus drainage or received aggressive medical treatment. Multiple organisms were cultured from sinus specimens in these cases. Three of the surviving patients improved shortly after the start of treatment; another, after a week of low-grade fever.

Prolonged nasotracheal intubation presumably causes sinusitis through direct irritation of the nasal mucosa, leading to edema and occlusion of the sinus drainage paths. It may be difficult to diagnose sinusitis by physical examination in a septic or obtunded patient, but CT of the sinuses is helpful. All nasotracheally intubated patients should receive topical decongestants and vasoconstrictors, and CT should be done at the first evidence of sepsis. Aspiration cultures should be obtained in all suspected cases to permit appropriate antibiotic therapy.

► The remarkable feature of this study is that 43% of patients who required nasotracheal intubation for more than 5 days developed nosocomial sinusitis. This diagnosis is probably frequently overlooked in the workup of fever in patients who are in the intensive care unit. The authors suggest that topical decongestants and vasoconstrictors may be useful for all nasotracheally intubated patients; however, there is no evidence that such prophylactic use will prevent this complication.—D.S.

Bacterial Changes in the Urine Samples of Patients With Long-term Indwelling Catheters

Robert B. Breitenbucher (Hennepin County Med. Center, Minneapolis)
Arch. Intern. Med. 144:1585–1588, August 1984   9–5

The author prospectively studied changes in bacterial flora in urine samples obtained monthly over a 1-year period from 15 nursing home patients with long-term indwelling urethral or suprapubic catheters. The patients were matched as closely as possible and then placed into 2 groups: those who received no prophylactic antibiotics (group 1) and those who received orally administered sulfamethoxazole (400 mg/day) combined with trimethoprim (80 mg/day) (group 2).

Polymicrobial isolates accounted for 86% of the specimens with 2 to 6 species identified in each of these specimens. Changes in bacterial flora were continual in both groups. When considering only those changes in species numbering more than 100,000/ml, there was a mean of 2.0 changes in flora per month for all patients (range, 0.5 to 4.7 changes). The average change per month was 1.5 for group 1 and 2.2 for group 2. When changes in species, quantity, and biogram were included, there was an average of 3.2 changes per month. The interval between catheter changes had apparent effect on the number of changes in bacterial flora. *Pseudomonas aeruginosa, Providencia stuartii,* and *Citrobacter diversus* were cultured significantly more often in group 2 patients ($P < .003$, $P < .023$, and $P < .007$, respectively). Five of 7 patients in group 1 and 5 of 8 patients in group 2 developed urinary tract infections. In only 3 cases (1%) organisms of established urinary tract pathogenecity were present that were not susceptible to ampicillin or gentamicin by routine disk diffusion.

Because of the rapidity of bacterial flora changes, routine monthly cultures have little predictive value in patients with long-term indwelling catheters. In addition, the findings do not support the practice of daily administration of sulfamethoxazole and trimethoprim as a prophylactic measure in such patients.

▶ A long-term indwelling urinary catheter seems to acquire its own microbial flora in which the microorganisms are both numerous and diverse. The authors only considered microbial isolates numbering more than 10^5/ml. This criterion, however, is arbitrary in this setting since it was devised for patients with a normal urinary stream. Theoretically, any isolated organism, sampled directly from the bladder without urethral contamination, should be considered significant. In any case, this study shows the futility of a number of commonly used modalities in such patients. Specifically, there was no value in using this antimicrobial regimen, changing the urinary catheter, or periodic culturing of the urine.—S.G.

Hospital-Acquired Bloodstream Infections With *Staphylococcus epidermidis:* Review of 100 Cases

Samuel Ponce de Leon and Richard P. Wenzel (Univ. of Virginia)
Am. J. Med. 77:639–644, October 1984   9–6

Much of the increase in gram-positive bacteremias at the authors' center is attributable to coagulase-negative staphylococci. The findings in a prospective series of 100 patients with nosocomial coagulase-negative staphylococcal bloodstream infection were reviewed. The underlying disorders are listed in the table. Nearly three fourths of the patients were hospitalized

---

Diagnosis	Number
Prematurity	20
Cardiovascular disease	20
Trauma	13
Solid tumor neoplasms	10
Gastrointestinal disease	7
Congenital anomalies	6
Hematologic malignancy	5
Burns	4
Renal transplant	3
Others	12
Total	100

(Courtesy of Ponce de Leon, S., and Wenzel, R.P.: Am. J. Med. 77:639–644, October 1984.)

---

in critical care units at the time of bloodstream infection. A similar proportion had previously received antibiotics in hospital, and a previous episode of bacteremia was documented in 16 cases. Most patients were neonates, infants, or persons older than age 50 years.

The overall hospital mortality was 34%. Most deaths occurred in the first 3 weeks after the initial positive blood culture was obtained. A single positive blood culture had the same clinical import as multiple positive cultures. Twenty-two patients had evidence of septic shock; half of them died in the first 3 weeks after the diagnosis of bacteremia. Vascular-catheter cultures yielded coagulase-negative staphylococci in 56.5% of 46 cases that were cultured. Most patients received more than 1 antimicrobial agent.

Mortality due to coagulase-negative staphylococcal bacteremia in this series was similar to that reported with *Staphylococcus aureus* bacteremia. Patients with a single positive culture for coagulase-negative staphylococci require close evaluation. Opportunistic infections of this type are a true threat to hospitalized patients, and positive blood cultures should not be dismissed as a contaminant.

Opportunistic Infections in Endogenous Cushing's Syndrome
Barney S. Graham and W. Stuart Tucker, Jr. (Vanderbilt Univ.)
Ann. Intern. Med. 101:334–338, September 1984   9–7

Reports of opportunistic infection in patients with endogenous Cushing's syndrome are infrequent, in contrast with glucocorticoid-treated patients. Six such cases have been added to 17 in the literature. The authors' patients included 5 men and 1 woman aged 24–68 years, presenting in 1975–1983 with both opportunistic infection and endogenous Cushing's syndrome. Five patients had ectopic ACTH production by a malignant tumor, while 1 had bilateral adrenal hyperplasia. The mean peak morning plasma cortisol was 117 µg/dl. All 6 patients were moderately glucose-intolerant, but ketoacidosis was not noted. Lymphopenia was a common finding. Three patients died of *Pneumocystis carinii* pneumonia. One patient each had cryptococcosis, *P. aeruginosa* meningitis, and disseminated aspergillosis. Three patients also had oral candidiasis. Five had serious bacterial infections. All 6 patients died of infection, 5 with uncontrolled steroid levels at the time they died or were moribund. One patient who was treated for ectopic ACTH syndrome survived 7 months before dying of disseminated aspergillosis.

The commonest infections in these cases have been cryptococcosis, aspergillosis, nocardiosis, and pneumocystosis. Peak morning plasma cortisol levels were higher in patients with pneumocystosis and lower in those with cryptococcosis. Patients with hypercortisolism must be monitored for infection. Fourteen of 23 patients have had malignant tumors, and 5 of them had received cytotoxic chemotherapy, 2 before the development of opportunistic infection. Fourteen of the 23 patients died of infection. Six of the 9 survivors had extreme hypercortisolism controlled before the terminal stage of infectious illness. Patients with endogenous Cushing syndrome and opportunistic infection usually will not survive unless extreme hypercortisolism is promptly controlled. Extreme hypercortisolism should be considered an immunologic and endocrinologic emergency.

Postoperative Pneumonia: Determinants of Mortality

Louis F. Martin, Eleanor F. Asher, Joseph M. Casey, and Donald E. Fry
Arch Surg. 119:379–383, April 1984

9–8

Postoperative pneumonia continues to be a major cause of mortality on surgical services. Nosocomial infections of the lower respiratory tract develop in about 0.75% of all patients on surgical services, according to the National Nosocomial Infections Survey (NNIS). The determinants that affect survival in patients in whom postoperative pneumonia develops are not clear. A retrospective analysis was conducted in 136 patients (135 men) treated at the Louisville VA Medical Center; postoperative pneumonia developed in all 136 after major operation between 1974 and 1980. These patients represented 1.3% of all operative cases, yet comprised 10% of the total 614 deaths occurring during the study period. The average age of the patients in whom pneumonia developed was 66 years. Significant determinants of death included the presence of gram-negative pneumonitis, emergent operation, respiratory-acquired pneumonia, postoperative peritonitis, and several factors that suggested host defenses were overwhelmed (remote organ failure, positive blood culture results, or spread of infection to the second lung).

The 1.3% incidence of postoperative pneumonia was associated with a mortality of 46%, but the overall operative mortality was only 6.0%. The definition of postoperative pneumonia used in this study was partially responsible for this high mortality figure, because interest focused on those pneumonia infections that altered the patient's hospital course. Although postoperative pneumonia is a nosocomial infection, the data cannot be compared directly with the findings in the NNIS study because only those patients who had major operative procedures were included; patients with any sign of an abnormality on the preoperative chest x-ray examination was eliminated. Also, the study population consisted of patients hospitalized in a VA hospital whose admission policies give priority to elderly, indigent persons needing immediate medical care.

The patients seemed to experience pneumonia via several different pathophysiologic mechanisms. For example, 41% of the patients had atelectasis that preceded the development of invasive pulmonary infection. Failure to maintain an adequate tidal volume either during anesthesia or postoperatively because of pain, increased intra-abdominal pressure, or sedation results in a collapse of airways that may aid in the growth of microorganisms. Nineteen percent of the patients had multiple operations before infection, and 50% of this subset had atelectasis prior to confirmation of pneumonia. Gross aspiration occurred in 34% of these patients despite the use of awake intubations, gastrostomy tubes, and other devices aimed at reducing the incidence of aspiration. The contribution of aspiration to the development of pneumonia is considerable. Patients in short-term care hospitals, especially those who are debilitated or elderly, have a high rate of colonization of the upper respiratory tract with gram-negative organisms.

In this study, 35% of the patients had pneumonia while they required respiratory assistance for hypoxemia. These patients also had a significantly higher risk of death than did those in whom pneumonia developed while they did not require mechanical ventilation. Intubation of the trachea eliminates the protective mechanisms that the proximal airway provides and increases the incidence of aspiration.

Comparative Study of *Legionella micdadei* and Other Nosocomial Acquired Pneumonia

Jennifer E. Rudin and Edward J. Wing (Pittsburgh)
Chest 86:675–680, November 1984
9–9

Infection by *Legionella micdadei*, or Pittsburgh pneumonia agent, has occurred in both immunosuppressed and immunocompetent hosts, although less often than infection by *Legionella pneumophilia*. An outbreak of 27 cases of pneumonia due to *L. micdadei* occurred at Montefiore Hospital, Pittsburgh, between 1979 and 1983. Twenty-two cases were diagnosed by culture. No case of nosocomial Legionnaire's disease occurred in this period. Infections by *L. micdadei* decreased after measures were taken to reduce colony counts in hot water tanks at the hospital.

Mean patient age was 59 years. All patients but 1 had serious underlying disease; most frequently chronic renal failure and collagen vascular disease. Twenty-three patients had received corticosteroids, 17 with other immunosuppressive agents. Patients typically had fever, dyspnea, and a dry, nonproductive cough of abrupt onset. Most had pleuritic pain. High, spiking fever was characteristic of *L. micdadei* infection. The laboratory findings reflected the underlying illness. Twenty-five patients received erythromycin. Two with dual infections received erythromycin and another appropriate antibiotic. Six patients died despite appropriate treatment, including the 2 with dual infections. Two late responders required trimethoprim-sulfamethoxazole for final recovery. Two cases were diagnosed postmortem; the patients had not received erythromycin.

Pneumonia due to *L. micdadei* is often an acute nosocomial disease occurring in immunocompromised patients. Fluorescent antibody staining and culture of sputum are effective diagnostic methods. Mortality is high, but erythromycin is effective when given in an early stage of the illness. Mortality in erythromycin-treated patients in this series was 24%. Two patients failed to respond to erythromycin but recovered when given trimethoprim-sulfamethoxazole.

Mediastinal Infection After Open-Heart Surgery
Robert Rutledge, Robert E. Applebaum, and B. Justin Kim
Surgery 97:88–92, January 1985   9–10

Mediastinitis that develops after cardiac operation is a serious complication associated with high morbidity and morality rates. A review was made of the experience with 29 patients identified among 2,031 having valve replacement, coronary bypass operation, or combined procedures between 1956 and 1981. Prophylaxis was with penicillin G and streptomycin before 1972, and with cephalothin or cefazolin between 1973 and 1979. Since then, penicillin G and streptomycin were administered preoperatively, and streptomycin and oxacillin were given postoperatively.

The incidence of mediastinitis was 1.4% (29 of 2,031 patients). Only patients having triple valve replacement were at a significantly increased risk. The mean interval from operation to infection was 11 days. Mortality has declined in more recent years, but the incidence of mediastinitis has not changed significantly. The overall mortality was 52%. All patients with mediastinitis caused by *Candida, Proteus,* or *Klebsiella* died. Mortality was 35% in the 17 patients having mediastinal exploration. Mortality was 65% in patients having valve replacement, and nil in the group having coronary bypass operation only. In 12 patients pneumonia developed after mediastinitis was diagnosed, and 9 of these patients died. Five of the 6 patients who had prosthetic valve endocarditis in association with mediastinitis died.

Mortality from mediastinitis has not change substantially in recent decades, but a significant number of patients can be cured. Prolonged intensive care is necessary. Mediastinal exploration should be performed with wide debridement and continuous closed irrigation. Wound coverage with muscle flaps has been recommended if closed irrigation fails. Open wound packing has also been successful, but hospitalization is prolonged. The open method is used by the authors only when extensive purulent destruction of bone is present or the closed method fails.

Nosocomial Hepatitis A: A Multinursery Outbreak in Wisconsin

Bruce S. Klein, Jacqueline A. Michaels, Michael W. Rytel, Keith G. Berg, and Jeffrey P. Davis
JAMA 252:2716–2721, Nov. 16, 1984   9–11

Day-care centers appear to represent a major source of hepatitis A infections of uncertain origin in this country. A multinursery outbreak of hepatitis A associated with exposure to premature infants infected at a neonatal intensive-care nursery is reported. Seven premature infants contracted asymptomatic hepatitis A while in the intensive-care nursery in a 4-month period in 1981. Fifteen secondary cases occurred in the next 2 months, 6 in family members of nursery infants, 5 in nurses at that nursery, and 4 in nurses and a physician at 2 other nurseries that had received an infected infant. An epidemiologic study failed to reveal a common vehicle, but it seemed likely that hepatitis A was transmitted in at least two generations of illness in infants at the intensive-care nursery. A case-control study suggested that hepatitis was transmitted by nurses at that facility.

This occurrence suggests that asymptomatic premature infants infected with hepatitis A can be a source of infection in nursery infants and personnel and in the community at large. There is evidence that infected infants in this study exposed nursery personnel. It is possible that the virus was introduced via blood transfusion. Nurses were implicated epidemiologically as vehicles of spread of hepatitis A virus between infants with first-generation and those with second-generation illness. Simple control measures, such as hand-washing between patients, can minimize cross-contamination with bacterial or viral pathogens, such as hepatitis A virus.

▶ Nosocomial hepatitis A has rarely been reported as a complication among patients or personnel caring for infected patients. This report is one of several epidemics which have emerged in the recent past (Goodman, R. A., et al.: *Am. J. Med.* 73:220–226, 1982; and Nobel, R. C., et al.: *JAMA* 252:2711–2715, 1984). These outbreaks have been primarily documented among neonates or incontinent patients. Occasionally the source of the hepatitis A virus has been from contaminated blood, even though the viremic phase of hepatitis A is brief. Because blood may be obtained from one donor and divided into multiple "packs" for neonates, a single contaminated unit may serve as the vehicle for multiple cases.

In general when patients with hepatitis A are admitted to a hospital, the bulk of virus excretion in stool has already occurred. These reports support the need for continued observation of good handwashing techniques, especially after handling stool and especially for hospital personnel caring for patients in neonatal intensive care units.—D.S.

10 Miscellaneous

Impact of New Cloning Techniques on Diagnosis and Treatment of Infectious Diseases
N. Cary Engleberg and Barry I. Eisenstein (Univ. of Texas, San Antonio)
N. Engl. J. Med. 311:892–901, Oct. 4, 1984   10–1

Cloning can provide an inexhaustible supply of a given product such as an antibody. Absolute isolation of molecular elements is achieved, and unwanted reactivities can be eliminated. Gene cloning permits the isolation of unique DNA sequences or gene products from similar elements in the donor species. The sensitivity and specificity of a given application of a cloned reagent are controlled by the user and are not limited by the purity of the reagent. Cross-reactivity essentially becomes a property of antigens rather than of antibodies. Monoclonal antibodies can prove rapid identification of clinical isolates and permit early diagnosis of many infections. Monoclonal antibodies can be used to improve the accuracy of serologic methods for quantifying pathogen-specific antibodies in patient serums.

The cloning of human B lymphocytes may provide biologic products for passive immunization against specific pathogens or for neutralizing or eliminating microbial toxins. The purity and presumed safety of human monoclonal antibodies may make them preferable to current antiserums used in immunoprophylaxis and immunotherapy. Monoclonal antibodies have been used to transfer protective immunity to animals challenged with viruses, bacteria, and parasites.

Cloned DNA is expected to be useful as a specific reagent in diagnostic hybridization assays. Further, the polypeptide products of cloned genes may be used as purified antigens for immunodiagnosis or for production of recombinant vaccines. New approaches such as recombinant RNA technology and monoclonal antibody-targeted drug delivery hold the promise of important new clinical applications.

▶ The space-wars technology of gene cloning is becoming more and more of a reality. As new developments occur, it is important to have an understanding both of the promise and the problems that are likely to be encountered with the use of these new reagents. A sound understanding of the subject will allow the physician to separate the wheat from the chaff in the promotional material likely to bombard our offices from the myriad of companies actively working to develop these reagents and biologics.—D.S.

Mechanisms of Fever Induced by Recombinant Human Interferon

Charles A. Dinarello, Harry A. Bernheim, Gordon W. Duff, Hung V. Le, T. L. Nagabhushan, Nancy C. Hamilton, and Flavio Coceani

J. Clin. Invest. 74:906–913, September 1984   10–2

Fever has been a prominent aspect of interferon administration. Human protein impurities might be responsible for fever in persons given cell-derived human interferon, but recombinant human interferon, free from extraneous proteins, produces fever in nearly all recipients. An attempt was made to determine the mechanisms of this fever. Recombinant human interferon is produced in *Escherichia coli,* and contaminating endotoxin therefore was considered as a cause of fever in recipients. Both rabbit and mouse pyrogen assays were used.

Polymyxin B, which blocks endotoxin fever, had no effect on the pyrogenicity of human interferon in rabbits. Interferon also produced fever when injected into an endotoxin-resistant strain of mice. No circulating leukocyte pyrogen (LP) was found in rabbits with interferon-induced fever, and human mononuclear cells incubated with interferon in vitro did not release LP. Interferon stimulated prostaglandin E_2 (PGE_2) release from rabbit hypothalamic tissue in vitro. Intracerebroventicular injection of human interferon into cats produced both fever and a rise in PGE_2 concentration in the cerebrospinal fluid. Both effects were reversed by indomethacin administraton.

These findings suggest that the fever induced by combinant human interferon is not due to endotoxin, but that the material is intrinsically pyrogenic because it induces PGE_2 release in the hypothalamus. Interferon may cause fever by raising the thermoregulatory setpoint via a change in arachidonate cyclo-oxygenase products, as does LP. The myalgia and weight loss associated with fever from both infection and interferon therapy may reflect a common mechanism.

▶ This is an important observation in that we have for years believed that all exogenous pyrogens worked by inducing the production of endogenous pyrogen (Interleukin-1) by host mononuclear phagocytes. This paper clearly demonstrates that recombinant-derived interferon produces fever in the absence of endogenous pyrogen production.—S.M.W.

Hemodynamic Characteristics of Patients With Hypothermia Due to Occult Infection and Other Causes

D. Lynn Morris, Henry F. Chambers, Mary Gayle Morris, and Merle A. Sande (Univ. of California, San Francisco)

Ann. Intern. Med. 102:153–157, February 1985   10–3

Hypothermia in inner-city populations may often be related to alcohol or drug abuse or exposure of the elderly, but severe infection and bacteremia also may be responsible. An attempt was made to distinguish cases associated with severe infection in a series of 85 consecutive hypothermic patients presenting in a 6-month period in 1981–1982. Hypothermia was defined as a core temperature of 35 C or below. Thirty-two patients had right heart catheterization shortly after admission, because of respiratory failure, persistent hypotension, or oliguria.

Exposure with ethanol or drug ingestion led to hypothermia in 42% of cases, and severe bacteremia alone in 39%. The clinical and hemodynamic variables are compared in the bacteremic and other cases in the table. There were significant hemodynamic differences between the 2 groups, and no overlap was found when the systemic vascular resistance and cardiac index were determined within 4 hours of admission (Fig 10–1). The mean cardiac index was 7.1 L/minute/sq m in patients with bacteremia and 2.8 L in those without bacteremia. The mean respective values for systemic vascular resistance were 486 and 1760 dynes/s/cm^{-5}.

Hemodynamic parameters can distinguish between patients with infection-related hypothermia and those with hypothermia from other causes. Patients with infection seem unable to maintain systemic vascular resistance by vasoconstriction. Myocardial contractility appears not to be significantly depressed until a profoundly low temperature is reached. Mortality is high when severe infection is present, and broad-spectrum

CLINICAL AND HEMODYNAMIC VARIABLES AT ADMISSION OF PATIENTS WITH HYPOTHERMIA RESULTING FROM INFECTION WITH BACTEREMIA OR OTHER CAUSES*

	Bacteremic	Non-bacteremic	P Value†
Patients, n	33	52	
Temperature, °C	31.4±3.6	31.7±2.4	0.75
Leukocyte count, $\times 10^3/mm^3$	14.0±9.7	13.8±4.9	0.82
Respiratory rate, *min*	19.9±7.5	17.0±8.5	0.35
Heart rate, *min*	97.6±37.9	101.7±23.2	0.46
Right atrium pressure, *mm Hg*	5.8±3.1	6.4±2.7	0.20
Pulmonary capillary wedge pressure, *mm Hg*	10.4±5.8	11.2±4.2	0.12
Arterial pH	7.41±0.16	7.33±0.12	0.09
Arterial Pco_2, *mm Hg*	29.0±12.7	34.4±14.2	0.27
Mean arterial pressure, *mm Hg*	60.2±15.9	70.7±16.5	0.08
Systemic vascular resistance, *dynes·sec·cm^{-5}*	486.0±125.0	1759.9±331.0	0.001
Cardiac index, *L/min·/m²*	7.1±1.9	2.8±0.7	0.006

*Values, where indicated, are mean ± SD.
†Using $a = 0.05$ and Bonferroni's adjustment for multiple independent comparisons, a P value less than 0.01 is considered significant.
(Courtesy of Morris, D.L., et al.: Ann. Intern. Med. 102:153–157, February 1985.)

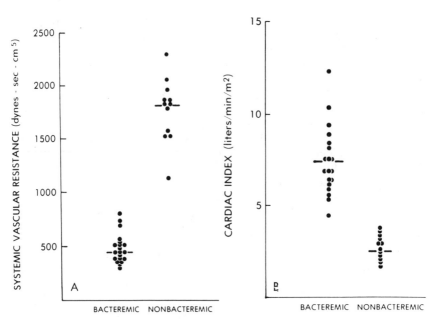

Fig 10–1.—Systemic vascular resistance (**A**) and cardiac index (**B**) as recorded within 4 hours of hospital admission in hypothermic patients with and without bacteremia. Horizontal bars represent mean values. (Courtesy of Morris, D.L., et al.: Ann. Intern. Med. 102:153–157, February 1985.)

antibiotic therapy may be indicated until infection can be excluded, particularly in patients with suspicious hemodynamic findings. Routine cardiac catheterization is not warranted in this setting if done only to identify bacteremic patients.

▶ This is an interesting and well done clinical study. The differentiation between alcohol or exposure-induced hypothermia and bacteremia-induced hypothermia is important. Unfortunately, the usual clinical parameters one employs to help differentiate infected from noninfected patients, such as temperature and white blood cell count, do not help in this situation. However, there are striking hemodynamic differences which should make differentiation of these patients more apparent.—S.M.W.

Hyperimmunoglobulinemia D and Periodic Fever: A New Syndrome

Jos W. M. van der Meer, Jiri Radl, Chris J. L. M. Meyer, Ralph van Furth, Jaak M. Vossen, Janny A. van Nieuwkoop, and Sacha Lobatto

Lancet 1:1087–1090, May 19, 1984   10–4

The authors present 6 patients of Dutch ancestry with long histories of recurrent fever of unknown cause, clinical features similar to familial Mediterranean fever (FMF), and no precipitating events. High fevers (39 C) preceded by chills were the main features of the attack with headaches and lymphadenopathy. Abdominal pain was less frequent and less severe than in FMF, and there was no periodicity of the attacks. Treatment with colchicine resulted in remissions. Immunoglobulin studies showed that all patients had raised serum IgD levels, and only 1 of 8 FMF patients had a raised serum IgD level. The IgA level was slightly increased in 3 patients, whereas 1 patient had depressed serum IgG level. None of the patients had paraproteinemia, and no homogeneous Ig component was found on agar electrophoresis. In all serum samples tested by immunoelectrophoresis, the IgD precipitin line was asymmetrical. Large numbers of IgD positive cells were found in 5 bone marrow specimens. Lymph node biopsy specimens showed plasma cells positive for immunoglobulins. Immunofluorescence studies on skin rash biopsy specimens showed perivascular depositions of IgA and C3 but not IgD. Lymphocyte transformation tests were normal.

The clinical picture resembled that of FMF, i.e., periodic fever, a positive family history, leukocytosis during an attack, and remission of symptoms after colchicine was given. However, lymphadenopathy is rare in FMF; serositis, which is frequent in FMF, was not common in these patients. Increased serum IgD levels were striking in these patients but not in FMF patients. The role played by IgD in the pathogenesis of the periodic fever in these patients is still speculative.

▶ The authors describe a new syndrome which is clearly not FMF. However, anyone who deals with patients who have fever of unknown origin has seen patients with features similar to these patients, and it will be interesting to see if this work can be confirmed.—S.M.W.

Acute Bronchoconstriction Induced by Cotton Dust: Dose-Related Responses to Endotoxin and Other Dust Factors

Robert M. Castellan, Stephen A. Olenchock, John L. Hankinson, Patricia D. Millner, Joseph B. Cocke, C. Kennety Bragg, Henry H. Perkins, Jr., and Robert R. Jacobs
Ann. Intern. Med. 101:157–163, August 1984   10–5

Current occupational health practice in the United States includes limiting the concentration of gravimetrically measured lint-free cotton dust in work areas of textile mills; however, previous reports have shown that cotton dust is not uniformly potent. To define the particular characteristics of cotton dust that are related to its acute pulmonary toxicity, acute ventilatory changes were measured in 54 healthy, adult human volunteers exposed on separate occasions to dust from several different commercially available cottons. Spirometric tests were done immediately before and 6 hours after exposure to card-generated cotton dust from 5 different cottons of several grades and growing regions. During exposure, airborne concentrations of viable fungi and bacteria (total and gram-negative), vertically elutriated gravimetric dust, and vertically elutriated endotoxin were measured.

On the basis of gravimetric elutriated dust, the dust from California strict middling cotton had no effect on forced vital capacity (FVC), forced expiratory volume in 1 second (FEV_1), or maximal flow at 75% of expired vital capacity (FEF_{75}) while dust generated by carding Mississippi strict low middling spotted cotton caused marked acute reductions in all spirometric indices. Correlation coefficients for individual exposure indices with acute FEV_1 responses showed significant relationship between gravimetric dust index, total bacteria, gram-negative bacteria, and elutriated endotoxin but not with viable fungi. The highest correlation was seen between the endotoxin exposure and acute FEV_1 response ($r = -0.94$; $P < .00001$). Total bacteria and gram-negative bacteria were more highly correlated with FEV_1 response ($r = -0.71$ and -0.91 respectively) than was the gravimetric dust index ($r = -0.34$, $P < .05$) which was the least correlated.

These results suggest that gram-negative endotoxin may play a major role in acute pulmonary response to inhaled cotton dust. Newer studies have shown that the number of gram-negative bacteria on parts of field cotton plants rise sharply after the first frost, which may relate to less marked human airway response to dust from California grown cotton which is rarely frost-killed.

The Occupational Safety and Health Administration has established a health standard incorporating a permissible exposure level for textile mills based on gravimetric concentration on vertically elutriated airborne cotton dust. The findings on this study suggest that vertically elutriated airborne endotoxin concentration may be a more appropriate exposure index on which to base a health standard. However, an inexpensive and rapid but quantitatively accurate and reproducible assay for endotoxin is yet to be delivered.

▶ Those of us who have spent a major portion of our academic careers studying bacterial endotoxins have made many hypotheses linking these ubiquitous materials to human disease. I am glad to see that the search for a pathogenetic role for endotoxins continues.—S.M.W.

Persistent Neutrophilic Meningitis: Report of Four Cases and Review of the Literature
James E. Peacock, Jr., Michael R. McGinnis, and Myron S. Cohen (Univ. of North Carolina)
Medicine (Baltimore) 63:379–395, November 1984   10–6

Four cases of persistent neutrophilic meningitis (PMN) were encountered. Routine bacterial pathogens were excluded in all cases. Aspergillosis was diagnosed in 1 case, nocardiosis in 2, and zygomycosis in 1. Several saprophytic intracellular bacteria have been shown to produce meningitis characterized by persistent cerebrospinal fluid (CSF) neutrophilia in both immunologically intact and immunocompromised hosts. The most prominent causes have been *Nocardia, Actinomyces,* and *Brucella* species. Involvement of the CNS occurs in as many as 40% of cases of nocardial infection, but CNS actinomycosis has become rare in the antibiotic era. Other causes of PMN include mycobacterial infection, fungi such as *Aspergillus* and *Zygomyces* species, and *Pseudoallescheria boydii*. Partially treated pyogenic meningitis can present as persistent neutrophilic disease. Fastidious microbes such as *Listeria monocytogenes* and *Leptospira* species may produce an ill-defined meningitic syndrome. Noninfectious causes include endogenous chemical meningitis, immunologic disorders, drug-induced hypersensitivity syndromes, and occasionally carcinomatous meningitis.

The nature of the conversion of a host-cell response from neutrophilic to mononuclear remains uncertain. Most of the infectious agents implicated elicit an initial neutrophilic host response which is supplanted by a mononuclear response in cases of persistent disease. Continued generation of neutrophil chemotactic factors may explain why this conversion fails to occur in some instances. Special CSF studies, such as detection of the metabolic byproducts of various organisms or of antibody, may be diagnostically helpful. Radiographic studies are not very helpful except for identifying a coexisting cerebral mass lesion, or showing the pressure or absence of other inflammatory parameningeal foci. The role of invasive biopsy procedures remains controversial. Empirical treatment may be warranted if progressive disease fails to respond to routine antibacterial measures. Amphotericin B, with or without a sulfonamide, should be considered in the immunocompromised host.

▶ In this report, patients were deemed to have persistent neutrophilic meningitis and selected for the continued presence of >50% PMN on repeat CSF examination at least 1 week after initial cerebrospinal fluid examination showed neutrophilic pleocytosis (>50% PMN), hypoglycorrhachia, and high CSF protein concentration. In each case, the patient manifested symptoms of meningitis and the initial CSF smear and culture were negative for bacteria. Saprophytic bacteria, e.g., *Nocardia asteroides* and *Mycobacteria,* and fungi accounted for almost all the cases (23 of 27).—M.K.

Effects of Postcesarean Section Febrile Morbidity on Subsequent Fertility
David J. Hurry, Bryan Larsen, and David Charles (Marshall Univ.)
Obstet. Gynecol. 64:256–260, August 1984   10–7

Little attention has been paid to the possible long-term effects of pelvic infection after cesarean delivery on future fecundity. The authors reviewed the records of 1,319 patients who underwent cesarean section to determine the relation between postoperative febrile morbidity and fertility during the 5 years after operation.

Of the 925 primary cesarean sections, 472 were performed after the membranes had been ruptured for 12 hours or longer. Of these patients, 200 (42.4%) developed postoperative infection, compared with 70 (15.5%) of 453 patients in whom the membranes had been ruptured less than 12 hours. The difference in overall infection rates between primary

---

FIVE-YEAR FOLLOW-UP OF 1,131 PRIMARY AND REPEAT
CESAREAN SECTIONS*

	No. pregnant	Pregnancy rate
Not infected after section	728/816	89.2%
Infected after section	278/315	88.3%
Puerperal endometritis	217/237	91.6%
Pelvic cellulitis	51/55	92.7%
Pelvic abscess	10/23	43.5%
All patients	1006/1131	88.9%

*Fifteen of the 1,146 potentially fertile patients had intervening tubal ligations.
(Courtesy of Hurry, D.J., et al.: Obstet. Gynecol. 64:256–260, August 1984. Reprinted with permission from The American College of Obstetricians and Gynecologists.)

(29.2%) and repeat (13.7%) cesarean section was significant ($P < .005$). After correction of data for voluntary infertility, the table shows that puerperal endometritis and pelvic cellulitis had little effect on the rate of pregnancy during the 5 years after cesarean section; however, postoperative pelvic abscess was associated with reduction in fertility, as only 10 pregnancies occurred among 23 affected patients. This rate of pregnancy was almost half the rate observed in other patients ($P < .005$). Of the 13 patients with pelvic abscess who failed to conceive, 4 had tubal ligation with the oviducts showing no evidence of previous salpingitis, 2 had peritubal adhesions, and 6 had cornual or interstitial occlusions. Specimens of the oviduct obtained from women who had puerperal endometritis and puerperal cellulitis showed normal histologic patterns, indicating that these conditions do not necessarily result in infertility.

Postpartum infection is associated with primary cesarean section and prolonged rupture of the fetal membranes. The infection can lead to pelvic cellulitis and diffuse pelvic suppuration, resulting in intra-abdominal abscess involving the ovaries and fallopian tubes. Infertility ensues as peritoneal adhesions isolate the abdominal ostia of the fallopian tubes from the ovaries. Formation of pelvic abscess may be responsible for secondary infertility in a third of women infected during cesarean section.

▶ The determination of postoperative infection following cesarean section is difficult, especially in milder forms of infection. The authors used as their major criterion "postoperative febrile morbidity," which is based on fever, with some signs pointing to the pelvis. The diagnosis of infection, however, was not verified in most cases by positive culture or other objective criteria, which is difficult, if not impossible, in this setting. Hence, it is not clear that all patients were indeed infected, especially those with low-grade fever and mild signs. Nevertheless, it is reassuring that the most common forms of postcesarean section complication, namely puerperal endometritis and pelvic cellulitis, were not associated with any loss in fertility. The most serious complication, pelvic abscess, did compromise fertility but only in about half of the women in this group. Even in the setting of emergency cesarean section for premature rupture of membranes, the outlook for future conception is quite good.—S.G.

Direct Fluorescent Monoclonal Antibody Stain for Rapid Detection of Infant *Chlamydia trachomatis* Infections
Thomas A. Bell, Cho-chou Kuo, Walter E. Stamm, Milton R. Tam, Richard S. Stephens, King K. Holmes, and J. Thomas Grayston (Seattle)
Pediatrics 74:224–228, August 1984   10–8

Chlamydia trachomatis is a frequent cause of neonatal conjunctivitis and early infantile pneumonia in the United States, and has also been associated with nasopharyngitis. A fluorescein-labeled species-specific monoclonal antibody to *C. trachomatis* can be used to detect chlamydial elementary bodies in smear specimens obtained from the genitals of adults. This approach was evaluated as a means of rapidly diagnosing *C. trachomatis* infections in infants. Thirty-nine infants, aged 3 months or younger with purulent conjunctivitis was studied; 14 mothers had genital *C. trachomatis* infection during pregnancy. Three infants were treated unsuccessfully with topical application of antimicrobial drugs. The *C. trachomatis* 2Cl hybrid cell line was used to produce ascites fluid in Balb/c mice. Immunoglobulin from the fluid was purified for use in immunofluorescence staining.

Chlamydial elementary bodies were easily recognized by their apple-green fluorescence. The number of elementary bodies in smears tended to correlate with the number of inclusions in cell cultures. Complete concordance between findings in conjunctival smears and culture results was observed for all 55 specimens from inflamed conjunctivae in the 23 infants with unilateral and the 16 with bilateral conjunctivitis. *Chlamydia trachomatis* was isolated in 16 infants, including the 3 given topical antimicrobial therapy. Some nasopharyngeal specimens produced culture-negative but smear-positive results. Correlation also was imperfect for oropharyngeal specimens.

The direct fluorescent monoclonal antibody stain technique is a sensitive, specific means of diagnosing *C. trachomatis* infection in infants. It can be completed within an hour of specimen collection. The inflamed conjunctiva is sampled in patients with conjunctivitis and the nasopharynx in those with pneumonia without conjunctivitis. Sampling both sides of the nasopharynx should increase the rate of detection of *C. trachomatis* in patients with pneumonia.

▶ This paper presents a significant advance in the rapid diagnosis of *Chlamydia trachomatis* infection by the use of a monoclonal antibody. It is simple, specific, and speedy. When generally available, it should increase the diagnostic accuracy for the infections caused by this organism.—G.K.

Corneal Ulcers Associated With Contact Lens Wear

Paul G. Galentine, Elisabeth J. Cohen, Peter R. Laibson, Charles P. Adams, Rollande Michaud, and Juan J. Arentsen (Wills Eye Hosp., Philadelphia)
Arch. Ophthalmol. 102:891–894, June 1984   10–9

Most complications associated with contact lens wear are minor, but bacterial or fungal keratitis is an exception and represents the most serious complication. The authors reviewed the records of 322 patients admitted with the diagnosis of ulcerative keratitis between January 1978 and July 1983 and found 56 cases (17%) associated with contact lens wear. Therapy was begun with cefazolin sodium and gentamicin sulfate or tobramycin sulfate until culture and sensitivity results were available. The patient population included phakic and aphakic patients wearing a variety of extended- and daily wear soft contact lenses and daily wear hard contact lenses.

Six (55%) of the patients using daily wear soft lenses gave a history of break in lens technique, usually insertion of a nondisinfected lens, shortly before onset of symptoms. Of the extended-wear lens patients, 25% reported a recent lens manipulation before ocular symptoms developed. Cultures were negative in 27 patients and positive in the rest; 67% of the patients with negative cultures and 41% of those with positive cultures had received topical antibiotic therapy.

Pseudomonas was the most common pathogen recovered and was found in 13 cases (23%); staphylococci were present in 11 cases (20%). Follow-up of at least 3 months was obtained in 52 patients; 30 (58%) had a final visual acuity of 6/12 or better, and 8 (62%) of those with *Pseudomonas* regained a visual acuity of 6/12 or better. Six (11%) of the 56 patients required penetrating keratoplasty to regain useful vision; 4 of these had *Pseudomonas* ulcers.

Bacterial keratitis should be suspected in any patient with contact lenses who has a red or painful eye, especially with corneal ulceration or infiltrates. Ulcers caused by *Pseudomonas* can progress rapidly and may even threaten the integrity of the globe. All corneal infiltrates should be scraped for appropriate smears and inoculated on recommended mediums. Due to the potential of rapid progression with gram-negative infection, initial subconjunctival antibiotic therapy (somewhat controversial) and fortified antibiotics used topically every 30 minutes are indicated.

The contact lens-wearing patient must be instructed to seek immediate ophthalmologic attention when redness or pain develops, to ascertain the presence or absence of serious complications and to initiate therapy, if indicated.

▶ Infectious disease specialists are usually among the first to encounter the complications of new devices. Hickman and continuous ambulatory peritoneal dialysis catheters as well as the vast array of short-term hemodynamic monitoring intravascular devices have all warranted their share of reports on the incidence, etiologic organisms, and management of implantable device-related infections. The increasing use of contact lenses, especially extended-wear soft contact lenses, serves as the impetus for this report. The high incidence of *Pseudomonas aeruginosa, Staphylococcus aureus,* and *Staphylococcus epidermidis,* as well as the frequency of gram-positive/culture-negative infections, (probably due to the widespread early use of topical antibiotics) are noteworthy.—M.K.

Association of *Ureaplasma urealyticum* in the Placenta With Perinatal Morbidity and Mortality

Ruth B. Kundsin, Shirley G. Driscoll, Richard R. Monson, Ching Yeh, Stella A. Biano, and William D. Cochran
N. Engl. J. Med. 310:941–945, Apr. 12, 1984   10–10

The pathogenicity of *Mycoplasma homonis* and *Ureaplasma urealyticum* in the obstetric setting remains unclear. The authors cultured placentas from 144 neonates dying perinatally, 452 admitted to an intensive care unit, and 205 control neonates. Seventy-five stillbirths and 69 perinatal deaths were included in the first group. The placentas were cultured for ureaplasmas, mycoplasmas, chlamydiae, fungi, aerobic and anaerobic bacteria, and cytomegalovirus.

Ureaplasma urealyticum or *M. hominis* were isolated from 21% of placentas from premature and term infants dying perinatally, 25% of those admitted to intensive care, and 11% of control infants. Both gestational age and birth weight were inversely related to the isolation of ureaplasmas. The presence of ureaplasmas was significantly associated with chorioamnionitis. Colonization by *U. urealyticum* was closely associated with low birth weight, as were spontaneous membrane rupture and preeclampsia. Diabetes was negatively associated with low birth weight.

The presence of ureaplasmas in the placenta suggests their transcervical migration from the lower genitourinary tract. The present findings of a strong association between ureaplasmas in the placenta and low birth weight suggest a causal relationship. Future work should focus on the pathophysiology of the inflammatory process in the fetal membranes elicited by *U. ureaplasma,* which may link them to premature births. Elimination of *U. urealyticum* from the genital tract before conception might offer significant improvement in perinatal outcomes.

Cardiovascular Abnormalities in Kawasaki Disease

V. M. Novelli, A. Galbraith, P. J. Robinson, J. F. Smallhorn, and W. C. Marshall (London)
Arch. Dis. Child. 59:405–409, May 1984   10–11

Kawasaki disease is an acute, febrile illness affecting chiefly infants and young children. Its cause is unknown, but an infectious etiology has been suggested. The disease is considered a manifestation of systemic vasculitis, probably immune complex-mediated, with a predilection for the coronary arteries. Coronary artery aneurysm formation and thrombotic occlusions may produce myocardial ischemia and sudden death. Fatalities have been reported in 1%–2% of cases.

Cross-sectional echocardiography was used to assess cardiac involvement in 18 consecutive patients seen in 1981–1983 who met criteria for Kawasaki disease. The mean follow-up period was 12 months. The children had a mean of 4½ EKGs each. Significant cardiovascular complications were found in 55% of the patients. Six had coronary artery aneurysms involving the proximal left coronary artery in 4 cases and both main coronary arteries in 2 cases. The aneurysms were detected in the subacute phase of disease, always in infants younger than age 1 year. Higher peak platelet counts were present in the patients with aneurysms. Aneurysms regressed in 4 cases during a mean period of 7.5 months. No patient had clinical evidence of myocardial ischemia, and there were no deaths. Two patients had small pericardial effusions that resolved without treatment. Eight patients had systolic hypertension during the course of the illness. Two required treatment with β-blockers and vasodilators; these patients had elevated plasma renin and aldosterone values.

Cross-sectional echocardiography is suggested for all patients with Kawasaki disease at the time of diagnosis and again 4 weeks after the onset of fever. A follow-up study should be done at 3–4 months. Patients with coronary artery aneurysms should be assessed at least every 3–6 months, and all children should have long-term follow-up. Most patients appear to have a good prognosis, but infarction and sudden death have occurred years after the illness had apparently subsided. Persistent hypertension should be treated.

▶ Coronary artery aneurysm is an unusual manifestation of any illness, but as pointed out in this article, it occurs quite commonly in Kawasaki disease. Of note is the fact that in most patients the aneurysms spontaneously regressed.—S.M.W.

Effect of Selective Decontamination of the Digestive Tract on Colonization and Infection Rate in Multiple-Trauma Patients

C. P. Stoutenbeck, H. K. F. van Saene, D. R. Miranda, and D. F. Zandstra (Univ. of Groningen)

Intensive Care Med. 10:185–192, July 1984   10–12

Infection is still a major cause of morbidity and mortality in severely injured patients. Selective decontamination of the digestive tract (SDD) attempts to eliminate aerobic gram-negative bacilli and yeasts, leaving the anaerobic flora to prevent overgrowth of resistant gram-negative bacilli. An open trial of SDD was carried out in 122 patients admitted with multiple injuries to intensive care who stayed there 5 days or longer. Fifty-nine earlier patients received no antibiotic prophylaxis, whereas 63 later patients received 50 mg of cefotaxime per kg from admission until potentially pathogenic organisms were absent. The oropharyngeal cavity was decontaminated with Orabase paste containing 2% polymyxin E, 2%

tobramycin, and 2% amphotericin B. The gut was decontaminated with the same nonabsorbable antibiotics administered via gastric tube four times daily. A combination of 100 mg of polymyxin E, 80 mg of tobramycin, and 500 mg of amphotericin B was used on each occasion.

The two patient groups were clinically and demographically comparable. Colonization rates in the oropharynx were significantly lower in SDD patients after 2 days, and no secondary colonization was evident. Rectal colonization declined significantly after 5 days, but 9 patients had secondary colonization with potential pathogens sensitive to the antibiotics used. The infection rate was significantly lower in the SDD group (16% vs. 81%). Cefotaxime proved to be appropriate in all but 2 patients in the SDD group with wound infections. A majority of infections in both groups were endogenous. Positive surveillance cultures of tracheal aspirate and catheter urine were significantly less frequent in the SDD group than in the control group.

Selective decontamination of the digestive tract is an effective means of preventing secondary colonization of the tract by gram-negative pathogenic bacteria in critically ill patients with multiple injuries. Systemic prophylaxis is also needed to prevent early endogenous infections. The emergency of resistance against systemic agents may be prevented by SDD.

▶ Undoubtedly, infection plays a major role in severely traumatized patients. Host defenses are depressed as a result of severe trauma, and use of antibiotics encourages emergence of resistant organisms. Whether the oral decontamination approach used in leukemic patients (an issue still not settled) can be applied to trauma patients is an intriguing possibility. Unfortunately, this paper tests two variables, namely, decontamination with oral antibiotics and active prophylaxis with a parenteral agent, cefotaxime. Another problem is the use of retrospective controls. In any case, it is intriguing that the decontamination/prophylaxis group had significantly fewer infections. A major concern, not addressed in this paper, is possible emergence of highly resistant microorganisms in the unit itself, particularly since tobramycin is included in the oral antibiotic mixture. The problem, of course, is that oral decontamination prevents endogenous infection, but it does not interdict exogenous infection which, if associated with resistant microorganisms, could be devastating to the severely traumatized patient. In any case, this approach deserves a more extensive trial.—S.G.

Subject Index

A

229

Index to Authors